SECRET NATIVE AMERICAN PATHWAYS

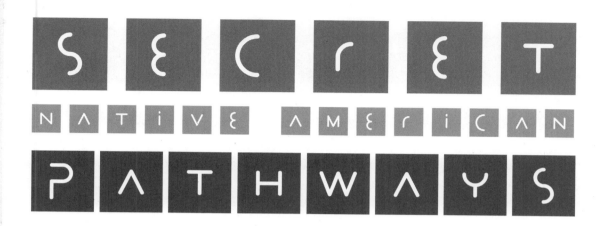

a
guide to
inner peace

THOMAS E. MAILS

Author of *Fools Crow: Wisdom and Power*

Council Oak Books
Tulsa Oklahoma 74120

Secret Native American Pathways: *A Guide to Inner Peace*
©1988 by Thomas E. Mails. Preface ©2003 by Sally Dennison. Index and
"Museums and Research Facilities" ©2003 by Council Oak Books, LLC.
Published 1988. Second Edition 2003

Book design: Melanie Haagie
Cover photo: ©2003 www.PhotoSpin.com
Illustrations: Thomas E. Mails
Typographic specifications: Body text set in 12 pt. Hiroshige,
display type is set in Stealth and Barmeno

Printed in Canada

LIBRARY OF CONGRESS CATALOGING-IN-PUBLICATION DATA

Mails, Thomas E., 1920-2001
    Secret Native American pathways: a guide to inner
peace/ by Thomas E. Mails
    p. cm.
    ISBN 1-57178-125-0
1. Rites and ceremonies—United States. 2. Indians of North
America—Rites and ceremonies. 3. Indians of North
America—Religion. 4. Peace of mind—Religious aspects.
88-070671   CIP

Council Oak Books
2105 E 15th Street, Suite B
Tulsa, OK 74104

www.counciloakbooks.com

4 3 2 1   06 05 04 03

Also by Thomas E. Mails

The Cherokee People
Fools Crow: Wisdom and Power
The Mystic Warriors of the Plains
Dog Soldiers, Bear Men, and Buffalo Women
The People Called Apache
Fools Crow
Sundancing at Rose Bud and Pine Ridge
The Pueblo Children of the Earth Mother Vol. 1
The Pueblo Children of the Earth Mother Vol. 2

Acknowledgments

I would like to thank Fools Crow, Archie Sam, Renzie Gordon, and the Pueblo people who must remain unnamed for their invaluable help, and I thank the Newberry Library at the University of Chicago for permission to use the Edgar Payne papers.

CONTENTS

Council Oak Books was only a couple of years old in 1987 when I pulled from the stack of submissions a manila envelope from Thomas E. Mails of Lake Elsinore, California. He had heard about Council Oak through a friend of my mother's, the Cherokee author and columnist, Joyce Sequichie Hifler. Mails had two projects to propose.

The first was a complete illustrated history of the Cherokee people, originally produced under contract to Doubleday but returned to Mails when Doubleday fired his editor and cancelled the project. The second was unusual for Mails, an outgrowth of his years of getting to know various native people, including the Sioux holy man, Frank Fools Crow.

Council Oak wound up publishing both books, the latter in 1988 as *Secret Native American Pathways: A Guide to Inner Peace* and the former as *The Cherokee People,* in 1992.

Tom Mails came to Council Oak late in a long writing career that was unique in several ways. An artist and a Lutheran clergyman, he had no formal training as an anthropologist or ethnographer. However, from childhood, he was fascinated by American Indian artifacts. He not only drew and painted them but also conducted research on their uses in traditional life. Many of the most beautiful of these were ritual objects. Little by little as he learned more, he began in his art to reconstruct Native American life-ways — some vanished, some vanishing, some still thriving on the periphery of modern life. At the same time, he began to delve into the history and spirituality of native peoples.

His search led him to seek out works by white men and women who had written of their encounters with North America's native cultures in the eighteenth, nineteenth, and early twentieth centuries. More importantly, it led him to visit the reservations, pueblos, and communities of contemporary Native Americans.

What he saw and heard from the natives themselves, especially the elders and holy men and women, became the basis for much of what he wrote and illustrated in his books. Although, or perhaps *because,* he was a Lutheran minister, Mails approached the spiritual beliefs of the native peoples with the utmost respect. Medicine men like Fools Crow (for whom he ghost-wrote an autobiography from taped memories) trusted Mails and allowed him to witness private ritual practices.

Mails never discounted the amazing things he witnessed as "trickery" or the spiritual knowledge his informants revealed as "superstition." With unabashed enthusiasm, he recorded what he saw and heard in faithful detail.

Throughout his career Mails was criticized by anthropologists and some Native Americans. The anthropologists faulted his lack of formal education in their field and his opinionated approach to his subjects. He didn't write like a scientist but as an enthusiast with a keen eye for details.

Some American Indians were extremely suspicious of the white Christian outsider who made money writing about their people. Late in his life, Mails often managed to run afoul of one faction of a pueblo or tribe when he took the side of another faction—usually the more traditional one — in a dispute.

Still, his works have been used by Native Americans and non-natives alike as important sources for traditional practices that might well have died out completely had it not been for Mails' visual and verbal records, painstakingly compiled over a lifetime. Filmmakers, including those who produced *Dances with Wolves,* used Mails' books as resources. Also, he delighted in reporting that, in some cases, Indians used the books as well, to help them resurrect tribal ceremonies he had recorded in interviews with tribal elders, ceremonies that had been lost through acculturation to the white man's world.

Mails' most widely distributed volumes have been the large, lavishly illustrated books such as *Mystic Warriors of the Plains, The People Called Apache, Sundancing: The Great Sioux Piercing Ceremony,* the two volumes of *The Pueblo Children of the Earth Mother,* and *The Cherokee People.* He researched, wrote, and beautifully illustrated each book, bringing native ritual and everyday life more vividly alive than any other writer/artist before or since.

Also, despite his detractors, the popularity of his books helped whites and Indians alike to gain a new appreciation for traditional ways of life that were dying out.

When *Secret Native American Pathways* was published in 1988, the idea that American Indian traditionalists actually wielded powerful medicine was startling to us at Council Oak. Even more startling was Mails' suggestion that non-natives like Mails himself could be empowered to overcome the problems of the late twentieth-century world by using ancient tribal rituals in suburban homes and urban apartments.

Tom Mails immediately appreciated the control Council Oak allowed him over the editing and design of his books. Because he had many more years of experience than we did with the publishing establishment, we thought he could teach us a thing or two.

While we were in the process of editing *Pathways*, he showed up on our doorstep. Not wanting to trust his irreplaceable artwork to any shipping service, he had driven his van, loaded with the original paintings and drawings for *The Cherokee People*, all the way to Tulsa from Southern California.

My husband, Gene, and I offered Mails the guestroom at our house. After a dinner out with my Council Oak partners, Michael Hightower and Paulette Millichap, we came back to the house, and Tom and I started going over the edits for *Pathways* — hundreds of edits, one line at a time.

As I recall, we didn't begin until 10:30 that night, normally my bedtime. Mails was still on Pacific time. Even though I had the age advantage (I was 41 and he was 66), after one hour into the editing I was struck by numb exhaustion, but Tom was still going strong, his eyes bright, his mind moving sharply from one detail to the next.

By 2:00 a.m., with many pages left to edit, I was frankly amazed. Tom seemed every bit as fresh as he had the afternoon before, when he rolled into Tulsa in his van. And he had been amazingly lively then, especially considering that he'd been on the road for two days. I couldn't figure out where he was getting his energy. He didn't act like a man on speed, only alert and steady, as though he'd just had a good night's sleep.

Editing, we came upon a passage about Fools Crow and a ritual he had once shown Mails for keeping oneself sharp and energetic through many hours without rest.

I looked up at him, saying, "You must have done this ritual before we started working tonight."

Mails didn't admit to anything, only gave me a mischievous smile and went on with the work.

That was the beginning of a new awareness for me, a real appreciation of a kind of spiritual power that I had never directly encountered until then.

I am certainly not unique in my response. Tom Mails' books have brought this same awareness and appreciation to thousands of non-natives like myself. Because he approached the material from the perspective of a practicing and seminary-educated Christian, he was quick to see the similarities between Native American and Christian beliefs, even as he was writing with fascination and enthusiasm about rituals quite strange to most Christians.

His enthusiasm for the people and practices about which he wrote was infectious, while his background enabled him to bridge the often-cavernous gap between traditional American Indian cultures and American Judeo-Christian culture.

Tom Mails died on November 18, 2001. He was 79. His books changed me and everybody connected with Council Oak, just as they changed the world for all who read them.

Secret Native American Pathways is the one book that encapsulates Mail's appreciation for the spiritual power and inner peace that is the great gift of traditional Native American life. Such gifts, he believed, should be available to all seekers. Council Oak has kept the book in print these past fifteen years because it has continued to find an audience in a twenty-first century world that sorely needs the spiritual re-orientation offered here.

As we present this new, updated edition, with the welcome addition of an index and a list of resources, we trust that yet another audience will treasure the pathways Mails has uncovered for us all.

—Sally Dennison, Ph.D., 2003

CHAPTER ONE

Finding the Pathways

I was transfixed as I watched and listened to the serene old man sitting cross-legged in the wild grass of the sun-drenched prairie. He was dressed in his familiar black cowboy hat, faded yellow and purple striped shirt, and jeans. Off to our left, the wind stirred in the leaves of the cottonwood trees. He paid no attention to our surroundings as he sang softly in a melodious and surprisingly strong voice, his eyes closed, his face etched like the craggy South Dakota badlands but not thickened with anxiety, and his arms and hands extended to the side with palms upturned in supplication. He nodded continually, and glints of sunlight caught on his copper-colored forehead, high cheekbones, and the classic arch of his nose.

He seemed to have forgotten that I was there, and that was understandable, for what was going on was a personal and encompassing thing between his Creator, Wakan Tanka, and himself. He had not lighted the small branches stacked in front of him, yet as he chanted his song for the fourth time, they burst into flames. The wood crackled, and as its musky odor reached me, his eyes opened. He stared blankly at the fire for a moment, and then passed his right hand over the flames. The smoke turned yellow. He did it again, and the smoke turned black. And a third motion caused it to turn white, and, a fourth, red.

I knew these were the sacred colors of the four cardinal directions from which powers and wisdom come to the Lakota. But how and why did he do this? I had watched intently, and he had put nothing in the fire to change its color. In a moment, I ceased wondering about that, because wild birds and animals — creatures who both feared and preyed upon one another — began to arrive: a fox, a family of raccoons, squirrels, groundhogs, a badger, four crows, two hawks, sparrows, meadowlarks . . . each one sitting down or standing near him and utterly unafraid of the fire or the other creatures while they waited for him to finish.

Now the different-colored smoke materialized in the air above his head, and suddenly Fools Crow was arrayed in an ancient, blue-painted, Lakota war shirt, with hair-locks and fringes. His hands dripped blue paint, and his face was thickly coated with the color. He began to sing again, and four plumes of colored smoke entered the top of his head then emerged from the midsection of his body. Feathers of the black eagle appeared inside the swirling smoke and spun slowly around. Cottonwood leaves, whose pattern had given the Indians of the plains the idea for their tipis, also appeared in the smoke. Fools Crow reached out and caught several of the feathers. The smoke eddied away. Fools Crow touched each creature on the head and held a brief conversation with it in his Lakota language. The creatures left, the fire died down, and his war shirt and paint vanished. He was wearing his faded striped shirt and cowboy hat again.

"He was a worker of miracles . . . a rare channel or tube . . ."

He glanced over at me, knowing I would be amazed. "They bring me messages from Wakan Tanka and the directions," he said matter-of-factly, "messages about things my people need to know to prepare for the future."

I shook my head back and forth . . . but not in disbelief, for I had already seen this aged man do incredible things. He was a worker of miracles or, better said, a rare channel or tube through whom Wakan Tanka worked miracles, although Fools Crow would not call them such. Later, he would say that when "The Highest and Most Holy One" acts, it is only the carrying out of a promise. The "miracle" would be if he failed to do what He said He would.

It was the spring of 1973, and I had traveled fifteen hundred miles from my home in Los Angeles to the Pine Ridge Reservation in South Dakota to visit the most amazing and soul-stirring person I had ever encountered. He was then a venerable eighty-three-year-old man I had first met two months before at the Lower Brule Reservation; at that meeting he had begun to transport me back to days that sat lazily on the rounded edge of prehistory becoming history. I was here at this time because I had to see him again and because he had asked me to write his story — not the full story of his astonishing life, but only those things he thought the outside world ought to know right then. The other things he would tell me were to be held back until another day . . . until today in fact, when, as he put it, I would know in my heart the time was right to make them public. At one time, I thought that would be when he had departed from this earth, but now I know better, for Fools Crow has already slipped into a transformed mental and spiritual state wherein, while yet physically alive, he is being embalmed in a holy atmosphere that prepares him for eternal life with Wakan Tanka.

"Since 1958 I have been a Lutheran pastor . . ."

Since 1958, I have been a Lutheran pastor, as well as an author-illustrator. I have written eighteen books in the religious education field, seven coffee-table-sized historical books and one smaller book about native North Americans. These include works about Plains Indian tribes, Apache, Pueblo, and Cherokee, as well as the story of Fools Crow, who is a venerable Holy Man and current Ceremonial Chief of the Teton Sioux. I have, at the same time, also established close personal relationships with a number of Indians. Most of these friends are deeply spiritual people, and I have shared with them many wonderful spellbinding mysteries and miracles. Some of these mysteries and miracles I write about here. Among the other things I especially prize are the name Wa-o-ki-ye (One who helps), given to me during a ceremony at Rosebud by the Rosebud Sioux; the fact that on occasion the Indians say special prayers for me at their ceremonies; and the knowledge that my books are often used in the classes of Indian schools. I cherish also the opportunities I have had in lectures to pass on to non-Indian individuals and groups some of the wondrous things I have seen and learned.

While I find Indian life-ways particularly fascinating and educational, what has impressed me greatly is the fact that each of these tribes just mentioned has survived circumstances so grievous that one would think the people should have been forever immobilized or shattered. But they haven't been. Instead, they have triumphed over one adversity after another. What secrets enabled them to do this? In every instance it has been *the walking of pathways* that led to so remarkable an inner peace that I felt compelled to learn their secrets for myself. The answers are unexpected, surprising, electrifying, awesome, and fascinating. One of the most intriguing discoveries readers will make here is how far ahead of their time the ancient Indians were in employing techniques and having insights and understandings that are only now being recognized as valuable in the modern world: the use of holistic healing, acupressure, imaging, becoming, creative and productive time-use concepts, consciousness-expansion, and the use of crystals.

In this respect, corporations, faced with increased competition and sluggish production growth, have turned to the New Age movement for employee motivation, but they are missing something perhaps even more valuable that is native and has been underfoot and present all of the time — an untapped resource of inestimable value. Group cohesion and positive thinking are the foundations of ancient American life. The realization of end-state visions, management of internal resources, and organizational alignment are natural components of Native American orientation. These things can be learned fairly rapidly. Also, in the Native American way, action control is every bit as important as mind control. People are happy to do what they do because the proof of its worth is found in the doing.

"In these spellbinding interims, he would relate to me secret things . . ."

Over the long months we labored to put together Fools Crow's story (which was published in 1977 by Doubleday under his name), Fools Crow often instructed me to turn off the tape recorder and not make notes while we continued talking. In those spellbinding interims, he would relate to me secret things — some of which I am revealing here — and along with those revelations, I was allowed to observe many of the secret things he did.

Those who have been in Fools Crow's presence have commonly described it as a religious experience. He is a renowned healer and is one of the few among his people who is properly called a "holy man," for Wakan Tanka has used him to dispense blessings that go far beyond healing. He is a seer and a transcendentalist. His mind, heart, and soul are in communion with the highest heaven and with the spirits Wakan Tanka has begotten and appointed to serve him. Yet Fools Crow's exalted position among traditional Lakota people comes from his remaining on their ordinary plane. While one arm and hand have reached constantly up toward the abode of the Creator, the other arm and hand have just as constantly reached out to his fellow people and all other created things. By intense and constant purification, he has become a gleaming tube through which Wakan Tanka has been pleased to work mightily for the well-being of all creation.

What cannot be missed about Fools Crow is that since the moment when Wakan Tanka first called him to service as a youth, he has been an advocate of peace among men, and he himself has been a stronghold of inner peace. Not once in his life has he felt the need to resort to drugs, liquor, strong words, threats, or violence. Being near him is like being near an energy source whose calming heat and light come reaching out in successive waves to make you its willing captive.

It is not surprising that over the decades from 1929 until now a steady stream of Indians and non-Indians has made pilgrimages to Fools Crow's humble home on the windswept South Dakota prairie and has come away touched by a power that has influenced them for life. Some have gone only to see him and to feel the force. Others, feeling lost, have gone to learn what they must do to find their way. Hundreds have gone to be healed — and they always were, either spiritually or physically. Of course, most of his healing practice lies in the past, for, having achieved a life span more than double that expected by the average resident of the Pine Ridge and Rosebud reservations today, Fools Crow is ninety-seven and in the metaphysical process of moving on. His power has slowly shifted into a neutral state and only enough of it remains to warm him and those who are truly close to him. When the time comes that he does enter his departing sleep — for that fleeting moment before he will be awakened by the hand of Wakan Tanka and told to rise — those present may not be surprised if his body undergoes some unusual transformation and there is some divine sound, for that seems inevitable.

Did I really see the colored smoke, the fire, the animals and birds and all the rest, or was it an illusion born out of desire? That afternoon, I asked Fools Crow about it.

He said, "Wakan Tanka gives me the power to make any person who believes in Wakan Tanka, The Highest and Most Holy One, see what I see happening to me."

"He was talking about thought transference . . . during my subsequent visits with him, I would see him do it on several occasions . . ."

He was talking about thought transference and mental projection. This was especially interesting for me, since it was not an aspect of belief I had paid much attention to. However during my subsequent visits with him, I would see him do it on several occasions, and in some of them, he would reverse the process by transferring to himself the thoughts and pictures of what was happening to others.

Oh yes! I should tell you that while Fools Crow came to his praying place empty-handed that day, on the way back to his house he handed me four of the black eagle feathers he had grasped. Once at the house, I gave them to Kate, his wife, to put away. This is another aspect of Fools Crow's power — something material always manifests itself in connection with the mental process.

The day after the wondrous event just described, Fools Crow and I sat side by side in a small clearing in a wooded place near his two-room plywood home, and I asked him what Wakan Tanka had given him that made his power so effective and had brought such remarkable serenity and endurance to his life.

Without hesitation he answered, "Inner peace." Coming from a man whose people had for more than a century suffered profoundly under confining reservation rules, this answer seemed wholly out of place. How, I wonder, could inner peace exist among a people with a reputation for savage warfare? How could inner peace exist among a people deprived of dignity, hope, and the opportunity to contribute to our society and achieve in it?

He saw my puzzled expression and knew what I was thinking. Folding his hands, he brought them up to his mouth and stared at the ground for a long time. Then he commenced a low chant. "Ah e, Ah e," he sang, following it with Lakota sounds as old as the earth. Four times he sang, then he pointed a wrinkled finger at the sky.

"Anyone who follows these same pathways can have the same inner peace and love I have, as well as the powers that come with them."

"The wise old ones among my people," he said, "were taught in the beginning that inner peace and love are the greatest of Wakan Tanka's gifts. No matter what else has gone on, the tribal elders have lived by this teaching and have not let the rest of the people forget it. We know there can be no lasting or worthwhile happiness without inner peace and love. With these we walk in a warm relationship with Wakan Tanka, and we put the well-being of other people and of all of nature first. We cling to this like a person clings to a raft on a roaring river. We know no fear, and our inner selves are serene. That is what I was taught, and it is what I have lived by. I have never hurt or hated another person, and I have never needed excitement or liquor to make life worthwhile. Whatever I had was always enough, and whatever happened, I never felt that Wakan Tanka treated me unjustly. I have followed the pathways of inner peace and love, and I have found that the flowers and trees that line these ways and the sun, moon, and seasons above and around them are my teachers. The spirits in the four directions are my main helpers — that is why the colored smoke comes to me and passes through me — and the spirits of the creatures who dwell along the pathways are my other helpers. Anyone who follows these same pathways can have the same *inner peace and love I have, as well as the powers that come with them."*

As I savored Fools Crow's words and promise, I observed how divinely quiet it was in that remote part of Pine Ridge . . . there was no automobile traffic, no airplane rumbling overhead, no madding crowd. A distant cowbell tinkled, and a bird or two chirped, but that was all I heard. For a fleeting instant I caught the sweet smell of new-mown hay carried to me in a small basket of wind from a neighbor's farm.

I was warm and I felt very good. I took a deep breath, folded my hands behind my head for a pillow, lay back on the grass, and began to compare what I had just heard with the dominant thoughts of the non-Indian world . . . ideas which are quite popular in our culture encourage us to "look out for Number One" and to ignore the past, to live as if one's own heritage didn't matter.

But if looking out for one's self is so worthwhile, why is it that the world is so lacking in both inner and outer peace? So many people are detached from their moorings, desperate for love, empty and lonely and still searching for "beauty" and meaning in life.

"I know that ancient and present-day Native Americans can help a modern world redirect and even resurrect its life."

The serene old Sioux Indian sitting next to me that day had the answer, for he had come through many a maelstrom, yet he had none of these problems. Perhaps he can teach us something. I know that ancient and present-day Native Americans can help a modern world redirect and even resurrect its life.

I feel that mechanization and computerization are making America more humanly empty. Much of this diminishment comes from a neglect of the study of history.

I am told that humanities professors in our colleges and universities are compelled by short classes to skim or skip entire segments of history. We need to correct this situation so that balance is maintained in the educational process. In the meantime, we should not let the situation keep us from becoming true students and determining for ourselves what the originals, including Native Americans, had to say and how valuable these teachings are.

The ramifications of this neglect of history have become so serious that the French and English governments are presently legislating the restoration of the study of history to a central place in all state-supported schools. All problems have historical roots, usually deep ones. In fact everything has historical roots. The noted archaeologist Sir Flinders Petrie sagely remarked that most people live only on the one-dimensional plane of the present, while the historian lives on several planes at once and, in so doing, adds to his understandings the dimension of time.

The Native American view is that we do not appear suddenly out of nowhere. To demonstrate this, they use the idea of the whole of life lived in a circle or hoop. Later, I relate Fools Crow's explanation of exactly how this works. In essence, the circle helps us understand that the past has, like a loving mother and father, delivered us to the present, and it is in our blood, *the vibrant core of our makeup*. The Native Americans believe we should be knowledgeable about this. For likewise, we who have inherited from others are each day mothers and fathers who are passing on our inheritance — further developed and shaped through us — to future generations. We achieve much of our self-worth as persons by the devotedness and concern with which we do this. Living "just for me" can become an easy way out of responsibility, but all such an attitude really does to those who hold it is to leave them companionless and to their own devices. The Native American way makes no such mistake.

Both Fools Crow and I would argue that, where longevity is concerned, the past and the future give the present its most worthwhile meaning and enable us to articulate for ourselves and others the inner peace we cherish and know we need. The Native Americans say that if we are wise, our petitions and our peace will be rooted in the past, nourished and improved in the present, and aimed at the future.

I fully agree with the premise that worrying about the future won't help, but planning for it and bearing a responsibility for it certainly do. What the Native Americans offer is not just for today. It continues. Their peace abides, and theirs are not short-term solutions, for the solutions have already proven themselves over the centuries.

During the months I prepared *Secret Native American Pathways*, I asked more than five hundred non-Indian adults the same question: "If I could at this moment offer you a choice between lasting inner peace and $50,000 a year for the rest of your life, which would you choose?" Without hesitation the firm reply was always, "Inner peace. If you don't have that, what do you have? Nothing else can take its place."

"Anyone who follows these same pathways can have the same inner peace and love I have, as well as the powers that come with them."

". . . you can have that inner peace by simply reading this book and following its instructions."

If your answer is the same, you can have that inner peace by simply reading this book and following its instructions.

What I write about in *Secret Native American Pathways* has much to do with the difference between concern with *outer space* and *inner space*. In our present time, the emphasis is heavily upon the former . . . but with a predictable result . . . human beings and human needs are relegated to second or third place. The ancient Native Americans emphasized *inner space* — first and foremost providing for the inner person. They believed that as long as concern for human needs held first place, all else essential to a full and expectant life would follow. Their emphasis was also upon the group rather than the individual. Each person worked for the welfare of the whole, and in turn the whole worked for the welfare of the individual. No one stood alone in petition or endeavor. "Is it not better," they would say, "for one hundred to pray for one that for one to pray alone for himself?" When inner peace prevails within individuals, there is also a special peace between those who have it. Inner peace is a remover of barriers and a maker of bonds.

Traced in these pages are the tranquil, although for us sometimes unorthodox, pathways some Native Americans followed to find what was essential to overcome their problems and to fulfill their deepest needs and desires. Long, long ago, and countless centuries before Christianity reached North America, the *Above Beings* carved out these pathways for the Indians to follow, yet it is evident they were put here for everyone's use. You may for the moment doubt this and wonder whether ancient routes laid down for unsophisticated and superstitious peoples can actually serve those of us who live in a more enlightened and modern world. They surely do, and in my concluding section I show you how you can follow them and achieve the same triumphs and inner peace.

Would you like:

To be happy?

To be creative?

To redefine your worth and plot new direction for yourself?

To feel understood and be part of a group that accepts you warmly?

To be possessed by a love that no one can take away from you?

To be more beautiful physically and spiritually?

To be constantly aware of and in harmony with the splendid natural world in which we live?

To give to others the most priceless gift there is?

To make loneliness a friend instead of an enemy?

To be ready for whatever comes and to meet any challenge?

To overcome any adversity?

To always bounce back from seeming defeat?

To conquer any guilt, fear, or anxiety?

To avoid burnouts and overloads?

To know how to cooperate effectively with others?

To be free of the desire for constant excitement, drugs, or other stimulants?

To be satisfied with needs instead of wants?

To sleep like a contented child?

To sail serenely along in our hectic, complex, and increasingly impersonal computerized world?

To be positive, secure, and strong in any circumstance?

To have unshakable personal worth, self-esteem, assurance, and dignity?

To expand your mind and your psychic powers?

To pray effectively?

To give thanks effectively?

To know the source of prophetic powers?

To know the source of physical and spiritual healing for yourself and others?

To put aside all fear of death?

"... all of these ... can be yours ... in a surprising and delightful way."

Any or all of these powers and more can be yours, and in a surprising and delightful way. Moreover, in achieving them you will also gain a *remarkable inner peace* — the most precious, durable, and sustaining jewel a person can possess. With it, whatever else you lack ceases to matter. Without it, whatever else you have will not sustain you. Eventually, most people come to know this truth, for all experience teaches it. Experience also teaches that we have no second chance in life — happiness should not be squandered, neglected, or put off.

~ ~ ~

An aura of mystery shrouds the ancient Native American world, and in approaching it, non-Indians are confronted by life-ways that seem so different from our own that they appear walled off and beyond our reach. The seemingly primitive aspects — brilliant and sometimes frightening costumes, determined dancing, pounding drums, hissing like dry-grass rattles, pungent incense, and primordial chants — tend to mesmerize us and leave us spellbound, but distant. Nevertheless, I promise you that this is a world we can touch and take into ourselves, making its essence, or spirit, our own. The point, however, is not to copy the ritual life of the Native Americans. Those who do not have Indian blood should not seek to become Indians, because they cannot. You will enter that world of mystery in the pages of this book, and you will find within it and claim for yourself love, breathtaking truths, extraordinary beauty, tranquility, hope, boldness, and sensitivity. As *you* walk the ancient pathways, you will come upon wondrous sources for coping and survival in any circumstance, and you will encounter wellsprings whose sweet nourishment will recharge and strengthen you whenever you need it.

When you employ these things, an accumulation of relief will come, and sometime before the ends of the different pathways are reached, you will find yourself infused with a new and potent peace that is at the same time a fabulous power. I caution, however, that reading about the pathways will not be enough. You must walk them, pick up what you find along the way, and make it your own. What is set forth here are only ways of beginning. Understanding how and why they work and discovering the proof of their potency will come as you practice what you learn in the challenging arena of daily life . . . at home, on the freeways, at work, at worship, and at play. Best of all, you will enjoy doing so, for while the ways are old, they possess constant challenges and a wondrous freshness that will keep you excited and filled with hope. Your family, friends, and fellow workers will notice the difference in you and will enjoy it with you. Native American pathways are contagious. A sense of accomplishment will attend your every step and continue to beckon you onward to the top of a peaceful and shining mountain.

"They followed fixed courses to specific goals."

Actually, the pathways walked by the Native Americans were and are of two kinds: *central* and *peripheral*. The central pathways were annually celebrated national ceremonies, and it is fair to wonder how a non-Indian can follow and make use of Indian ceremonies. The answer comes with recognizing that each of the ceremonies was made up of individual parts and ideas that equipped the participants to think through and meet particular challenges. In this regard, I cannot stress enough that the essence of an Indian ceremony lies in its parts. In evaluating ceremonies, non-Indians have often made the serious mistake of looking only at what a ceremony accomplishes when in fact is *the parts and their sum* that give the ceremony its value. Also, in those instances where a yearly cycle of several ceremonies was strictly followed, the sum of the rituals prepared the nation as a whole to face the challenges of life that were certain to come. The *peripheral* pathways were those walked by individuals, both holy persons and others, in their personal relationships with the Above Beings. Notice in particular that in neither of the pathways did the Native Americans wander aimlessly; *they followed fixed courses to specific goals.*

A warning is in order here . . . the pathways were not designed for people who yearn for what they believe were the simple days when life was less complicated than it is today. This is a sad misjudgment of the Indian. His daily life was simple compared to ours, but the simplicity ends there. Ceremonial practices were astonishingly involved, and anthropologists and ethnologists have written endless books about them without beginning to plumb the depths.

Not all of the Native American pathways are described herein, but there are enough to enable you to do the job at hand. Also, there are intriguing and sensual aspects of Pueblo religion that I do not cover here because of their sexual emphasis. Prudishness has nothing to do with this, for these are sensible and healthy customs when properly understood, and they have to do with proper application and understanding of procreation and renewal. The problem is that although the subject can be effectively treated in personal discussions, when it is only written about or witnessed without knowledge of its justification and sensibility, it can easily be misunderstood.

~ ~ ~

This book is divided into three parts, beginning with Chapter 2. In part one, I begin with a brief summary of each tribe's history so that readers will know something of the people we are talking about, can compare their own problems to those of the Native Americans, and will realize that if the Native Americans were able to overcome such difficulties, the chances are very good that we can, by employing the same means, overcome our own.

In stating this, please accept that I do not consider the Native Americans devoid of faults common to all peoples. I know their shortcomings as well as most ethnologists. But when there are much greater things to be learned from them, little is gained by dwelling upon the negative aspects of their lives.

"The Native American approach offers a way to take immediate action in any circumstance."

The Native Americans were taught to deal first with their individual problems and to recognize that once these barriers to inner peace were removed, inner peace would come to them in abundance and remain with them. The idea parallels that of Philippians 4:7, 8 (RSV), where we learn the result of thinking on certain things: *whatever is true, whatever is honorable, whatever is just, whatever is pure, whatever is lovely, whatever is gracious, if there is any excellence, if there is anything worthy of praise, think about these things. What you have learned and received and heard and seen in me, do, . . . and the God of peace will be with you . . .* By following similar pathways, native Americans did not suffer the agonies of those who, having convinced themselves they have attained through some esoteric exercise a state of mental peace, sometimes fail to measure up to challenges and are overwhelmed by guilt and shame. The Native American approach offers a way to take *immediate action in any circumstance*, although there are times when inaction may be the action that is best, for a well-planned retreat can often win a war. Their solution has been to prepare in advance, and boasting of nothing, when a problem arises, tackle it immediately. Being thus occupied, one remains positive and confident, and has little time for fear, regret, or remorse. He or she stands on solid ground, confronts the problem head-on in the open, and overcomes it. The Indians learned that action comes before motivation, that it is usually after we get involved in a task that we become keenly motivated. When we don't like doing something, we tend to put it off — and if we wait until we are in the mood, we may wait forever.

For these contests, the ancient Native Americans employed some very effective spiritual weapons. For instance, they were convinced that Above Beings created us and continue through lesser powers to create, sustain, and watch over us. They were also convinced that while the Beings are infinitely superior to mankind and the rest of creation, they desire a warm and enduring relationship with all they have created, and most importantly, they do not withhold themselves from anyone who sincerely wants them and knows they need them. In the beginning of time when each of these peoples first appeared on the surface of the earth, the Above Beings provided them by various means with instructions as to how they should worship and live to survive and to continue the relationship. Eventually, these instructions became the basis, or pathways, for the tribal myths and legends replete with fascinating insights and mesmerizing guidance for ritual performance.

In most instances, the Above Beings worshiped by the Indians consisted of a Supreme God who was head of a triune Godhead like that of Christianity, and served by lesser deities, not properly called gods, whom the Godhead created and had ultimate authority over. I do not give credence to the Native American religious view because of this, for they stand very nicely on their own.

My personal and literary research substantiates my belief that most Native American tribes worship the same God as Christians do, and many of the Native Americans resoundingly claim this is so. The only difference is that while Christians learn of God through the Bible, the Indians learn of him through nature and legends. When we get down to the core of their religious views, we find that their traditional ways of worship and their religious practices are not so different from ours as is commonly supposed.

The tribes did, of course, have their personal names for God, and I make occasional reference to those names herein. However, to simplify things I have chosen to refer to the Godhead as the Above Beings, and I use this title throughout the book.

"Secret Native American Pathways is not intended to be a religion, and certainly not to be a replacement for yours . . ."

Secret Native American Pathways is not intended to be a religion, and certainly not to be a replacement for yours if you already have one. It will, however, provide an excellent complement to your religious thoughts and practices. They were and are in most respects a beautiful people whose lives were in nowise dominated by warfare and savage acts. The life-ways described here will prove this, and we should be thankful for what they can teach us. I will admit, however, that there is some small reward in recognizing that Native Americans were and are finite and fully human. It lets us know that we too, as finite beings, can ascend to the same inner peace they attained.

In Part Three, I describe the major pathways the Indians followed to reach inner peace and reveal some of their intriguing thoughts and practices regarding these. It is important to recognize while reading this part that the Native American method is virtually the opposite of that of Zen and other similar systems which teach that you must first achieve a state of mind in which inner peace prevails and then employ this state to order and control your life.

Another important weapon in the Native Americans' spiritual arsenal was the knowledge that the whole of creation, animate and seemingly inanimate, is *alive*, and is interrelated for mutual sustenance like the strands in a spider web, with each strand able and expected to make its individual, unique, and vital contribution to the whole. Furthermore, each part must respect the others, must be concerned for their welfare and reproduction, and must not willfully hurt them.

Foremost, they were convinced that as they sought inner peace they did not find it — *it found them!* Therefore, they did not make inner peace a *goal*, for as they walked along the various pathways, making and claiming one new discovery after another, inner peace *materialized* at a time they least expected it. Manifesting itself suddenly, an engulfing wave washed over them. One moment they did not have it, and the next moment an enlightening, warm, loving, and powerful peace that became the most welcome guest they ever knew *had them*.

In Part Three, I show in detail how anyone can walk the ancient pathways, make the same discoveries, and choose which of these to employ for different problems and to achieve the results they need. *Please resist the temptation to skip ahead to this part.* Meet the Native American people first, get to know them, and learn something of how they think. Notice how all of their religious acts are carried out with grace and beauty and that their thoughts are noble, exalted and majestic. Understand their motivations . . . for only then will Part Three be plausible, workable, and meaningful for you.

Please do not let the seeming foolishness of some of the Native American ways hold you back. Most of us know that it is often delightful and productive to explore, test, and be different . . . to now and then experiment and do "foolish" things . . . especially when, although they can be shared and developed with others, we can also do them privately. Remember always that such foolishness has worked wonders for the Native Americans for thousands of years, and know that when it works for you, it will have been well worth doing. *The proof for you lies in the results!* Sometimes the Above Beings show us their capricious nature by asking us to do outlandish things, testing our willingness to entrust ourselves to them.

Expect strange and wonderful things to happen to you as you walk the ancient pathways, for you are about to have experiences that will raise you up to new plateaus of expanded life. It is an amazing voyage. We start slowly and the pace is moderate as we move through history and into the material *about* the pathways. We need some basics, a foundation to build on. *But then you will begin to become a part of it,* and that is when the excitement enters in. Believe, and you can do it! Most of the things you will find along the pathways are straightforward in their application. Others are more mysterious and daring. Yet even these become understandable and workable as you begin to take unto yourself the spiritual Native American's mind. The modern intellect does not encourage us to think of such inanimate things as rocks as having life — yet consider what is happening today with people who use crystals, and ponder the experiences, insights, and rewards people cheat themselves out of by being hesitant and doubting. Leave caution behind now. Soon you will read about more of the perceptive and mysterious things revealed by Fools Crow and by my Cherokee friend Archie Sam, and you will realize that with the power received from the Above Beings you can accomplish most of these wondrous things for yourself.

"Archie Sam talks about bringing back the dead so we can visit with them and discuss our problems."

Archie Sam talks about bringing back the dead so we can visit with them and discuss our problems. You too can do this, and you'll laugh when I show you how simple it is. Learn how to treat rocks as though they are alive, and see what happens to you when you do. Learn to wear exotic masks — but not to hide anything. Wear them to enhance your imagining, your becoming, and your control over your life. When you fashion your own prayer sticks, or pahos, and place them as directed, notice how that focus enables you to handle them. Believe as the Hopi Indians do, that Sun will come by as he travels to pick up the spirits of the pahos and carry them away to the Beings who will answer your prayers, and see how that simple belief in itself will transform you into a more positive person. Think of yourself as being part of nature and see what that does to you. Whether nature itself is actually conscious of this relationship is not the point, although nature is programmed to do naturally what we human beings must rationalize ourselves into doing. By thinking this way, you will become gentler with nature and more considerate of it. You will want to conserve it for yourself and for future generations. You will become partners, and you will work together for the well-being of all, yourself included.

"You will be given eyes to see things you never saw before, and never thought you could."

A relationship like this with nature played a giant part in the maintenance of inner peace for the Native Americans, and when they added to it a lifestyle that provided adequate exercise, it produced active life spans that, in early times, frequently exceeded those of the whites. Prehistoric Native Americans did not become toil-worn and disease-marked in middle age. They were not old at forty, and they aged gracefully, seldom knowing what senility was, for it seldom occurred. Nor, except for the perils of war and the epidemic diseases brought in by outsiders, did they, as most of the outside world was doing at the time, live constantly in the midst of death.

Remember that it is not the tangible, but your state of mind that matters here . . . not so much what you do as how the doing of it sharpens your mental process, expands your capabilities, and elevates you. Blessed are those who believe without seeing. What you believe changes you, for in measuring up to your beliefs you become what you want to be, and, because of your efforts and your unwavering faith, you reap endless benefits. You will have a new sense of direction, of purpose, of inventiveness, of creativeness, of accomplishment, and then victory after victory! Before long, your touch will be more sensitive and your taste more sublime. You will be given eyes to see things you never saw before, and never thought you could. You will hear rich new sounds coming from objects and places heretofore invisible and silent. Native American pathways enable us to break the skepticism barrier, take action, and slip into the flow of inner peace. Expect good and extraordinary things to happen to you as you walk and make use of the Native American pathways, and they will!

There are, however, final questions you surely will ask: Do the pathways always work perfectly? Should you expect that you will triumph gloriously in every instance of battle against stress in your life?

Both Fools Crow and I will tell you that, while we are the Above Beings' instruments and can accomplish extraordinary things, we are not gods. Therefore, the Native American pathways will not make you independent of being *dependent* upon the Above Beings, and they will not enable you to sail blissfully through everything. What they will enable you to do is have inner peace, survive everything, and prosper.

Heed also the cautions of physicians and psychologists when they tell you that some parapsychology practices can be damaging if misapplied. People who are emotionally unstable should not attempt to solve their problems by using the mind expansion and certain of the more powerful pathways described in Parts Two and Three of this book — although many of the less powerful pathways will prove very helpful in emotional situations. In addition, never forget that the healing material is, in life-threatening situations, intended to augment and not replace professional medical treatment. Guard especially against shutting down pain that signals a serious problem in the body.

"It is a peace that . . . is filled with power and action."

You must understand that the inner peace the Above Beings will give you as you follow the pathways in this book is absolutely unique. It is a peace that passes understanding, and not the kind of peace the world thinks in terms of. It is not passive, it is filled with power and action. In its essence, it is a totally secure relationship with the Above Beings that frees you from all fear, so that — fearing nothing — neither life nor death, nor things past nor present, nor things to come, where personal relationships, healing, creativity, and achievement are concerned, you will act decisively, bravely, and boldly. When opportunity comes, you will seize it and make the most of it. With this peace, you will be tranquil within, not sedentary — a doer and a contributor to a worthwhile, hope-filled, and joyful life for yourself and for others.

PART ONE

Tribal Histories

CHAPTER TWO

Gentle Pueblo

The Ancient Ones

Archaeological discoveries have enabled us to trace the ancestors of the Pueblo Indians as far back as the year 100 B.C., and scholars have given these ancient forebearers the title *Anasazi*, "the Ancient Ones." They were cave dwellers who lived in the present-day states of Arizona, New Mexico, Utah, and Colorado. Theirs was an enviable life — untroubled, simple and tranquil. When they foraged for food during the clement months, they left the caves, and as they wandered, build crude and temporary brush dwellings that offered little more than shelter for the night and shade for the day. They were basket makers, and they used atlatls, boomerang-like rabbit-throwing sticks, clubs, snares, and nets for hunting and defense. For the most part, they kept to themselves, lived quietly, preferred peace, and did not make war on neighboring peoples. Work was done with stone and wooden tools, and it was shared by the sexes — women handled the domestic chores, and men served as hunters and defenders. House construction was a joint effort. Clothing was simple. Musical instruments consisted of drums, flutes, and rattles. Only a few of their religious items and some pictographic rock art have been found, but there is enough of this to reveal the beginning of what became an ongoing spiritual and ceremonial development that would reach its highest point centuries later, just prior to historic times.

The nature of this religious material tells us that the primary foes of the earliest Anasazi were a harsh environment and the caprices of

nature. Since fear of the unknown is the natural child of such antago-
nists, it was inevitable that from the very beginning they would turn to
the Above Beings for guidance and protection. In this relationship, the
Anasazi founded their lives upon what they were taught. The Above
Beings and their teaching stories soon became the touchstones for survival and understanding, and all aspects of existence were rooted in
them.

About 500 A.D., southern neighbors brought corn to the Anasazi,
and they quickly became a farming culture with permanent villages
made up of recessed pithouses. For the performance of ritual, subterranean kivas — both clan-sized and community-sized — were dug in
the ground. In the Anasazi mind, to enter one of these was to enter the
womb of Earth Mother, who was the giver of life and renewal. Rock art
of the time indicates that ritual and ritual costumes became more fixed
and elaborate. Katcinas, of whom more is said later, participated in the
rituals. Jewelry and costumes were more sophisticated. The bow and
arrow appeared in Anasazi country around 600 A.D., and the hunting
task became easier.

The Ancient Ones had few concerns about linear time and thought
in terms of seasons. They moved slowly and adapted or adopted traits
with seeming detachment. But as their population grew, geographic
expansion became unavoidable. Over a period of many years, the
people grouped themselves into six regions within the area where they
already resided. The best known of these today are Chaco Canyon in
northwestern New Mexico, Kayenta in northeastern Arizona, and Mesa
Verde in Colorado. Here they built complex and ingenious stone communal structures and huge kivas. They achieved a highly developed
ceremonial life and farmed using irrigation.

Eleven happy and undisturbed centuries passed. Then, the picture
changed considerably as something happened to set in motion an
altered and intensified contest for survival. Sometime before A.D. 1200,
the Anasazi relocated in nearly inaccessible coves and caves that
nature had carved into the almost sheer cliff faces of their regions. Here
they constructed magnificent dwellings of stone and timber that could
serve as fortifications against the roaming, fierce, and aggressive new
tribes such as Apache, Navajo, and Ute. Life became doubly hard for
the Anasazi. Not only must they be constantly on the alert, they had to
climb up and down the cliff faces to hunt, obtain adequate water, and
tend their fields — all of which were only available on the mesa tops
above and in the valleys below. In winter, the caves were cold and
dank, and huge amounts of firewood had to be hauled in. The old and
infirm could not climb. The very young had to learn not to play too

close to the harrowing cliff edges. The few remaining mesa-top villages were consolidated into walled towns. Understandably, archaeologists who later examined the ruins of these dwellings changed the name of their residents from Anasazi to Pueblo or town builders.

Battered by these new stresses, the people intensified their religious life. Cliff dwellings often had dozens of kivas in their plazas, and some cliff structures were built solely for religious purposes. Material culture kept pace, and splendid pottery and woven garments came into being. Nevertheless, the people moved again — even the great citadels of Mesa Verde were completely abandoned by A.D. 1300 — migrating south into Arizona and New Mexico, joining their relatives who already lived there and leaving behind thousands of impressive ruins. New consolidations took place along Arizona's Little Colorado River, which became Hopi land, and in New Mexico at Zuni, Acoma, Laguna, and along the Rio Grande River.

The Hopi Story

We can center ourselves in the Hopi story, for their lives are representative of Pueblos in general. Where spiritual matters are concerned, until recently they have been the most open to anthropologists and ethnologists. Sometime around A.D. 1100, their rock and adobe villages existed in places in present-day Arizona called Awatovi, Kawaika-a and Sikyatki. Excavations there showed that all life centered itself in ritual, and it appears that, despite the harsh aspects of the land, the people were relatively happy again.

Pueblo cliff dwelling

But the happiness did not last, and the ability of the Hopi to survive was to be tested again and again. From 1276 to 1299, drought plagued the area, and prosperity gave way to grim efforts for survival. Spanish explorers made their first appearances in the Southwest in the early 1500s, committing inexcusable atrocities at the pueblo of Acoma and among the Eastern Pueblo towns. But they found Hopi country to be inhospitable and unredeeming. For the most part, the Spanish left the people alone. Nevertheless, the psychological effect of their appearance in Hopi land, coupled with word of what they did to the eastern cousins, was profound, and the introduction of Spanish missions after 1629 began a far-reaching modification of Hopi life. The Eastern Pueblo revolt of 1680 brought a temporary end to Spanish rule, but the fearful Hopi nevertheless abandoned their lowland locations and moved to the more defensible mesa tops, where Hopi villages are still found today. While the dwelling structures they erected there were impressive, existence was at its bleakest. Nothing could be grown on the arid mesas; men had to climb up and down and travel long distances on foot to tend their corn and bean crops, and women had to make difficult, daily trips to haul huge loads of water and firewood. Time-consuming hikes had to be made to the mountains for structural timbers. Epidemic diseases brought in by outsiders periodically reduced the Hopi population, with the smallpox invasion of 1813 being particularly severe. Navajo, Apache, and Ute pressures restricted any attempts at geographic expansion to more hospitable sites.

Smallpox Devastates Population

When Mexico gained its independence in 1821, Spanish rule ended for the Hopi. But the Mexicans gave no aid to them, and nothing was done about the Anglo-American mountain men who began to move into the area, occasionally raiding Hopi gardens for food — and killing Hopi men who dared to object. The United States terminated Mexican sovereignty in 1848, and shortly thereafter, American forces subdued the warlike Navajo and ended that threat for the Hopi. But smallpox returned with white traders, and in 1854 and 1865 bludgeoned the Hopi with devastating blows. More droughts added to the damage.

Christians Attempt to Convert Hopi

The Mormon missionaries arrived in 1858, and missionaries of other denominations followed, all doing their best to shame or coerce the Hopi into conversion to Christianity. For example, the Hopi believed, as other Indians did, that the hair of the head was part of the soul and that its length and continuing growth exhibited the spirituality of the bearer. Stories are told about some missionaries who, ostensibly for hygienic reasons but more truly to break the Hopi spirit, used barbed wire to tie the hands of Hopi children behind their backs so they couldn't resist while their hair was cut short. It is not hard to imagine what else went on.

The first United States agent came to Hopi land in 1869, and in 1882 established a 3,863-square-mile reservation that included the three mesa-top villages. The total Hopi population for the year 1891 was 1,994. Obviously it had been greatly reduced by drought and disease.

The first American tourists to visit the Hopi villages after 1882 were surprised and delighted to find that life there was about the same as when the Coronado expedition first found it in 1540. In fact, half of the twentieth century would pass before distinct white influences could be seen in Hopi country. Even today customs and architecture that existed at the turn of the century are present to a remarkable degree. The population has continued to grow; in 1948 there were 4,407 Hopi.

Life Was a Cycle

Life for the Hopi was a cycle, and the year was a cycle. For all things in the universe, there was no beginning and there was no end. A Hopi died, only to be born again in an underworld where life went on much as it had on the earth's surface. In this comforting knowledge, the Hopi found a general security and every reason to follow month by month the ancient Way that promised them an always-fulfilling existence. Life was never easy, but that was best, for it kept the people aware that they were dependent upon the Above Beings. Besides, comfort brought pride, pride invited dissension, and dissension assured division. The welfare of the entire village came first, the individual came last, and each village had the

Hopi Katcina

strength of its whole upon which any one Hopi could draw and depend. Prayers and acts were multiplied by the number present, and even those who had died and were reborn into the Underworld had ways of adding their strength and advice to that of the people on earth. Deities watched over every aspect of life, and they provided the Hopi with all they needed to know to obtain their help in proper season. It was and still is a good Way. Not surprisingly, Christian missions made slow progress with the Hopi, and outsiders who went to Hopi country continued to be impressed as they found a people immersed in a spiritual existence that, despite problems and challenges, had continued without serious deviation for two millennia.

There were to be, however, portentous changes in secular life. In 1887, a government school was established at Keams Canyon; attendance was compulsory, and as previously mentioned, hair was cut. Missionaries worked a division among the Hopi regarding this and other aspects of traditional life, and over the years, the secular education pattern of the Hopi children was considerably transformed. Moral questions were always resolved in favor of the missionaries, and severe punishment was dealt out to those who violated the new codes. To keep tradition, the Hopi had no option but to live double lives, behaving in one manner for the whites and secretly continuing the old and preferred ways at home and in the kivas.

Before white contact — and continuing in the religious realm even afterwards — the Hopi began teaching the customs and beliefs of their people to their children at an early age. From the age of a few months, children were taken to see every public ritual that took place in the village. The child grew up with the Katcinas, whose enthralling nature is explained shortly, and the Katcina and life were always inseparable and considered as one.

Hopi history was told in traditions and stories that described life before emergence from the Underworld — the exit having been through the small sipapu hole in the kiva's floor — the long years of wandering before the Hopi settled permanently, and finally the origins of their many religious ceremonies. These revelations were

Ceremonial bear-paw mitten   handed down by word of mouth from one

generation to another by elderly men versed in the lore of the Anasazi-Pueblo. Children were taught until they could repeat each legend with complete accuracy. Some stories told recently have been compared with those recorded by the Spanish in the sixteenth century and are the same, even in the minutest details.

With the advent of government schools and other white influences, the behavior and belief situation of the Hopi did change appreciably, but the most important phase of a child's education still began before the age of ten when boys and girls were initiated into the tribe's Katcina Cult. A few years later, they took the second step, joining one or more of the several secret societies. On reaching adolescence, a boy took his third and climactic step by passing through the Tribal Initiation and being admitted to the Soyal Rite, which

Ceremonial prayer hoe

opened the annual cycle of ceremonial observances. The girls took part in the boy's rite vicariously, and a steady immersion into the religious life infused and circumscribed Hopi existence. Within this same sphere, the major portion of adult education would take place — and an encompassing and magical education it was, full of the unexpected and the mysterious. We could say it was full of the miraculous, except that the Hopi, like other Indians, did not consider the extraordinary acts of the Above Beings in response to ritual to be miracles; the "miracle" would be if the Beings did not do what they promised. Yet this was not an aspect of life the Hopi questioned, for its efficacy lay in the fact that it had always been done in a prescribed way. Through this Way and the blessings it had brought, the people had survived since their Anasazi beginning.

In the traditional Hopi view, nature and gods were of one mind and one purpose. Seven principal deities possessed the basic power that regulated and sustained life. Some dwelt above, some dwelt in the underworld. An all-powerful one named Co-tuk-inung-wa created the earth. Muingwu controlled germination, lived in the Underworld, and was the guardian of life. Gna-tum-si created life. Baho-li-konga was a great serpent that controlled life-blood, vegetal sap, and water. Masau'u controlled death. Omau was the force that controlled clouds and rain. Dewa was the sun or father. Other than the original or chief Katcina Spirits, Katcinas were human spirit intermediaries who carried the humans' messages to the deities and returned as bearers of blessings. The spirits of some nonhuman beings served also as messengers, as did *pahos* (prayer sticks) and other ritual paraphernalia.

Stripped to its essence, the Hopi religious position was that all created things — human and nonhuman, animate and inanimate — had individuality, and each thing had its proper place in relation to all other phenomena, with a definite role in the cosmic scheme. But, whereas the nonhumans fulfilled their obligations more or less automatically under the divine law, humans had specific responsibilities that must be learned and fulfilled in the traditional Way. Much of the child's training was devoted to learning that Way. The Way consisted of the manner of acting, feeling, and thinking in every role that a human being was required to assume in the life cycle from birth to death. The welfare of the tribe and that of the individual, in that order, depended upon the responsible and wholehearted fulfillment of the role. Responsibilities increased with age, and they reached their peak in ceremonial participation, with the heaviest burden being carried by the village chief and the next heaviest by the clan chiefs. The matriarch played her consistently vital role in the all-important matrilineal system. As one might assume, the Way taught young people to respect their elders and to look to them for advice and the solutions to a happy and productive existence. They knew that experience and the lessons of history counted. The Hopi were sensible enough to recognize the values of the present, and they were confident and future-oriented as well. But by nature, they adhered strongly to the principle that famed anthropologist Louis Leakey espoused, "Human salvation comes through humanity's past." In this regard, elders were never retired from active service and remained essential to the fulfillment of everyone's life.

Ceremonies Physical and Psychical

It does not surprise us to find that religious life consumed as much as sixteen days during some months and that, besides the major ceremonies, there were countless individual religious acts to carry out each day. The rules for ritual observance had two aspects, the *physical* and the *psychical*. If either was neglected or any regulation was broken, failure would result. Participants in ceremonies must perform the proper acts and observe the tabus, and they must exercise control over their emotions and hearts, exulting only at those moments when it was traditionally appropriate, as when the snakes were ritually purified in the Snake Ceremony. Consciousness was expanded, and participants felt and learned things beyond the realm of ordinary man, but such control only came to a person through firm devotion and, in some instances, a lifetime of ceremony and prayer.

In the scheme of control, prayer was thought of as a form of willing something into being. Hence, by performing ritual acts that included prayer, the Hopi believed that human beings, in conjunction with the Katcina spirits, could control nature to a limited extent and that if man failed to carry out his responsibility in this wise, the universe itself might cease to function properly. Obviously, the individual Hopi felt personally valuable and important. After all, much of the success in the perpetuation of life depended upon them. So they had individual pride, a sense of place and a feeling of real worth. The movement of the sun, the coming of the rain, crop growth, and reproduction as a whole were all linked to man's correct, complete, and active fulfilling of the rules. If the Hopi wished these things to take place, they must carry out their roles individually and collectively. So, while particular emphasis was placed upon individual freedom, Hopi behavior was checked by fear of nonconformity. A person seldom dared to depart from the convention-al modes of behavior.

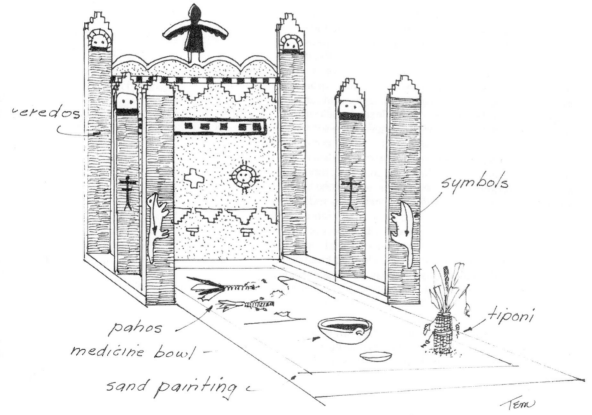

A simplified Pueblo altar made with boards that can be used as a design guide for personal purposes

The Hopi Today

As of today, the Hopi situation continues to be altered by outside pressures, and significant changes have taken place in their secular life. Until the 1940s, elementary day schools were located near the villages but at the foot of the mesas. Children could walk to school and in the afternoon return home to their families. The parents were also able to visit the schools and take part in the educational system. More recently, modern educational facilities and teachers' quarters have been built at points far enough away to require busing. Thus, the bond between home and school no longer exists. Teachers seldom visit the homes, and the consequences have been serious for the Hopi, who seek to center their lives in communal living. Unless there has been a recent change, there is no high school on the Hopi Reservation, and Hopi youth who wish to continue their educations are forced to leave home during this critical period in their lives and live in boarding schools in places like Phoenix, Arizona, and Riverside, California. Other aspects of the secular life of the outside world continue to prey on the Hopi, and constant attempts are made to disillusion the Hopi about their traditional religion. Homes away from the mesa-top structures are modern and comfortable; tribal dress is mostly confined to ceremonial occasions. Such conveniences as pickup trucks have become necessary, and, in some homes, television is thoroughly enjoyed, even though it is divisive in terms of exposing the people to conflicting worlds. The arts flourish, and many Hopi have acquired international reputations as artists and craftspeople. They do superb silverwork, weaving, pottery, and painting. There is a civic and arts center on the reservation, and tribal affairs are conducted there in a businesslike manner. Despite the suffering and hardships they have endured, the Hopi continue.

CHAPTER THREE

Imperial Cherokee

The Cherokee Indians are both the best known and the least known of the Native American tribes. Today their tribal rolls number more than 150,000 members. Beyond this, there is an even greater number of people with small percentages of Cherokee blood living in various parts of North American who are proud enough of their heritage to proclaim it at every opportunity.

A Civilized Tribe

To say they are the best known and the least known may seem a contradiction, but it is true. They are best known because of their amazingly rapid transformation from the ancient culture to white ways between 1700 and 1825, when they became what whites referred to as the first "civilized" tribe. And they are the least known precisely because of this rapid transformation. So quickly and completely was the old religious and material culture modified and then discarded that any evidence of it passed into oblivion. For lack of such evidence, it seems as though the Cherokee suddenly appeared out of nowhere. Once their transformation was complete and their removal from the ancestral lands in the southeast to present-day Oklahoma and northwestern North Carolina was accomplished, interest in them subsided as though nothing in their continuing culture warranted further investigation.

Until recently, searching for information about the prehistoric Cherokee was like approaching a blackboard upon which the entire history of the people had once been written, yet all but the period from 1700 to 1840 had been wiped away, leaving behind only pale traces of the time periods before and after . . . something had been there, but the viewer could only wonder what it was. The ample descriptions of the Cherokee during the years 1700 to 1840 assure us they were originally — and must be today — an extraordinary people whose full history should be made known.

A summary view of their reconstructed history indicates that the Cherokee were once part of the powerful Great Lakes Iroquoian family. Then, at an unknown and distant point in time, some form of discord caused the Cherokee to separate themselves from the other Iroquoians and to migrate slowly southward through what are today known as the states of Ohio, Pennsylvania, and Virginia.

Finally, the more than twenty thousand Cherokee found a suitable new home. They quickly laid claim to a vast wilderness empire, which, in terms of present-day states, included western North Carolina, South Carolina, Virginia, West Virginia, northern Georgia and Alabama, all but the western parts of Tennessee, and those parts of Kentucky that adjoin Tennessee.

Archaeologists are making efforts to determine precisely when the Cherokee first settled in southeastern North America. At the present time, the date appears to be about 1300. The 240-year period from then until the explorer Hernando DeSoto made contact with them in 1540 might best be described as a formative one during which the Cherokee established themselves in their new home and began to shape their civilization.

As time went on, the Cherokee culture came to resemble the more established tribes of the Southeast as they adopted many of the traits common to their Indian neighbors. Along with other practices, they used the pottery techniques of the Catawba Indians and wove Mississippian-style, double-weave basketry. Moreover, it is probable that some of the Indians who were displaced by the Cherokee merged with them, creating an amalgam of cultures.

Cherokee Civilization Flowers

Eventually, the Cherokee flowered into a major nation with a vibrant material and spiritual life. Their society was not on as grand a scale as that of the Mayans and Aztecs, yet it was grand enough to impress anyone, including those white traders who came among them at the beginning of the eighteenth century. These traders found the Cherokee living in four main divisions in the forested country. The fertile-soiled land teemed with wildlife and natural foods, springs and streams. The domain was, in fact, so rich that nearby nations were contesting with the Cherokee for it. These encounters were so fierce and enduring that the region was known as "The Dark and Bloody Ground."

Although widely scattered, Cherokee towns and villages were located close to rivers or creeks where the land was level and fertile. The locations were chosen for crop cultivation, as sources of fish and shellfish, and as places that attracted deer, elk, bear, bison, and fowl. Most importantly, the rivers and creeks were needed for the performance of the purification rituals that were so vital to the Cherokee manner of worship.

Wars Threaten Cherokee Survival

The first real test of the Cherokee's ability to survive stress came in 1740. According to traders' reports, the "hot wars" with other Indians had led to the destruction of several of the finest Cherokee towns, and the borders of Cherokee country were steadily shrinking. This foreboding period caused great introspection among the Cherokee people, and the traders were led to wonder whether any Cherokee town or citizen would long survive. But survive they did, and life went on.

Cherokee life as a whole was continually active, with religious thought and performance dominating other pursuits. An examination of ancient Cherokee life reveals that the people had a dynamic culture, the composition of which was the result of diverse contacts, mergers, and frequent changes. This fact above all gives us our first hint about the Cherokee adaptability that welcomed and made the best use of what change offered. As their story continues, we see this promising factor showing itself again and again.

Cherokee settlements were made up of groups of near relatives that included members of at least four clans. While there were always cultivated fields outside the palisade walls, for security purposes the earliest towns and villages also enclosed a large field. In both the interior and exterior fields, each family in each clan had its own section marked off by ridges of earth, lines of stones, or ownership sticks. Under the direction of the village leader, all men and women cooperated in the working of every section. Men toiled in the fields, hunted, fished, built the houses and civic/religious buildings, made civic decisions, and ran the religious festivals. Male priests trained boys as priests and also as hunters. Men participated in peace councils and trading; men were the defenders of the village. Women ruled the houses, and their many duties included caring for the home; raising children; assisting in planting, cultivating, and harvesting; preparing food for domestic and ritual purposes; carrying water; gathering wood; making and caring for clothing; cooking; making baskets and pottery; and performing in certain ritual dances on festival occasions. Selected women shared in council decisions, and Beloved Women determined what would happen to Indian captives.

White traders described the adult male Cherokee as frank, honest, and in warfare, fierce, cunning, and unforgiving. He was a lover of freedom and jealous of his rights. He adored his wife and children, loved and respected his parents, and in his home, harsh behavior was rare. The women were mild mannered, amiable, modest and industrious. Exceptional beauty was common among the young women. In truth, the women were so attractive and had so many desirable traits that trader after trader found himself anxious to take one for a wife . . . and those early intermarriages were the beginning of something that would ultimately transform the nation and redirect its history.

Cherokee houses were one- or two-room frame structures with mud-daubed walls and gabled roofs. Every town had in its center a circular cone-roofed, fifty-foot-diameter Town Council House that sat on a man-made earth mound and was fronted by an open Sacred Square. Here the old men and head warriors met to discuss civic and religious matters, and they gathered here with all of the men of the town or village for social purposes and diversion. Here too the entire community assembled to feast and dance. This council house was the hub of the settlement. In the center of the house, a Sacred Fire burned continually. The house was furnished with soft couches, which the people either sat or lay on, Roman style. All seats were assigned according to rank, and clans sat together. The great religious ceremonies of the community were always held here.

By 1600, Cherokee government was already highly developed. We can begin to see clearly the true greatness of the Cherokee nation, as well as another facet of their personality that made adaptation to rapid change possible for them. In their enlightened system of government, we find a concern for individual freedom and human rights, a sense of shared responsibility, and an awareness of consequences for acts that mark the best of both democratic and republican control. These qualities opened them up to the adoption of the principles they encountered in the fledgling federal government of the Americans.

The Cherokee Heptagon

At the top of the Cherokee social structure was the national capital, followed by the town, household, and clan. Situated on a high mound in the national capital was the huge, sumptuously furnished Heptagon, a seven-sided building with a cone-shaped roof. It was here that national festivals were celebrated, here that major war parties assembled before going off to war, and from here a measure of control was dispensed to the entire nation. In the center of the Heptagon, the Most Sacred Fire of the nation burned continually. Sacrifices of tobacco and venison were made to the fire, which was kindled anew each year. Directly in front of the Heptagon was a large Sacred Square where ritual dancing and sacred games took place.

Red, White Organizations

Since the Cherokee lived in alternating states of war and peace, they developed a tribal government consisting of the White (Peace) Organization and the Red (War) Organization. The White Organization was made up of officials aged fifty or older, many of whom were priests performing both secular and religious functions. They ranged in authority from the splendidly attired Great High Priest, whose Cherokee name was *Uku*, to the lesser officers needed to carry on the minor functions of state. In addition to administering civil law,

Cherokee high priest and sacred fire

White officials owned the prayers for invoking blessings from the Above Beings, Sun, Moon, and the other protective spirits who, assuming it was the will of the highest powers, could prevent or take away illness, wounds, and even death. Only White officials could remove uncleanness from polluted persons and restore them to normal life. White officials and their belongings were sacred and not like the other citizens.

The Red Organization consisted of a set of officials who corresponded in rank and duties to the White officials, except that their function was exclusively military. The Red Organization was subordinate to the White, since the Great High Priest could make or unmake the war chiefs.

Usually, Red officials acquired their ranks as a result of bravery in battle and were surnamed Raven, Wolf, Fox, or Owl, for these were the foremost symbols of cleverness and bravery. Red officials were honored with victory and scalp dances, and they sat in places of honor in the Town Council Houses. Since war involved killing, and bloodshed was a polluting agent, many of the ritual acts associated with war were designed to deal with and remove the effects of uncleanness. Purification was always required after a battle, and divination with crystals and sacrifice to the Sacred Fire were standard parts of every war expedition.

An assemblage of Beloved Women was present at every war council. These women served as counselors to the male leaders, and, in addition, they regulated the treatment dealt to prisoners of war. Wives of the priests were also women of rank and wore distinguishing dress.

Two Sects

In 1835, those aged Cherokee whose primary sources took them well back into the 1600s said that as far back as their history could be traced the nation had been divided into at least two sects regarding their beliefs about Divine Beings. The first sect was made up of the majority of the people who believed that more than two Beings came down from above and formed the world. They then created Sun and Moon, whom they appointed lords of all lower creation, returned to their own place above, and paid no attention to this world. Sun then completed the work of creation, formed the first man and the first woman, caused the trees and plants to grow and produce fruit, and continued to order, watch over and preserve everything on earth. The smaller sect believed there existed above Three Beings who were always together and always of the same mind. They created all things, were present everywhere, and governed all things. These three sat on three white seats above, and all prayers were directed to them. They had messengers who came to this world and attended to the affairs of men.

The difference between the sects consisted only in the objects of worship, not in outward form of ceremonies. Both sects agreed that in the beginning all creatures and objects were innocent and harmless — that even snakes had no poison, and such weeds as became harmful to health were at first created harmless.

Six National Festivals

In ancient times, the Cherokee nation held an annual series or cycle of six national festivals. Each had its own rituals and order of progression. The festivals were held at the National Capital, where virtually the entire population of the nation assembled in response to a summons sent by the Uku through his seven counselors. On such occasions, generosity and good will were the rule, each home in the National Capital was open, and every hospitality freely given.

The first festival of the cycle was the Great New Moon Feast, which took place on the appearance of the first new moon of autumn. Second came the Cementation and Propitiation Festival. It occurred ten days after the New Moon Feast. The third festival was the Exalting (or Bounding) Bush. Fourth was the Festival of the First New Moon of Spring, celebrated about the time the new grass began to grow. The New Green Corn Feast was fifth; it was held when the young corn first became fit to taste. Sixth was the Ripe (or Mature) Green Corn Feast, following the New Green Corn Feast by some forty or fifty days when the corn was hard and perfect for eating.

Besides these major festivals, numerous minor rites were celebrated in both the National Capital and the different towns and villages. All told, the ceremonies performed by the Cherokee consumed an enormous amount of time, and we are forced to wonder whether there was nearly so much time left for warfare as commonly portrayed in films and literature.

Suppose we return now to the period before 1700 and, knowing the greatness of the civilization as it came to be, see how the Cherokee, having accomplished so much, could have changed as quickly as they did, giving up their great ancient ways and embracing the ways of the whites.

After the meeting with the DeSoto expedition, life for the Cherokee proceeded much as it has been described until 1667, when a British trading and exploratory expedition led by Henry Blatt came to visit the tribe. That was the pivotal year in Cherokee history because it marked a turning point — the beginning of white movement through the area. Other traders from Virginia and South Carolina quickly followed Blatt. By 1690, a trader named Daugherty was residing with the Cherokee and had established a pattern of close fraternization that was to have a profound effect upon Cherokee development. The proud Cherokee felt they had nothing to fear from a few traders who were in Cherokee country, where the Cherokee culture was powerful and mature. They were a grand and glorious people, blessed by the Above Beings, and riding the crest of a wave of influence and prosperity.

Cherokee Adaptability

While the Cherokee had an adaptable nature that usually stood them in good stead, it proved this time to be a flaw. They were most curious about the views, habits, and skills of these newcomers. They thought there might be something here that the Cherokee nation could use. They couldn't read the traders' devious minds and didn't know anything about what was going on in the outside world. The wisest course, they concluded, would be to keep the whites around and make them feel useful and wanted.

Thus, innocently on the Cherokee's part, began their unraveling and the conversion from a profoundly spiritual, warring, hunting, and semi-agricultural nation to a wholly sedentary group of agriculturalists that would follow, to a considerable extent, the white manner of life. Difficult as it may be to comprehend how the Cherokee could give up a rich and satisfying culture, the answer becomes indelibly clear as the next 125 years roll rapidly by.

By 1700, metal weapons and cutting tools were replacing the old stone and bone implements. Not long after that, the use of shell, stone, and feathers for the arts was discontinued. A steady stream of white traders continued to infiltrate the country, and they brought with them white agricultural methods, guns, metal ornaments, trinkets, and whisky. Many of these traders took Cherokee wives and settled down in Cherokee towns. Before long, their mixed-blood descendants were engaging in raising stock and the typical pioneer industries of the white colonial settlers. Within a few decades, these descendants would also become the ruling class in Cherokee society, replacing the old form of White and Red Government. They would exert enormous influence on the transformation of the native culture.

Festival Procedures Change

Certainly, early on in Cherokee/white relationships, the full-blood Cherokee was straining mightily to hold onto traditional life while the white traders sought to end it.

During the early 1700s, the resistance of even the most fervent Cherokee began to buckle, and as inevitably happened in instances of white intrusion into Indian lands, the people let the whites and mixed bloods talk them into altering their festival procedures. For a while after that, national events continued to be celebrated in the Capital, the only exception being those instances of domestic or sectional sickness when families, and occasionally groups of families, were permitted to perform the rites in their own homes or towns. But as white power and the number of mixed bloods continued to increase, the power and appeal of the Capital declined.

The mixed bloods were not insensitive to what was happening, but the mixed-blood youth had a white or partially white parent to convince him that the old ways were heathen and counterproductive. Early in the historic period, these children were persuaded to abandon the ritual life. The full bloods tried to hold on, but even among them — at first individuals and then the towns as a whole — people began to act on their own and according to their personal convictions. Ultimately, most everything the Cherokee did became so modified and mixed up that the old ways came close to losing their effectiveness entirely.

Cherokee Cooperatives Disappear

Gradually and steadily, the Cherokee were surrounded by and forced to become part of a white man's world upon which they were increasingly dependent for food, shelter, and clothing. To the east were the English colonists and what were becoming Americans, to the west were the French, and to the south were the Spanish — all three contending for trade advantages and for every inch of Cherokee land. The old cooperative efforts of the Cherokee became obsolete, and by the end of the eighteenth century, the neighborhood cooperatives were nearly gone. Skins and textiles as mediums of exchange were replaced by white currency. Most produce was handled through white markets, and Cherokee young people began to learn the white man's trades. As white exploitation and control of the natural resources continued, the old Cherokee economic system collapsed. Except for deer, rodents, and birds, the wild game was disappearing. Fishing was subjected to severe restrictions, and even the Cherokee's efforts to raise livestock were hampered by regulations. Forest areas were denuded of trees as lumbering interests bought up and then exploited timber rights. Mining and chemical interests moved in to excavate the ground and to pollute and poison the plants and streams. Finally, waterpower interests came to build dams across the beautiful valleys, and numerous lakes appeared where formerly Cherokee homesteads had stood.

Clan-Tribe/Matriarchal System Changes

Government too was changing; the old system of clan/tribal loyalty was giving way to demands for a republican form of rule, and the people were emerging from the matriarchal system that had been the basis of the society for centuries. Into this flawed political scene stepped the ambassadors of the English and French, whose divergent interests acted to pull the Cherokee even further apart. Both sides encouraged the Cherokee to dispute among themselves for tribal control and, by this ploy, kept the tribe in a constant state of turmoil. Ultimately, the Cherokee sided with the British, and that led to problems with the white colonists who were beginning to lobby and work for an independent country of their own. Cherokee settlements also remained squarely in the way of the relentless incoming tide of white settlers. The inevitable result was a series of wars with the whites that lasted from 1756 to 1794, culminating in the virtual annihilation of the Cherokee settlements. As if this were not bad enough, the outbreak of the American Revolution embroiled the Cherokee in a storm of opposing forces. Because of their existing blood feud with the Americans and their long relationship with the British, the Cherokee joined the latter in what proved to be a fatal war against the revolutionists.

The Cherokee hunting grounds and territory had greatly contracted by now, and the Americans were able to surround and simultaneously attack them from all sides. By 1794, some Cherokee had already fled to the hill country of northern Georgia where, during a period of comparative peace and respite until 1838, they managed to build up a thriving community governed by mixed bloods as a dependency of the United States.

Intermarriage, Mission Schools, Whisky

Further changes were underway in the disposition of the tribe as a whole. The traditional faith of the people had been thoroughly shaken. Cherokee everywhere, especially school students, became prime targets for the persistent efforts of the Moravian, Presbyterian, Baptist, Methodist, and Quaker missionaries who began their work in Cherokee country in 1801. Even then, the results did not come quickly; years would pass before the missionaries could celebrate the first conversion of a Cherokee student.

Religious and domestic assaults, intermarriage, loss of confidence, whisky, the contributions of mixed bloods, and mission schools had a steadily deteriorating effect upon the Cherokee. By 1820, most Cherokee lived in log cabins, and some mixed bloods lived in great homes like those of the wealthiest whites. They were practicing all of the white ways of life, and little serious regard was being paid to what whites described as "heathen rites." An occasional war party went out, but when it returned from a successful expedition, there was no traditional rite of purification and thanksgiving, only boisterous joy and drunkenness. What whites described as "superstitions" remained, but even these were yielding to the influence of the missionaries' "proper religious instruction."

Traditional Cherokees clung to vestiges of their past. The Green Corn Festival was still well attended, and a Great New Moon Feast and other feasts were still held. Priests, whom the whites now called "conjurers," still led these and carried out some of the minor rites and exorcisms. Weather control was practiced, and the people continued to purify themselves by immersion in streams and rivers. All religious acts were, however, steadily modified and diluted; with the passage of time, some of them became unrecognizable.

John Ross and the Mixed Bloods

A republican government, which copied the main characteristics of the U.S. government, was set up in 1827 at a convention in New Echota, Georgia, and John Ross was elected Principal Chief, beginning his long and remarkable career as a Cherokee leader. Although a recalcitrant group of North Carolina full-blood Cherokee steadfastly refused to cooperate fully with white ways and authority, the other and most mixed-blood part of the tribe was rapidly becoming Anglicized. By 1830, the transformation of these Cherokee was nearing completion. Mixed-blood offspring had grown up to be prosperous merchants, traders, planters, slave owners, writers, tribal statesmen, and teachers who lived well and embraced the social mores of the whites. Missionary efforts intensified, and schools and churches were built throughout the nation. Mixed bloods were convinced they had achieved acceptance by the whites, that they had equality, and that they had finally become what the whites wanted them to be. Perhaps they even thought of themselves as white. After all, a goodly number did have more white than Cherokee blood.

Sequoyah

About this time, a brilliant but illiterate Cherokee named Sequoyah astonished Cherokees and whites alike by developing a Cherokee alphabet that put the tribe's language in written form, and in 1828, the first Cherokee newspaper was published. Within months, most of the tribe could read and write in their native language, and the Cherokee became the first Indian tribe in the United States to have a language and a newspaper written in its own alphabet.

Things seemed to be going well for the tribe. Recovery was in sight. But under the surface, the Cherokee situation was a perilous one. Georgia was protesting fiercely the idea of having a tribal government within her borders and was claiming the right to use force if necessary to rid the state of Indians. The Cherokee were seen as a handicap that prevented Georgia from progressing at the rapid rate of other states. As the new white settlers moved in, they joined in the clamor for Indian removal until it became a ringing din.

The Trail of Tears

The mixed bloods learned a lesson so bitter they would never forget it. They had made a fatal miscalculation. They had not thought the whites would do to them what they would do to the full bloods. To whites, though, an Indian was an Indian, and any fraction, however small, of Indian blood was sufficient to make that determination. In spite of the tremendous advances and concessions both the mixed-blood and the full-blood Cherokee had made, the powerful machinery of the American government began to turn, and in 1838, the removal called the "Trail of Tears" took place. Sixteen thousand Cherokees were brutally rounded up by U.S. military forces and marched in midwinter to Indian Territory, which today is known as the state of Oklahoma. Of this group, four thousand would perish in holding pens or along the way. The entire episode stands as one of the darkest and most shameful events in United States history.

Another one thousand mostly full-blood escapees and refugees huddled together in the lofty mountains of northwestern North Carolina, ultimately emerging to become the nucleus of the Eastern Cherokee. The survivors of the long march to Oklahoma are known as the Western Cherokee, and except for exchanged visits between relatives, the two branches cooperate in very little.

The Eastern Cherokee

Until 1935, the Eastern Cherokee attempted to retain a semblance of their ancient life-way. Although the annual festivals were terminated relatively soon, they kept up the ball-play games and the minor ritual dances, including the animal dances, and, in particular, performed a comical but sacred masked dance, the Booger Dance. Medicine persons continued to heal, prophesy, and make charms, although their numbers diminished year by year. By 1940, modern life had taken over. Reservation activities centered around what would become the city of

Cherokee, a commercial center that caters to a thriving tourist business through its superb annual pageant called "Unto These Hills," a re-created Cherokee village, outstanding museum, arts and crafts centers, and countless shops. In the outlying areas of the reservation are people who follow some of the old customs, and what they do is fascinating. But aside from that, very little consequence can be seen or learned about the Cherokee's ancient forebearers and the pathways they followed.

The Western Cherokee

The Western Cherokee underwent a considerably different metamorphosis. Settling down was marred by continual internal turmoil, for the division between the mixed bloods and the full bloods had still not been put to rest. The latter retreated to the back country of the new Cherokee territory in northeastern Oklahoma, while the mixed bloods adapted quickly to the ways of the white settlers, becoming in time at least as prosperous as the average non-Indian and, in some instances, more prosperous. By the turn of the century, they were well educated and excelled in every professional and political pursuit. Tahlequah was established as the capital city for the nation, and today it is a business center which features for both Cherokee and tourist an annual pageant, a museum, and a re-created Cherokee village. Among the renowned tribal members are humorist Will Rogers, admirals, army officers, senators and congressmen, writers, painters, sculptors, musicians, attorneys, physicians, and teachers. William Keeler, former Principal Chief, headed the giant Phillips Petroleum Company; Joyce Sequichie Hifler is one of the most gifted writers in the United States; Willard Stone was a sculptor of considerable repute; Ross Swimmer is the former head of the Bureau of Indian Affairs and now the Special Trustee for American Indians.

Sacred Fires Kindled

While the traditional people in the backwoods practiced little of the ancient ritual life during the turbulent years, around the turn of the century they established ceremonial grounds where Stomp Dances were held. Each of these grounds was a continuation of the Sacred Square and had in its center a Sacred Fire originally kindled from the coals or upon the ashes of the ancient National Fire lovingly transported by delegated men over the Trail of Tears. Of those grounds that have survived — and there are four today — each has its own chief and officers, and the members belonging to it gather there when the leaders call the people to dance.

Ancient Practices Continue

In addition, considerable numbers of medicine men and women continued to practice their trade in Oklahoma until 1945, and today, more people are active in ceremonial events than most outsiders suspect. They continue some of the ancient Cherokee practices — they keep the life-way going, and, as they dance, they venture in mind and spirit back to ancient times, reliving their proud, imperial heritage.

CHAPTER four

Marauding Apache

The Apache are usually portrayed as brutal savages whose only redeeming qualities were craftiness and endurance. Who would ever associate them with pathways, or love, or inner peace?

To my knowledge, only one motion picture, *Broken Arrow*, ever showed a human side of the Apache people, with Jeff Chandler playing the role of a wise and compassionate Cochise joining forces with a firm but sympathetic mail agent, Jimmy Stewart. Even here we saw little of the life-way. There was a glimpse of a stunning young Apache woman in her alabaster buckskin Sunrise Ceremony dress that hinted something beautiful was associated with it, but we never learned more. All of the western films put together have never shown us the true nature and life-ways of the Indians. (Compare, for example, what Indian films have taught us about Native American culture with what the masterful series "Shogun" taught us about the rich ways and thought patterns of the ancient Japanese.)

Small But Well-Known Tribe

Of all the Indian nations that inhabit North America, no name is better known than that of the Apache. Yet, records show that — excluding their Navajo cousins, but counting all men, women, and children — their total population never reached twelve thousand prior to this century. The Apache were separated into six divisions, which were further subdivided into virtually independent smaller groups that seldom cooperated in anything, certainly not in raids and warfare. Once settled in their geographic areas and somewhat isolated from one another, each group adapted to local ecological conditions and developed the linguistic and cultural characteristics that differentiated them in historic times.

Somehow — whether from their place of origin, by those adjustments made as they migrated, or through experiences undergone as they settled at last into their final ranges — the Apache learned that a desirable life could be led in localities that combined high, timbered mountains with lush valleys and nearby desert areas. It is believed they came first to the western Great Plains. Sometime later, they formed smaller divisions, which separated and searched for living areas that provided the desired environment and sufficient resources to support their populations. Finally, each division chose some of the most spectacular mountain country in North America. Contrary to how they are popularly depicted in film, the Apache are mountain people.

Mountain People — Six Divisions

The desert setting — where they are usually seen in films — became a resource area for food and a place the Apache learned to cross in traveling from one mountain range to another. Except in severe winters, the Apache were not by choice on the desert for long at any one time, but since it was essential to be there in natural growing seasons, they learned to exist in it incredibly well.

Perseverance is a key word in coming to know the Apache, since it is a clue to their basic nature. They learned to survive in every circumstance, and the practicalities necessary for their survival appear to have become an integral part of the very person and personality of each Apache. Perseverance is an important factor to bear in mind when we study their pathways and seek to make them our own. Scholars who analyze the Apache are invariably impressed with their historic tenacity and vitality in the face of adversity. This vitality weakened only during the darker days of reservation history when at various times a sense of utter futility forced them into periods of blackest and bleakest despair.

Today, there are six branches of the Apache tribe: Western, Chiricahua, Mescalero, Jicarilla, Lipan, and Kiowa Apache, each of which has been independent of the others and has developed certain characteristics that make it somewhat different from the rest. The

Western Apache live in Arizona at Fort Apache and San Carlos. In New Mexico, the Jicarilla are on the Jicarilla Reservation, and the Mescalero, plus some Chiricahua and Lipan, are on the Mescalero Reservation. The Kiowa Apache live in Oklahoma. Even where the branches have been mixed because of reservation grouping, ancestral identifications continue. For example, a Chiricahua remains a Chiricahua. In cases where members of one Apache branch have gone to live with another branch, apparently being absorbed in time into the dominant group, they still display a few characteristics that set them apart. Even the children of mixed marriages are usually viewed with suspicion, their inability fully to become members of either branch inevitably complicating their lives.

Whatever else they are, an Apache remains an intensely human and compellingly unique individual. Once thought to be on the way to extinction, the Apache have a resolute nature that is surfacing again today as they gain a solid foothold in the modern world. At the same time, they are clinging to their ancestral center and reinforcing some aspects of their native culture. Traditional roots, while badly abused in prolonged confrontations with other tribes and non-Indians, have never been severed.

Origins of the Apache

The Southern Athapaskan, or Apachean, are linguistically related to the Athapaskan-speaking peoples of Alaska and Canada. Most of the current estimates place their time of arrival in the American Southwest at between A.D. 1000 and 1500. Anthropologists have not yet agreed upon the exact route they followed and the pace of their migration. The evidence discovered so far seems to indicate that the Apache forebearers crossed the Bering Strait and slowly moved south and east. Some anthropologists have speculated that the migration began as much as three thousand years ago and that hundreds of years were consumed in crossing Alaska and Canada before the people moved to the western Plains and then, in the late 1500s, to southwestern North America.

Of course, the most recent discoveries of Indian remains on the North American continent keep pushing back the arrival date of the earliest Native American people. That date is accepted as thirty-five thousand years ago now, but in June of 1987, the exciting discovery of new evidence of ancient humans in Brazil's remote northeastern backlands was a stunning indication that humans may have lived in the Americas hundreds of thousands of years earlier than previously thought. Scientists digging there also say they may have discovered the world's oldest astronomical observatory. An international expedition has unearthed a stone tool, fossilized bone fragments, and teeth of extinct animals buried in layers of sediment beneath the rock floor of a cave in Central America, three hundred miles northwest of coastal Salvador, capital of Bahia state. The fourth layer is 350,000 years old or more. If confirmed, it would be the first proof of pre-Neanderthal man in the New World. The discovery would refute the theory that mankind came here from Asia not more than thirty-five thousand years ago, indicating that he could have crossed the land bridge from Siberia to Alaska as early as 500,000 years ago, then migrated south. It calls to mind the day Fools Crow scooped up a handful of dirt and said to me, "My people were born here, in this continent. They have always been here." Perhaps Indian origin and migration stories are more accurate than many specialists think.

Linguistically, the Southern Athapaskan are divided into two main groups: an eastern group, including the Jicarilla, Lipan, and Kiowa Apache — with the first two more closely related to each other than either is to the Kiowa Apache — and a western group with two major subdivisions, the Navajo and the San Carlos-Chiricahua-Mescalero. The Navajo are considered a distinct tribe. The term "Apache proper" refers to those Southern Athapaskan groups other than the Navajo who had become such an entity during the early years that some authorities once thought they had only a surface relationship with the Apache proper. But since subsequent studies have revealed deep and intriguing similarities, many scholars are increasingly anxious to make detailed comparisons between the Navajo and other Apache groups. For example, the Western Apache, Chiricahua, and Mescalero hold a Sunrise Ceremony that is quite similar in its details to the Navajo ritual for pubescent girls.

In 1680, there were about 5,000 Apache. The census of 1910 listed 6,119 Apache, excluding only the Kiowa Apache; the 1923 report of the United States Indian Office showed 6,630 Apache. The census of 1930, including the Jicarilla and Lipan, showed 6,537. The Indian Office Report for 1937 set the population at 6,916, exclusive of the Jicarilla. In 1988, the total population numbered about 15,000. The notorious Chiricahua, who in 1873 totaled 1,675, had by the year 1910 been reduced by wars and imprisonment to 258.

Geronimo and Cochise

The Chiricahua — most famous of the Apache because of the brilliant war leader Geronimo and the wise politician Cochise — lived close to the Mescalero. These two tribes were normally at peace, had a reasonable amount of contact and not infrequently offered a haven for each other in troubled times. In pre-reservation years, the Mescalero were known to the Western Apache only through the intermediate Chiricahua. During the U.S. Army campaigns against the Chiricahua war parties that had bolted from the San Carlos Reservation, Western Apache scouts were sent to the Mescalero Reservation in New Mexico and there saw the Mescalero for the first time.

The White Mountain and San Carlos sub-tribal groups had some social contact with the Chiricahua in the pre-reservation period and remained on friendly terms with them until 1870 or so, when many of the Western Apache warriors served as scouts with the U.S. Army in campaigns against the Chiricahua, the only Apache branch that fought the whites to any great extent. Several elements in Western Apache culture are derived from the Chiricahua, and some intermarriage took place between the two, resulting in a few members of both groups living in the other's territory. But there was no trading, for the Apache traded only with people unlike themselves. White Mountain Apache on the way to Mexico to raid were sometimes joined by a few Chiricahua, but nothing is said about joint war parties.

Apache sunrise ceremony girl

From 1875 to 1886, when the U.S. government attempted to settle the Chiricahua on the Fort Apache and San Carlos Reservations in Arizona, relations between the Apache groups were sometimes friendly but were also regularly disrupted by the breakouts of the Chiricahua. These breakouts brought inevitable troubles even to those who chose to stay behind peacefully on the reservations. In consequence, there were times of internal stress and bitterness, which varied in intensity according to the overall problems provoked. Even today, the memory of strife remains, and contact among the four Apache reservations of Arizona and New Mexico is infrequent, limited primarily to occasional social visits between relatives. Political cooperation is nonexistent.

As soon as the Apache were well established in the Southwest, they adopted an active life-way in relations with other tribes. Although the Navajo spoke a language intelligible to any of the Western Apache, relations between the two groups were sometimes hostile. During peaceful times, they traded; at other times, they raided one another and made war.

The Apache occasionally raided the Hopi and Zuni, but on the whole, relations between the two peoples appear to have been friendly. No intermarriage occurred between the Apache and these tribes. It is suspected that in early times there may have been some contact between the Western Apache and the Rio Grande Pueblo, but no one knows this for certain.

However, from 1690 to 1870, the Western Apache and the Chiricahua traveled south into northern Mexico to conduct regular raids against the Opata and the Mexicans. The main route to Mexico was through the Arivaipa and San Pedro valleys. Once in Mexico, the raiding parties fanned out in several directions to raid the towns and ranches in the huge territory of Sonora. In time, the Apache came to know it as well as their own land, and a raiding party might be operative in Mexico for as long as eighty days. This is not surprising, for Mexico proved to be a veritable cornucopia of easily obtained supplies.

Also south of the Western Apache were the Apache Manso and the Papago of the Tucson area, persistent enemies of the Apache because they joined the Americans and Mexicans in campaigns against the White Mountain and San Carlos sub-tribal groups. Between the Papago and Western Apache, a state of war always existed, with both sides continually launching raids and war parties.

Westward were more enemies: the Havasupai to the northwest and the Walapai to the west. These exchanged raids with both the Chiricahua and the Western Apache.

The Yavapai lived close to the Apache and were on friendly terms with them. They joined a few of the Apache bands in raids, traded with the Apache, and even intermarried with all but the White Mountain sub-tribal group.

No one seeks to explain the constant animosity between the Apache and their neighbors, and no one can justify its brutal aspects, or even know who began the hostilities in most instances. Perhaps the Apache displaced some of the tribes as they pushed into the Southwest, or else they caused enough shuffling of territories to spur anxiety and increase pressure. However, it was always the Apache's habit to raid, and raiding became part of their economic complex. At the very least, their attitude played its inevitable role in the maintenance of a hostile state of affairs.

Apache Habit of Raiding

By the 1850s, Mexico's control of her northern frontier had been weakened while American strength was increasing. It was a perilous time for Mexicans, and their understaffed northern presidios were not able to protect Mexican citizens against the marauding Apache, who moved quickly and repeatedly to take advantage of the situation. They struck deep into eastern and northern Sonora, gathering food, livestock, and other commodities. They stole or captured horses, mules, burros, cattle, clothing, blankets, cowhides, saddles, bridles, leather, guns, and metal that could be cut up for arrow points. The cattle were usually killed and eaten in Mexico, since the mobile Apache lifestyle was not conducive to raising stock. Life was so good for the Apache that there was no incentive to gain territory, to destroy property, or to exterminate the Mexicans, although those who resisted strongly were often slain. The Mexicans were viewed as an ongoing economic resource, and enough supplies were always left behind to enable the Mexicans to recover and go on producing items that could be appropriated by the Apache later.

Apache Reservation Established

In 1860, the situation changed appreciably. Concern about Apache raids caused the U.S. Commissioner of Indian Affairs to establish a fifteen-square-mile strip of land along the Gila River as an Apache reservation. But the few Western Apache who used the strip resumed their raiding as soon as the Civil War began. The Mescalero, Jicarilla, and Chiricahua were also active, and when gold was discovered in Western Apache territory in 1863, U.S. soldiers and citizens had an excuse to attack all Apache indiscriminately.

U.S. Poisons Apache Food at Peace Conference

On one such occasion, a large group of Apache was invited to a peace conference and fed poisoned food. The infuriated Apache responded so viciously that it seemed for a time that the whites would be driven out of Apache country. In 1863, Arizona was made a United States territory, and in 1865, Camp Goodwin was established on the Gila River in the White Mountain country. Until then, the large White Mountain sub-tribal group had remained comparatively undisturbed by the U.S. Army, although they were well aware of what was going on elsewhere, for they hastily accepted the army's offer of peace in a treaty at Camp Goodwin. By this tactic, they avoided conflict with the military and were able to continue their raids into Mexico. The treaty also led to the establishment of Fort Ord on the White River in 1868 and to the enlistment of White Mountain and Cibecue warriors as scouts for General George Crook in his campaigns against the Tonto and the Chiricahua.

By 1871, relations between the Apache and the Arizona citizens had become so bad that the legislature published a paper, which scathingly indicted both the Apache for their marauding ways and the military forces for their failure to protect the whites. "A savage war still exists herein," the paper said, "causing the murder of hundreds of our citizens and the loss of a vast amount of property . . . our people have made their homes here, and have no other, but unless protection is given to them, the constant decimation that is made will sweep from the country all traces of civilization, except for deserted fields and broken walls."

One can appreciate the gravity of the situation, yet no such expressions of concern were made for the Apache, whose culture and land were being taken away.

In 1871, spurred on by this report and those in other papers, a body of about 150 enraged citizens from Tucson, with the assistance of Papago warriors, slaughtered 120 defenseless Western Apache women and children at Camp Grant in what became known as the Camp Grant Massacre. In addition, twenty-seven Apache children were taken by the Papago and sold into slavery in Mexico.

All Apache Confined to Reservations

Public reaction to this outrage caused the federal government to inaugurate at least a new peace policy in Arizona, the intent of which was to provide better army control, put an end to white vigilantism, and terminate corruption by civilian Indian agents and white contractors. The policy called for the placing of all Apache on reservations as a first step toward "civilizing" them. Four areas were set aside in Arizona and New Mexico. Once the gathering of Apache got underway, General Crook was placed in command of army forces. While he was the first to decisively defeat those who resisted, he was also among the first to treat the Apache with understanding and sympathy. He doubted that the reservation policy would bring peace, for while most Apache came in, others did not trust the whites and stayed away. A new headquarters was established at San Carlos, but Apache raids continued, and there were legitimate fears that those Apache on the reservation would soon break out and join the raiders. Crook's answer was to round up all off-reservation Apache, and in 1872, he led a series of sweeps against the Tonto and dealt them a crushing defeat. Several hundred were killed in battles; the rest were captured and placed on reservations.

Geronimo Surrenders

At this point, the Department of the Interior came up with yet another unfortunate idea, typical of the way Indians as a whole were treated. In 1874, the Department decided to place all of the Western Apache, the Chiricahua, and the Yavapai on a single huge and barren reservation at San Carlos. The decision was disastrous, for it failed to recognize Apache divisions and cultural variations. Within three years, five thousand Indians had been crowded onto the reservation, and serious problems were manifesting themselves. There was distrust and suspicion. The Indians had no wish or reason to cooperate with one another, and they disputed constantly over how to react to white control. Some found the Spartan living conditions unbearable and made plans to escape. Others were tired of fighting and wanted peace. Some ethnologists believe that the reservation was in truth a not-too-subtle device for bringing about the extinction of the Apache. No doubt the Apache believed that also. Whites aggravated the situation with their continual internal struggles for control of reservation policies and by the use of corrupt merchants. Finally, the Apache exploded. Chiricahua began to break out and to kill and raid as in pre-reservation days, and soon the entire Southwest was again in a state of panic. In 1882, when General Crook sought to correct the situation, more Chiricahua fled, and soon it seemed that the removal program had backfired completely. Thereafter, periods of peace alternated with turmoil. The hostilities did not end until Geronimo surrendered in 1886 and the remaining Chiricahua were shipped off in railroad boxcars to Florida prisons.

There were a few small breakouts after that, but by 1890, the armed conflict between the Apache and the whites was over, and a new day of tenuous coexistence began to dawn.

In addition to what we have considered regarding Apache survival, we can turn to a *Century Magazine* article that was published in 1887. It presented an enlightening account of how Western Apache had appeared to the whites among them from 1871 to 1881: "At the San Carlos Agency, the Apache are seen to be slowly acquiring the arts of peace and will soon be a useful part of the agricultural population of that region." The Indians were "partly civilized, partly barbaric," with "the barbaric element still predominating." The government had "cultivated their martial feelings, and at the same time, turned them (as scouts) to its own account." The writer stated that this feat had "thereby lifted [the

Indians] a little in their ideas of sovereignty and self-government." Then he explained the value of this elevation by pointing out that the scouts were being encouraged to spy on their own families, "acting in the interest of the Government." Apache accused of crimes were being tried before a jury of Indians, with possible verdicts of three-year sentences at Alcatraz prison in California or even death. A guardhouse accommodated the lesser criminals, and "through one of the windows peered the face of an Indian sentenced for life. . . . Superstitions are shown in their dress and ornaments, or rather in the charms which adorn and compose these." The writer did not mention any wish to learn the meaning of these items or to ask why they were still being worn by a subject people.

Fort Ord became Fort Apache in 1879. When it was abandoned in 1922, the fort was turned over to the Department of the Interior and converted into the Theodore Roosevelt Indian School.

Today's Apache

Today, Apache individuals and families are involved in all of the gainful occupations and activities common to Americans. They also maintain contact with the past through ritual and healing, basket weaving, leather crafts, silversmithing, painting, and carving. The White Mountain, Mescalero, and Jicarilla reservations have entered the regular business world of America, and they are attractive and good places to live. They have excellent educational facilities and run their tribal affairs in an efficient manner. San Carlos has been less fortunate and remains the poorest reservation of the lot. Most Apache have been converted to one form or another of Christianity, yet in conjunction with this, the staunchly traditional people still follow their central pathway and some peripheral pathways to inner peace . . . and I am quite certain you will discover that these pathways presented in Part Two are not at all what you expect them to be.

CHAPTER five

Majestic Sioux

Mystery surrounds the origin of the majestic Sioux nation as it does the Cherokee. They had no written tradition, and it seems as though the dramatic change in their lifestyle as they migrated from eastern North America and settled upon the Great Plains erased from memory the ways of their people before that time. Quite probably, the dramatic and dashing Sioux culture the world came to know included extensions of ancient customs, but as of today, no one, including the Sioux, is able to separate that which is very old from that which is relatively new. To all intents and purposes, the Sioux are a ghost-people who took on human form in the late 1600s when first they moved as a nation into the buffalo country of Midwestern North America.

Seven Clans

Reports by early explorers state that the Western Sioux once had seven clans whose leaders held an annual meeting around a sacred fire and were known as the Seven Council Fires, a title that designated the seven divisions of the nation: Mdewakanton, Sisseton, Teton, Wahpekute, Wahpeton, Yankton, and Yanktonai. Each of these names was derived from a certain characteristic of the clan or the region in which they lived.

While the Santee, or Eastern Sioux, established themselves in what is known today as eastern Minnesota, the Yankton and the Yanktonai settled on the western border country of what is western Minnesota and the Dakotas. Beginning about 1775, the stronger Teton, who spoke Lakota, ranged across South Dakota as far west as the Black Hills and into North Dakota and northern Nebraska, becoming, once they obtained horses and guns from the whites, the strongest and fiercest of the plains peoples. Yet, they were a people of great spirituality.

Their invasion led inevitably to acute friction and warfare with tribes already well established in the region. They successfully fought the Crow, Kiowa, Ponca, Omaha, Arikara, and Cheyenne. By 1800, the Teton had forced these tribes to move to new locations, and until 1830, they reigned supreme. Life was good, but not easy . . . they relaxed, played, hunted, socialized, performed mysterious rituals, and consolidated their hold over the splendid country they now considered to be permanently their own. In the 1830s, they extended their hunting grounds into southern Wyoming. By then, the Teton had become willingly and totally dependent upon the hulking, humpbacked buffalo, whose number in those days was estimated to have been thirty to sixty million. The buffalo was a sacred animal, a unique gift from their highest God, Wakan Tanka, for it was a walking commissary from which they obtained their basic food and fashioned most of the items they needed to exist.

The Sun Dance Encampment

The buffalo foraged for grass and were constantly on the move, so the Teton moved with them. They broke this pattern every summer in July or August when each sub-tribe would assemble in a selected location for a great encampment lasting two weeks or more. A Sun Dance was usually held during this meeting. The warrior societies would reorganize; the feathered, quilled, beaded and painted costumes we are so familiar with would be worn; people would socialize; and the civil, or camp, chiefs would meet to discuss common problems and to plan for the year ahead. Included in the planning would be the assignment of general areas in which each of the villages making up the sub-tribe would travel, as conditions permitted, while they hunted for buffalo and other game. The chiefs might also decide where each of the villages would bed down for the winter so that individual areas would not be overcrowded or the wood supply exhausted.

Division into Villages

The great encampment would end with a communal buffalo hunt; then the mass of people would subdivide into small villages that would go their various ways. They would cross paths now and then as they moved, and they would sometimes help one another against enemy tribes. Otherwise, contact was maintained only through messengers.

The pattern of life from early spring until late fall was for each village to make camp for a few days while the men hunted, the meat was brought in and cured, and the hides were tanned; then the village moved on to a new location. Consequently, each village became, for the most part, an independent social and military entity.

The Sioux Way of Life

The hardy women did all of the backbreaking work around the camps and owned the lodges. As might be expected, they made the final decisions regarding home and family affairs. The men were hunters and warriors. Young children had the free run of the camp, and older children were diligently trained to become responsible adults. The people were profoundly religious, and all life centered in ritual. Few things were done without reference to Wakan Tanka and the other spirit powers he had begotten.

Looking backward from the reservation period, the Teton described their early life on the plains as a happy time. For awhile at least, they had been free people who decided their own destinies and, in those warmly remembered days, managed to fashion a life-way that still excites and enthralls nearly everyone who comes to know of it.

In that memorable period, there were several kinds of leaders for each of the nomadic villages, all of which held office only as long as the people agreed with their conduct and views. White men called them "chiefs," and the title stuck from common usage, yet few of them commanded among the Indians the absolute authority the title implies. Civil chiefs were elected for indefinite terms to manage the movements of the village from one site to another and control the encampments with the aid of the warrior societies, each of which had its own leaders or chiefs. There were also war chiefs, whose reputations — acquired in defense, horse raids, and war parties — qualified them to lead the other warriors.

In addition, there were a number of individuals called medicine men, medicine women, and holy men, with exceptional spiritual powers that gave them special status among the people. A medicine person was one who received the ability to become a channel through which Wakan Tanka healed — usually by the combined use of faith and herbs. A holy man was a medicine man who, in addition to the healing, became a channel through whom prophetic and visionary information was dispensed. Included among the latter were the famous Crazy Horse and Sitting Bull.

In 1830, the Teton began to war against the Pawnee and, for the next twenty years, would do battle with them at every opportunity. In

1840, some of the Oglala Teton sub-tribe shifted their hunting grounds westward into the country of the Snake Indians, adding them to their expanding list of foes. The Crow also foraged in this area, and while friction with them had lagged for a decade, this small but formidable tribe became the principal enemy of the Sioux.

At this point, the Sioux had their first serious conflicts with whites. Trappers working the far western mountain ranges assisted the Crow and Snake in warfare against the Sioux, angering them until they were soon driving out every white except those who traded for their buffalo hides and furs.

The Sioux would have been wise to run out the traders too, since competition among the fur companies caused the traders to bring cheap liquor to the Indians in an effort to get them drunk, and then cheat them. The ultimate result of failing to oust the traders was a continuing disaster for the whites and Indians alike.

Despite the efforts of the holy men to stop the whisky trade, many Sioux obtained liquor. For the first time in their history, brawls occurred between tribal members. Families were soon alienated, and in a particularly significant act, an aspiring young warrior named Red Cloud became involved in the killing of a chief named Bull Bear. Later, Sioux would remember this act, and Red Cloud and his friends would pay dearly for it.

Whites Bring Epidemic

Beginning around 1848, Sioux survival problems were further compounded when white traders brought an eighteen-month-long epidemic of cholera and smallpox. The disease devastated the Teton, and hundreds of them died horrible deaths, leaving a remnant of grieving survivors. Other problems were also afoot. Since 1841, the Sioux had watched with apprehension as the wagon trains of white migrants passed through their country on their way to the West Coast. At first, there was only a trickle; then the trickle became a broad river. By 1850, it had swelled to fifty thousand migrants a year, all devouring buffalo and other game while their stock consumed huge amounts of the vital buffalo grass. Next, the U.S. government began to establish forts in Sioux country. Soldiers manned these, and with this protection, white migrants decided it was safe to stop and settle down.

War at Fort Laramie

The Sioux knew something had to be done, and when the federal government spurned their pleas for help, they turned to Red Cloud, whose reputation as a war leader qualified him to lead them to war. In 1851, at Fort Laramie, Wyoming, an incident concerning a cow owned by whites led to a fight between the Brule Sioux and Lt. J. L. Grattan and twenty-nine of his men. Several Sioux were killed, and Grattan's entire force was wiped out. Word of this encounter spread like wildfire, and soon there were attacks and counterattacks by Indians and whites all over the territory. Finally, Col. William S. Harney and his troops surrounded a group of Brule warriors, killed 136 of them, and dragged the survivors off to Fort Laramie in chains. There were grim statistics for the Sioux nation, and the test of their ability to survive was underway. In Part Two, you will learn how they managed it.

Alarmed Brule and Oglala scattered like quail to the north and south, leaving the migrant trail along the Platte River undisturbed for several years. The whites took advantage of this, adding new trails that compounded the situation. In 1885, the trail from Fort Laramie to Fort Pierre was added to the 1830s trail along the Platte River, and with the discovery of gold in Montana in 1862, the Bozeman Trail was established, cutting through the very center of Teton country.

"In heart and mind, the Teton people were indivisibly united with their land."

In heart and mind, the Teton people were indivisibly united with their land. They smoldered within at these intrusions, needing only a spark to set off a raging fire of reaction. That spark was struck in 1862 in Minnesota, when such awesome violence broke out between the whites and the starving Santee Sioux as to send shock waves across the North American continent. Hundreds of people on both sides were slaughtered. When the Eastern Sioux were finally defeated, thirty-eight of their leaders were shamefully hanged side by side on a public gallows. Some of the horrified Sioux who escaped fled to the Dakotas, and the rest scattered to reservations stretching from Nebraska to Canada. Red Cloud thought a great deal about the white man's justice and concluded that the Western Sioux had little recourse but to fight for their very lives — which is exactly what they did for the next twenty-six years.

Sitting Bull and Crazy Horse

Not until 1890, at a place called Wounded Knee, would the struggle come to its ugly end. During this tumultuous period, names like Sitting Bull, Crazy Horse, Red Cloud, and General George Armstrong Custer would become famous, known to whites and Indians alike. After the shocking defeat of Custer on the Little Big Horn River, the Indians struck their camps and headed off in every direction to make pursuit by white soldiers as difficult as possible. Most of them, when government forces finally encircled them, gave up quickly and were herded away to designated reservation areas. Sitting Bull and some of his followers fled north to Canada and remained there four years before returning. Crazy Horse and his band ran until they were starved into submission. Once they surrendered, all effective resistance ceased, and the Sioux reservation period was underway.

The Sioux and whites began the agonizing and frustrating attempt of settling down side by side and adjusting to a new way of life together, but the odds were not even, for the task was by far more difficult for the Sioux. Details are scarce about the earliest years on the reservations, but we do know that for the anxious and bewildered Indians, it was mostly a time of despair — heightened when the revered Crazy Horse was stabbed to death at Fort Robinson on September 5, 1877.

Loss of the Sacred Black Hills

From 1877 to 1879, the Sioux were sent to stay in the damp and barren Missouri River bottomland while negotiations for the sale of their sacred Black Hills were carried on between Red Cloud and the U.S. government. In 1879, Red Cloud and his followers were moved to the present site of the Pine Ridge Reservation in South Dakota where they attempted to make a new beginning. In this same year, Red Cloud, without the general approval of his people, signed over to the government the rich Black Hills of South Dakota. This error, added to the killing he had once been involved in, became his unforgivable sin, and even today it tarnishes his once great name.

By 1876, treaties with the federal government had reduced the size of Sioux territory by half. In 1879, the various sub-tribes of the Sioux were rudely pushed onto scattered reservations in the remotest and least productive areas of South Dakota, North Dakota, Nebraska, and Montana. Some Sioux stayed in Canada, and their descendants live there today. Presently, about sixty thousand Sioux live on reservations, and more than twenty-five thousand live in the major urban centers of the United States.

Allotment Ends Traditional Sioux Government

For a brief time after 1879, the reservation-bound Sioux maintained their own form of government, subject to the approval of a U.S. government agent who presided over each reservation. In 1889, Congress enacted legislation designed to change this. Over a period of several years, land was allotted and deeded in trust to the head of each family, who was given a certain number of acres of reservation land which, on his death, would pass on to his heirs. Each family was also issued a few cows and horses, a wagon, pickaxes, shovels, sets of harnesses, and fifty dollars in cash with which to build and farm a permanent living place. In the government's mind — and in the minds of white missionaries — a thorough conversion of the Sioux, both religious and secular, was in order. The whites simply took for granted that the conversion would be accomplished in a very short period of time.

They gave little thought to whether this position was reasonable or fair. In battling back so fiercely to hold onto their land, the Sioux had committed an unpardonable crime in the view of the whites, and they were to pay a painful and enduring price for it. The trusteeship was intended to be only temporary, to last until the Sioux could govern themselves with elected officials. It was, in fact, designed to self-destruct in twenty-five years. But the Sioux were not schooled to handle such things, and little was done to educate them. At the end of its term, the trusteeship was extended for another ten years, then again for ten more, until finally the Howard-Wheeler Act was passed in 1934 to end it.

The Sioux chafed under government programs they seldom cared for or understood. Compounding this were the severe droughts of 1889 and 1890. Unlike the white farmers, the Sioux could not relocate. They were confined by force to their reservations. Meanwhile, white hunters readily reduced the remaining buffalo population. The government allowed this, the motive being that, without the buffalo, the Indians would have no alternative but to obey the government in order to survive. By 1890, only a few hundred buffalo remained. In February of 1890, the Dakota reservation was opened to homesteading by non-Indians, and the bewildered Sioux, whose pathways had been under steady assault, were ready to turn to anyone or anything that would offer them the slightest hope of returning to their old way of life. They prayed desperately and sought visions for guidance and deliverance. Fortune intervened in the person of a Paiute Indian named Wovoka who announced he had a portentous vision in which God told him how the Indians could be united in peace and prosperity and how they must learn to do a certain sacred dance called the Ghost Dance. When the news reached the Sioux, they accepted it eagerly, and the Oglala sent a delegation to Wovoka to learn about his vision and teachings.

Sioux Ghost Dance

The Sioux added two new dimensions to the Ghost Dance: a painted cloth or buckskin ghost-shirt that was believed to be bulletproof, and the conviction that ghost dancing would cause the whites to move away and the buffalo to return. Their faith was fruitless. Frightened white settlers, who vividly remembered the recent wars, called urgently for soldiers to protect them. On November 20, 1890, General John R. Brooke came to the Pine Ridge reservation with a heavily armed contingent. Thus the scene was set for the ultimate tragedy. It began when Sitting Bull was killed at his home and ended when a frightened and peaceful chief named Big Foot and his followers were massacred in snow left blood red at Wounded Knee. For a brief period after that, the alarmed and angry Sioux gathered and threatened to revive the war, but a Jesuit priest talked them out of it, and on January 1, 1891, armed Sioux resistance ended for all time.

Peaceful Pursuits

The historical review just presented is essentially the conventional one that allows outsiders to depict the Sioux as a bloodthirsty people. It is the popular picture held by the outside world today, and one that is amplified and perpetuated by writers, filmmakers, and many Western artists . . . all of whom recognize its commercial value and have not considered the disservice to the Sioux. Hence, it may also be difficult for those who cling to that popular picture to think of the Sioux in terms of spirituality.

Let us consider, however, the life-way of the Sioux and see how much time they actually had for warfare. We can begin with the Midwestern climate. In most years, six months of freezing temperatures and deep snow are followed by one month of slush and mud. That leaves five months of decent weather — not counting heavy summer rains, humidity, windstorms, and tornadoes — in which to travel.

In addition, we cannot forget that a large portion of the five clement months had to be given over to the gathering of foodstuffs by hunting, digging, and picking, then to the preservation of the food so it would last through the seven winter months. Hides and furs had to be tanned and prepared. Trade with other Indians and traders was vital. Since the game did not stand still and wait for the Indians to find it, considerable time was allowed for unpacking and making camp, as well as for hunting and preserving them, packing up and moving again.

Besides regular household tasks, horses had to be trained and watched over, and forage had to be provided for them. Babies were born and cared for. Children had to be taught, marriages performed, clothing repaired, and weapons kept in order. Councils needed time to consider tribal and personal matters. Warrior societies had to meet, plan, and initiate new members. The sick and wounded had to be cared for, the dead buried.

If it is true that the entire Sioux nation numbered no more than sixty thousand at any one time, no more than ten thousand warriors could have been in condition to fight. These were spread over what today is a two-and-one-half state area and were subdivided into many small nomadic villages. Since the foes of the Sioux were not exactly next-door neighbors in the conventional sense of the word, and although the war parties did at times enter Sioux country, the Sioux raiding and war parties were kept small in number; they had to travel considerable distances to battle and carry out horse raids. It is also known that even these skirmishes were routinely brief and indecisive. Add to this the fact that the counting of coup — the striking of a blow on an enemy with one's own hand or a slender coup stick — was considered a far greater honor than killing or even wounding and was so preferred a custom that it led many writers to describe Indian warfare as a game.

Rituals of the Sioux

Moreover, it should be recognized that, prior to the reservation period, much of the Sioux life-way was given over to religious ritual. In the spring of most years, preparations were made by each sub-tribe for a Sun Dance to be held the following July. This was a rite of renewal, rebirth, procreation, and thanksgiving, and everyone gathered at assigned places to celebrate it. The sixteen-day rite, considered in more detail in Part Two of this book, consisted of eight days of preparation, four days of performance, and four days of abstinence.

Men and boys took time to travel to rugged mountain locations to hold four-day vision quests, which provided guidance for their lives and spiritual helpers to assist them. They also participated in sweat-lodge rituals, in which the Sioux purified themselves and performed healings.

There were many kinds of dances: a rain dance, a Horse Dance, an Eagle Dance and numerous others that had been given by Wakan Tanka in the beginning of time as ways to obtain his special blessings. Two rituals of consequence, the Medicine Lodge Society's Grand Medicine Dance and the Feast of the Virgins, are described in Part Two.

"... it was common for people to give to the point of utter impoverishment."

Public giveaways were also part of the life-way; it was common for people to give to the point of utter impoverishment. In addition, each clan took the time for the care of orphans and the aged. Loving parents were proud to have daughters who visited the unfortunate and helpless to carry them food, comb their hair, and mend their garments. Any girl who failed in her charitable duties was, in tribal eyes, considered unworthy of the Sioux name.

The foregoing by no means exhausts all that the Sioux did in ritual and secular pursuits during the five clement months of the year, but even this much is sufficient to call into question the portrayal of the Sioux as a constantly warring and brutal people. Most of their time was spent on far more important pursuits, and it was not until they were driven to desperation by white intruders that they exhibited the warring tendencies and acts that are so well known to us through films and literature. The Sioux were a sensitive people who followed many peaceful pursuits and had a passionate desire for external and internal peace. Therefore, when I describe their central and peripheral pathways in the pages ahead, more of what they did and believed will be emphasized.

It might be assumed that, with the end of warfare at Wounded Knee and the beginning of the reservation period, the worst was over for the Sioux. But the worst was still to come, and along with it the true inner peace of the people emerged to sustain them.

In the fall of 1972, the resolute militants of seven national Indian organizations marched on Washington, D.C., and for several days occupied the Bureau of Indian Affairs headquarters. Then in February of 1973, desperate members of the American Indian Movement (AIM)

Young Sioux woman

began what would become a dramatic and dangerous seventy-two-day occupation of the historic Wounded Knee Village at Pine Ridge. Before this occupation was over, the entire country was looking on, and it was clear that something was terribly wrong at Pine Ridge and elsewhere among the reservation Indians. For nearly a century, the "out of sight and mind" Indians had been forced to live in circumstances that had brought them nothing but misery. The military clashes with whites that began in 1851 expressed much more than the contest for land. They also expressed a profound clash of cultures for, as previously mentioned, the intruding whites had determined that the immediate "civilizing" of the savage and heathen Sioux was their first order of business.

"Once the Sioux were pinned down on the reservations, the primary imperative of the government was to transform the Sioux into whites as quickly as possible."

Once the Sioux were pinned down on the reservations, the primary imperative of the government was to transform the Sioux into whites as quickly as possible. No one thought to ask whether the Sioux wished to comply or whether the whites by their own manner of conduct had earned the right to make such a demand. There was no moratorium period to quench the bitterness that existed on both sides. The government, with the enthusiastic support of Christian missionaries, simply bore in and began the compulsory education of children, while programming the adults to death with a dole system that would have cumulative and catastrophic consequences.

So effectively did the government do this that most whites assumed the "heathen" Sioux would quickly give up their Indian ways and become white men and women with copper-colored faces. Except for reservation agents and other government employees, only a handful of non-Indians went to the reservations to find out what was going on, so that early records are scarce, veiled, and unclear. We can only draw a summary picture: In the earliest part of the reservation period, the goal was to make the Sioux self-supporting through farming and education, although the education was carefully circumscribed. Indians were to learn, but only what the whites wanted them to learn. Higher education was never considered.

The allotment of lands has been mentioned, and that in itself led to incredible abuses. When corrupt government officials saw that the Sioux were not able to make what they considered to be efficient use of the land, agents were permitted to lease the land to whites. By 1916, most Oglala-owned cattle had been sold to whites, and eight percent of the Pine Ridge land had been leased at ridiculously low prices to white people for grazing purposes. The dole system continued, and no work ethic was established.

The government decided to do its first educating of Sioux children through the Christian church missions, believing they would be the most effective in civilizing them. However, the system of education — a totally different one than the Sioux were accustomed to — was to be rigid and vigorous. "The instruction," one missionary wrote, "of all Indian children in good schools, during a given period of each year, should be made compulsory. In that direction lies the one great hope of modifying and ameliorating the Indian character. It is uncertain, to say the most, whether the adult members of the wild tribes can ever be induced or constrained to raise themselves from their abject savagery to the level of any fixed idea of education. . . . But the rising generation is plastic, and can be molded effectually, and to higher uses. The education of children goes to the core of the problem. We must begin at the cradle if we would conquer barbarism and lift a race to a height beyond itself."

A typical article of the day carried in the November 4, 1876, Omaha *Herald* describes a group of Sioux whose train stopped over on its way to Oklahoma Indian Territory. Its concluding paragraph read as follows: "Several [white] ladies passed through the cars, two of whom were evidently officer's wives, and somewhat acquainted with the Indian language and customs. The Indians seemed delighted to see these white ladies and took pains to shake hands with them. American Horse's papoose was a chubby, sturdy little beggar, and when one of the ladies spoke to him, he set up a tremendous wail, *just as natural and lifelike as if he were human.*" [Italics mine.]

Is it not sobering to consider the atmosphere in which the Sioux future was set? But this was the atmosphere in the beginning, one that continued through most of the twentieth century. It is not surprising that the school dropout rate for Indians has always been and remains the highest in the country. How have they survived it?

In 1895, F. W. Blackmar of the University of Kansas wrote an article about Indian education in which he stated that a recently passed law for the compulsory education of Indians was a step in the right direction. This law, passed by Congress and approved in March 1881, provided for the enforced attendance of Indian children at schools established and maintained for their benefit. Blackmar went on to say that it was not supposed that parents of Indian children were capable of determining whether education was good for their children or not. The Indians "were too savage for that."

Unfortunately, Blackmar's opinions were to become the rule for early Indian schooling. Government-controlled schools became military in character, without tolerance and patience. Their primary goal was to humble the heathen and destroy every vestige of the Indian lifeway. As might be expected, they met with resistance at every turn from resentful students and parents; the educational system on reservations has only recently begun to emerge from this dismal situation.

The churches, most notably the Roman Catholic, did somewhat better than the government where education was concerned and provided the only source of acceptable education on many reservations. They did, of course, join in the attempt to stamp out tribal customs and culture — a course they have in recent years regretted and begun to change — but it should be noted that many of their Sioux students would become the community leaders needed to comprehend and work with government officials.

"As the years went by, most of the Sioux were baptized into one denomination or another."

As the years went by, most of the Sioux were baptized into one denomination or another. Some felt it was the expedient thing to do, since it was the best way to please the whites and thus receive rations; others felt that the Christian God presented to them was much like the Wakan Tanka they believed in already, so there was no problem. A few whites did appeal for justice and understanding. For example, as early as January 1891,

Sioux method of wearing protective-sage head, wrist, and ankle bands during the sun dance

writing in the *North American Review*, General Nelson A. Miles stated that "The Indians are practically a doomed race, and none realize it better than themselves. . . . The subjugation of a race by their enemies cannot but create feelings of most intense hatred and animosity. Possibly if we should put ourselves in their place, we might comprehend their feelings."

In another sphere, opportunities for corruption were so numerous that from the very beginning the Indian Service became a hotbed of graft and wrongdoing. With few exceptions, it attracted men more interested in making money than in serving the Indians, and government officials gladly opened the door wide to legalized robbers, tying the hands of those who would do justice. Most agents did their best to undermine the authority of chiefs and ignore leaders who resisted their demands, while at the same time they catered to lesser men who would do whatever they were told.

In addition, the agents struck hard at the most critical point, uniting with church authorities in a massive effort to extinguish the vital ceremonial life of the Sioux. As early as 1881, calling the Sun Dance "savage rites," a "barbarity," "this cruel spectacle," and "horrible," the whites moved to stamp it out by forbidding its practice on any of the Sioux reservations. Shortly thereafter, they condemned nearly all of the traditional rituals and practices, and those who violated the rule by practicing any of the rites were subjected to instant arrest and discipline.

Not for many years would anyone come to the reservation to ask why the Sioux performed these rituals in the first place and whether they might have important religious substance. By 1885, whites accepted that Sioux ceremonials were rapidly becoming things of the past, and the fact is that some of them are irretrievably lost. Yet, in an unexpected way, the attitude of the whites became the guarantee of the continuance of the most vital traditional rites, for the Sioux were not about to accept in totality the religion of a people who took their land by force and now held them captive. The holy men and medicine men and women living in the back country, away from the agency centers, became the determined perpetuators of the ancient ways. Thanks to them, the Sioux are today undergoing a cultural renaissance. Customs that were all but lost are being researched and reinstated, and the religious rites that have been kept in secret are being performed in public with greater intensity every passing year. The Sun Dance is one such ceremony. There are frequent Yuwipi ceremonies, healings, vision quests, and there are Spirit-Keeping rites. Puberty rites are being held for pubescent girls, and Heyoka ceremonies are being held to make sacred clowns. Attempts are even being made to revive the sacred Horse Dance, last held near Pine Ridge in 1931. I say more about some of these rituals in Parts Two and Three, and I promise you will find them enthralling and instructive.

PART TWO

Tribal
Pathways

CHAPTER SIX

Hopi Pathways

opi legends tell us that in the beginning, when the ancestors of the Hopi people emerged through the kiva's sipapu hole onto the surface of the earth, the Beings who created the people sent with them one central and several peripheral pathways, depositing along these paths the gifts the Hopi would need to survive . . . for the Above Beings were intensely aware of the hostile nature of the world the Hopi would be confronted by, even in the most ordinary circumstances.

Rituals That Are Preparatory in Nature

In its essence, the central pathway walked by the Hopi has been an annual cycle of rituals that are preparatory in nature and go hand in hand with specific planting, cultivating, and harvesting tasks. These rituals include acts having to do with the continuance and heightening of their spiritual awareness of everything needful to life and survival. In other words, both the material and the spiritual sides of life are addressed in the central pathways, although in truth the Hopi sees no distinction between the two, for the material life is itself infused with spirituality.

The annual series of rituals serves the basic purpose of helping the Hopi prepare for and think through all things needful for mental and physical survival in the inhospitable world in which they live. Being intimately acquainted with their world of frigid, stormy winters and blistering hot summers, the Hopi know from experience what dangerous events might occur, but they never know when they will occur or what strange turns and twists they might take.

Hopi kiva interior

The Above Beings taught them to gird their loins before any adversity struck so that they would be ready to meet it and deal with it. Only when something entirely foreign to the realm of their accustomed existence struck them were they unprepared and nearly done in . . . such as when smallpox was brought in by outsiders or when outsiders sought to replace Hopi culture with their own. These were alien events, outside the realm of what they were acquainted with and, therefore, mysterious and difficult to handle. The Hopi might be staggered or knocked down by adversity, but being strengthened and advised through rituals — given in advance what they needed to defend themselves — they immediately fought back and were soon on their feet and going again.

It should be borne in mind that no matter how difficult the problem, including those utterly foreign to them, there is no record of the Hopi having panicked. Here is another testimony to the depth of Hopi spirituality that has kept them calm and carried them through.

The individual rituals celebrated by the Hopi are incredibly complex, and there is no need to consider them in detail here. What we do need, though, is to examine and put to our use what they intend and what they accomplish.

Annual Cycle of Ceremonies

In general, the annual cycle of ceremonies opens in November with the New Fire Ceremony. At the Winter Solstice, an elaborate sun drama occurs, and there are rites for the food germ and warrior gods. In

January, a dance dramatizes the return of Sun, who is followed by Hopi clan-ancients in the form of Katcinas. Flute and buffalo rituals are also held. In February, the Hopi hold the Bean Planting Ritual and a ceremonial purification festival celebrating the return of the Katcina clan-ancients and other clan-ancients. In March, a mystery play dramatizes the growth of the corn (the play's purpose is to bring rain), and prayer sticks are deposited at important shrines. In May, there are public appearances by masked personifications of different Katcinas. In July, an elaborate celebration of the departure of the Katcinas occurs, and the Open or Masked Season for Katcina dances comes to an end. In August, they hold snake and flute dances. In September and October, Basket Dances celebrate the harvest, and the Closed Season ends. In November, the cycle of rituals begins again.

Hopi Katcinas

Katcinas have been mentioned several times now, and the most splendid, enchanting, and characteristic of the Pueblo ceremonies are those involving them. Hopi stories involving the origin of Katcinas vary somewhat, but it is generally accepted that when the Hopi emerged from the Underworld they brought with them a large number of living spiritual beings known as Katcinas.

According to one mythical account, the Katcinas accompanied the Hopi in their early wanderings until they settled at Casa Grande, where they were attacked by Mexicans. All the Katcinas were killed, and their spirits returned to their homes in the Underworld. To maintain contact with them, the surviving Hopi kept the masks and costumes of the Katcinas and developed the customs of impersonating them in rituals. By this means, Katcina-obtained blessings continue to be bestowed, principally in the form of rain, but also in the form of well-being. Both of these blessings are related to healing and fertility, and they assure the reproduction and perpetuation of all created things.

Placing pahos in an outdoor shrine

In another version, the loss of the original Katcinas occurred when the people began to take for granted the blessings bestowed by the supernaturals and even had the audacity to argue with them. So the Katcinas decided to leave. But first they taught a few faithful young men how to perform some of their ceremonies and how to make the necessary paraphernalia, assuring them that as long as the ritual details were followed to the letter and were performed with good and pure hearts, the real Katcinas would come and take possession of those who wore the masks. Rain and well-being would follow. Conversely, if rain did not fall, or if other serious problems occurred, it was proof that something had been done improperly or that someone was not pure in action or heart.

The Hopi dead are believed to return to the Underworld through the sipapu from which the people first climbed to the earth's surface. In the Underworld, the dead are in communion with the original Katcinas, and they carry on both a ritual and secular existence that is a replica of Hopi life on earth. One aspect is different. Each of the main Katcina ceremonies is held twice yearly at the villages, once in a major and once in a minor form. At the same time that the major form is being performed on earth, the corresponding minor ritual is being performed by the spirits in the Underworld, and vice versa. It follows also that the seasons are reversed. When it is midwinter in the Underworld, it is midsummer on earth. The one exception in living patterns is that the spirits eat only the soul of food; thus, weighing nothing, some spirits can be transformed into Katcina Clouds that bring rain and other benefits to the living. The dead are also invited to come back to the village on the fourth night of the Tribal Initiation Ceremony.

Zuni Pueblo Katcina hood masks

A belief in life after death may be the most pivotal concept in Hopi religion. This truth is manifested again and again in ceremonies. The modern Hopi recognize in man a double nature, corresponding to body and soul, and to the latter they give the expressive name *breath body*. It is the breath body that passes at death through the sipapu to the Underworld. When the body is prepared for burial, a prayer offering is tied to the hair in front, and the face is covered with a masklike layer of cotton. Openings are provided for eyes and nose, and the mask is tied on by a string that passes around the head at forehead level "to hide themselves in." To this string are fastened prayer feathers that the deceased will wear in the Underworld. As the mask is put on, the deceased is addressed as follows:

> *You have become a Katcina.*
> *Aid us in bringing the rain,*
> *And intercede with the gods to fertilize our farms.*

Black marks are made under the eyes, on the lips, forehead, cheeks, the palms of the hands, and the soles of the feet. Prayer feathers, sometimes a little food, and a small container of drinking water are placed on the chest. The body is wrapped in several blankets, which are secured by ropes, then is carried on the back of the father, another relative, or on a horse or burro to its final resting place.

With this faith firmly in hand, the Hopi consider death as little more than an important change in stature. There is no real loss to society or to the individual, for the dead are reborn to go on living in the Underworld much as they have on earth. As Cloud People (rain-bearers), they continue to serve the living in a vital way. By means of *pahos* (prayer sticks) they are also called back to serve as advisers to the living. In this regard, time as experienced in its most profound sense has less to do with the clock than with a mental state or with the psychological realities of life. Through this vital understanding, the Hopi have achieved a sense of self and one's place in society, as well as a feeling of continuity with the past. The individual is able to define himself in terms of his entire life span. It is here, interestingly enough, that the Hopi have actually profited from adversity. Having gone through a crisis of identity and emerged with a commitment to an ideology of life, they have a balanced perspective and are able to project themselves both into the distant past and the far future. By this, for the most part, they avoid doubt and indecision about their identities, and they extend back into the past and forward into the future in a balanced way. They struggle, but they avoid depression, and life is never an endless, bleak present with no hope of change. Their one addiction is to the belief in what they are, and in many ways they have done a better job of this than most other Indian tribes, thus retaining more of the ancient culture.

Two hundred and forty or more Katcinas are personified in ceremonies, although a few are the most popular and most frequently represented. Katcina types include animals and birds, Katcinas identified by a peculiar physical aspect or a special costume feature, Katcinas associated with certain sounds, Katcinas related to fixed seasons, melon Katcinas, rodent Katcinas, and so on. In effect, everything necessary to a full and fruitful life on earth and in the Underworld is represented. Only men, and specifically those who have been properly qualified by passage through the required tribal rites, can put on masks and costumes and impersonate Katcinas, but women also play vital roles in ceremonial life.

Hopi Shalako Katcina

Katcina personifications most often take the form of group dances, performed from daybreak to sunset with intervals for rest. The society members secretly rehearse the songs and dances for several days prior to a public performance, and then they are carefully painted and elaborately dressed in refreshed masks and costumes. In many cases, the costume and body paint are distinctive, but it is the mask that holds the power to transform a living man into a Katcina. While the society member wears the mask during the prescribed ritual, he is transformed into the Katcina, and he has all of the Katcina's powers and attributes.

Usually, although not always, the Katcina impersonators are masked, and they appear in proper season at all the eastern and western Pueblo villages, although in the Rio Grande area, non-Pueblo are not permitted to see them. In fact, non-Pueblo, including other Indians, are not even allowed in a Rio Grande village when a Katcina dance is being performed. Consequently, there is a dearth of eyewitness descriptions, although informants have revealed something of the dances.

At Hopi and Zuni villages, the masks, with the exception of clan masks, have been more openly displayed, and there is a mass of published material on their Katcinas.

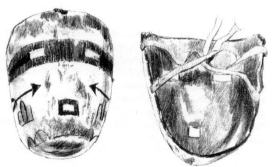

Hopi Pueblo Katcina face mask

The Cloud Katcina masks are manufactured by their owners. They are refurbished each time they are used and redecorated if a different style of Katcina is to be represented. In addition, new Katcinas are introduced periodically to deal with new situations, and some of the old ones occasionally become obsolete. The efficacy of the Katcina is usually the controlling factor in this, and a Katcina is called upon only as long as it brings benefits to the people.

There is almost no limit to the number of variations and innovations that are permitted. The principal exceptions are the few special types known as *Mon* (Chief) Katcinas, whose masks are permanent and never duplicated. In most instances, these belong to a specific clan, are regarded as the *wuye* (clan ancestors) and may be impersonated only on particular occasions. Some of the clan masks are never exposed in dances or copied for dances, but in the more esoteric ceremonies, they may be brought out and worn with the admonition to all witnesses that they must not describe the mask to anyone. The clan mask is in the keeping of the clan head or clan mother, who is required to feed the mask ritually each day and to know the prayers and songs connected with it.

The entire Hopi tribe is admitted at a prescribed time in life to what ethnologists call the Katcina Cult. Little children are taught to believe that the Katcinas they see performing are actually supernatural visitors with awesome powers. Since this pretense can only be kept up so long, sometime before the age of ten the child is initiated into the Katcina Cult, and thereby taught, as they see the masks removed, that men they know are actually impersonating Katcinas in ritual practices that have preserved the Anasazi-Pueblo for centuries. Adults accept the human dimension, but continue to believe that the impersonator becomes the actual Katcina. However, being accepted in all respects for who he is, the Katcina impersonator is called a friend rather than a god. During the Open Season, the Katcinas are present in the villages whenever rituals are performed. Otherwise, they dwell in Underworld homes in the mountains, lakes, and springs — more specifically on the splendid San

Francisco Mountain peaks just north of Flagstaff, Arizona. During the closed portion of the year, the Katcinas perform in their Underworld homes, and dances that do not require their presence on earth are held.

Hopi Secret Societies

In every Hopi pueblo, the populace is organized into a number of secret societies, each of which is responsible for a single ceremony. A particular clan has charge of each society and of its associated ritual and paraphernalia. The headman of a clan is usually the chief of his group's society, and he is the keeper of the most important object related to the performance of his society rite. This is the *tiponi* (fetish) that is made up of an ear of corn, feathers, corn and vegetable seeds, piñon seeds, and a variety of outer string wrappings. The Hopi call it the "mother" or "heart" of a ceremony. It is highly venerated, and when not in use, it is kept in a secret place in the clan house of the clan's headwoman. It is thought that all tiponis are redone by the headman during each annual performance of a rite. In particular, the old ear of corn is replaced with a new one, as are the feathers and the paint. It is said that each chief had a tiponi in the Underworld prior to emergence.

Corn / feathers / sticks / Cloth or ribbons / feathers / shells / clay base

Hopi tiponi

There is a fixed time of the year when a society is expected to perform the observance in its care. The time to begin some of the rituals is determined by the sun's position along the horizon at daybreak. Some are begun when a certain moon appears, some when a given number of days have elapsed after the completion of the preceding ritual. Leaders whose ceremonies are inaugurated by solar observation are notified at the proper times by the village sun watcher. Other society chiefs must determine their own starting dates. Ordinarily, the society members assemble in their kiva for the ceremonies, but lesser rites are sometimes conducted in the main houses of the clans in charge. Kivas are owned by the clans whose members built them, and there are as many kivas as there are clans in each village. Their identifying names are related to the controlling clan, and the headman of the clan is commonly both the leader of his group's ceremony and chief of his kiva.

As we proceed, please bear in mind that where pathways are concerned, it is the parts of the rituals that matter. Focus your thoughts upon what the participants think about and accomplish each day and not upon the ceremony as a whole.

Hopi Kiva Rituals

All major rituals of the Hopi that take place in kivas are of nine days' duration, and every ritual has its origin legend that is repeated in its songs and acts. On the opening day, the leaders proceed to their kiva and erect a *na'atsi* (standard). This is placed where everyone can see it, either on the south side of the entrance hatch or suspended from a rung of the kiva ladder. It gives notice to one and all that the society is in secret session. From this time on, none but members may enter the kiva, and all participants must refrain from salt, fat, and sexual indulgence. Any nonmember who breaks the entrance rule is forced to join the society.

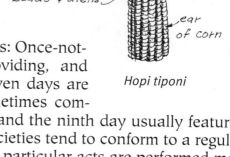

wing feathers

painted sticks

corn

ath feathers

seashells

beads & shells

ear of corn

Hopi tiponi

The first day of the nine-day ceremony is called *Yung-gya'a* (entering). It is important only in the sense that it is the beginning, and the full membership is rarely present. The next four days are numbered, and the last four days have descriptive names: Once-not-anything, Piki-providing, Food-providing, and Dance Day. Ordinarily, the first seven days are given to ritual, the eighth day sometimes combines public activities with private, and the ninth day usually features a public dance by the society. All societies tend to conform to a regular pattern, although the order in which particular acts are performed may vary widely.

Most of the secret ritual in the kiva is devoted to smoking, singing, and praying. Shell or gourd-rattle music and the manufacture of prayer offerings and other gifts, such as Katcina dolls, are part of the ritual. The prayer offerings are placed on the altar and at specified shrines, and one or two members are sent to make four circuits of progressively decreasing size around the village on four successive days. During each circuit, prayer offerings are placed at a number of sacred places.

At different times, society members impersonate deities to which the cult is devoted. In addition, an altar is erected, sand paintings are made, and medicine water is prepared.

The altar is set up at the north end of the kiva, and it has two parts. The first is a *reredos* (back screen), and the second consists of a group of ritual objects set on the floor in front of the screen. Each ritual has its own altar, design, and objects. The usual reredos is made up of a row of vertical wooden slats, together with clay tiles or flat stones that are all affixed to an upright wood frame. On these are painted symbolic or realistic representations of natural and supernatural things related to the ceremony in progress. Typical are corn, rain clouds, lightning, heavenly bodies, sacred animals, and cult heroes. The base of the altar reredos rests directly on the kiva floor. In front of it are placed tiponis and the effigies of sky and earth gods and cult patrons. A medicine bowl sits on a low pile of clean sand. Six radiating lines of sacred cornmeal are drawn out from the bowl to represent the six cardinal directions — north, east, south, west, up, and down. On top of each line is placed an ear of corn whose color corresponds to the direction with which it is associated. The north ear is yellow, the west is blue or green, the south is red, the east is white, above is black, and below is

Hopi altar and sand painting

speckled. Appropriate bird feathers, aspergilli, crystals, stone animal effigies, varicolored pebbles, and other objects are also placed along the lines.

When they make medicine, the officers of the society mix the ingredients while the other members sing sacred songs, shake their rattles, and beat on the floor of the kiva to let the people in the Underworld know the living realize the Underworld spirits are listening, sharing, and enacting the counterpart ceremony in the Underworld. Therefore, for the period when medicine is being made, the sipapu hole is uncovered; that is, the wooden plug that closes it is removed from its place in the board cover.

Zuni Pueblo altar showing method of placing pahos and medicine bowl

Water in which the medicine ingredients are mixed is brought from a special spring in a netted gourd. As the water is being poured into the medicine bowl, various objects taken from the radiating lines of sacred meal are dropped into it at intervals, and specified songs are sung. Sometimes a crystal is used to reflect light into the bowl. This is interpreted as a prayer for fertility, since there are several myths that describe how women became impregnated when a sunray fell on their vulvae. Sometimes smoke is blown into the bowl as a direct appeal to the home of the Clouds. Nearly always a member kneels and blows an eagle or turkey wing-bone whistle into the bowl to summon the deities.

Nearly every secret society is able to inflict a particular illness on others. This illness is called its *wuvata* (whip), and the ability to control it is inherent in the sacred paraphernalia of the society. Assorted ailments that are controlled include twisting sickness, lightning shock, weight loss, earache, rheumatism, snakebite, abdominal swellings, epilepsy, facial sores, head eruptions, running sores, and sore throat.

The whip strikes all who trespass on ceremonial secrets, but it may also afflict persons or things that come into contact with religious objects even in legitimate ways. To prevent this, the members of a society purify themselves by the Navotciwa Rite. They take a pinch of ashes in their left hand and wave it counterclockwise over a person or object while singing a dis-charming song. In particular, the Navotciwa Rite is performed at the conclusion of every ceremony so that the members can mix once again with the people without danger to themselves or others. There are additional methods of purification: prayer meal is used, and self-induced vomiting is common. On unmasking, the Hopi Katcina impersonator waves his mask around his head four times, and after that he waves a pinch of ashes around his head four times.

The Hopi believe that whatever causes a disease may cure it. Like cures like. Accordingly, those who suffer from an illness controlled by a given society will call upon that group to heal it. The cure is generally accomplished by waving ashes over the patient while the society's dis-charming song is being sung. As a rule, the cured person usually joins the society that cured him, either permanently or for a period of years.

Sometimes during the nine-day ceremony, one of the society chiefs directs the fashioning of a sand painting. Usually it is laid out freehand, but mechanical aids might also be employed. Portrayals are similar to those painted on the altar reredos. The colored sands are distributed Navajo-style by letting them trickle in a fine stream between the thumb and forefinger.

The kiva rites usually terminate on the eighth day at which time the altar is dismantled and the sand painting is destroyed. The next day, virtually the full membership appears in public in spectacular Katcina costume — often sprinkled with sacred cornmeal — and performs what is popularly called a dance, although the term is not always an apt description. In essence, this portion of the ceremony is a celebration of thanksgiving to the gods for what the society and people knew from the beginning day would be granted to them. The gifts prepared during the first four days are now given out to the people in acknowledgment of this. When this dance ends, all participating society members are expected to refrain from salt, fat, and sexual indulgence for four more days and to return to the kiva and remain there to avoid temptation. After this, they emerge and resume their secular activities.

Whenever a nine-day ritual is being held, there is always a festive attitude among the Hopi. The people exchange greetings and make offering presents consisting of prayer feathers and pine needles tied to twisted cotton strings called *breath lines*.

Pahos (Prayer Sticks)

Reference has been made to the *paho* (prayer stick), the most common form of prayer offering. It is inseparably connected with all religious ceremonies and prayers. It is, in fact, a prayer in itself, and it makes the spoken prayer associated with it effective. Pahos are manufactured in several forms. One form consists of two sticks, often painted green with black tips and tied together with cotton string cut to a prescribed length. The color green represents a mossy place and moisture. One of the sticks is male, the other female. As a rule, only the female is given a face, consisting of two dots for eyes and one for a mouth. A small cornhusk — shaped like a funnel and holding a little cornmeal, grass seeds, pollen, and honey — is attached to a pair of sticks where they are joined together by the tie string. These represent a prayer for a plentiful harvest. Added to the husk is a short, four-strand, cotton string, on the end of which are tied two small feathers. At the butt end of the sticks are tied a turkey-wing feather and a sprig of each of two specified herbs.

Hopi pahos

Other forms of pahos are made of flat pieces of board ranging from one to three feet in length and two inches or more in width, to which feathers and herbs are attached. Painted on the boards are symbolic figures of Katcinas, natural objects, animals, and reptiles.

Pahos used on altars are numerous, and they vary considerably in design. Some are long, thin sticks with cotton strings and feathers attached near the ends. Others are thicker sticks with a profusion of feathers tied on at their center. One type is bent over a cane or crook shape. Others are just straight rods. Some are long willow switches to the tips of which the feathers of the eagle, hawk, turkey, flicker, and other birds are tied.

Hopi pahos made of boards with painted symbols

All pahos have meanings that are understood by the society members, and they are employed accordingly. For example, a cane shape is usually a prayer to a very old person who has died and gone to the Underworld, but who, by the stick's presence, is now called back to share in the ceremony and to assist in the fulfillment of its purpose. All pahos are made with great care and solemnity, and they are prayed over each time they are used. There are specific ceremonies for making pahos. The kiva leaders meet to fashion them, and they always perform prescribed acts before the actual construction of the pahos begins.

There is a theory behind the making of prayer sticks and prayer feathers: A man makes a prayer stick because he wants something good, some benefit from Cloud, the Cardinal Point Chiefs, the Ice Chief or Planting One. From these and other chiefs all benefits proceed. A man makes a prayer stick exactly as prescribed because the wise old men of the ancient times said it should be made so. Feathers are used on prayer sticks, as well as prayer feathers, because they are light in weight and because Cloud and all the other chiefs desire them to make *Ka'lamonwu* (the prayer feathers hanging in front of the forehead).

The Hopi barters his prayer sticks and prayer feathers with the chiefs for material or other benefits, and he places on his prayer stick the prescribed feather and grass emblems that are related to the kind of benefits he desires. Feathers of the yellow bird, warbler, bluebird, turkey, eagle, hawk, duck, and owl are used. If a Hopi desires rain, he ties on a yellow bird or duck feather. A turkey feather is tied to every prayer stick. For the hot weather needed to make a good peach harvest, owl and yellow bird feathers are used. For hunting,

Hopi pahos

the feathers of the turkey and the yellow bird are attached, and also some of the grass that deer and antelope prefer. The feather of a blue-bird is a prayer for snow and ice.

The father of a young boy makes him a paho to which is tied the primary wing feather of the hummingbird. He places the free end of the string of this prayer feather against the base of a shrine (the feather points toward the sunrise) and prays for swiftness and endurance, so that his son's movements may be like those of the hummingbird — swift and tireless.

No paho is to be touched for four days after it is placed. To do so will bring terrible harm to the offender. Even after that it is to be touched only with the left hand, for the left hand is on the heart side of the body, and it does not grab as the right hand does. Also, it is cleaner, for it does not touch the mouth during the eating of food, and does not clean the body after waste is released. In healing, the Hopi medicine man always uses the left hand.

As Sun journeys across the sky each day, he sees the prayer sticks and prayer feathers and comes to them, inhales their essence, and then takes their breath body or spiritual likeness with him. He places each prayer in his belt and carries it with him as he goes in at the west to the Underworld at the end of the day. There he gives away all he has collected to Muyingwu, who knows all prayer sticks and prayer feathers. As Muyingwu takes them up one by one and looks at each, he says to the other chiefs, "This is for you, or you," according to the way the prayer sticks are designed. Those that are poorly made, or made by thoughtless men or men of evil hearts, he casts away, saying, "This is from an evil man, or a foolish one." The chiefs thank Muyingwu and the makers of the emblems. They decorate their foreheads with the feathers and then send along the benefits that the prayer-maker desires.

Assertions by highly qualified professionals that Anasazi-Pueblo migration and religious histories "have little or no historic validity" cannot be ignored, but they are troubling. The people and their religious practices did come from somewhere, and as yet the sciences have come up with remarkably few answers as to where.

Hopi paho made of boards with painted symbols

Somewhat regrettably, I feel, the sciences tend to think of spiritual and secular views and practices as evolving side by side as time passes. In this scheme, spiritual and secular developments are lumped together without distinction. According to the scientific viewpoint, as man adapts to his environment he invents out of his own limited facilities what he needs for survival; therefore, his religious life is not given by Above Beings — man makes it up as he goes along and is confronted with life's crises.

Hopi pahos

The Pueblos and other Indian tribes do not think of religious views and practices as evolving. They do recognize that certain minor additions to ceremonies have been made from time to time, but they accept that the essences and the vital parts were given to them by living supernatural powers — either at the beginning of time or early at specific periods and places in history. The Pueblos accept an historical emergence from the Underworld, the existence of the chief Katcinas, the inception of the clans, and more. The fact that kivas came into being at a later date would hardly be a problem for them, since they would answer that these were built for ritual practice when the Anasazi were instructed to build them by the Spirit Powers.

Amazingly complex rituals are performed, not just because they work today, but because they have always worked. It is known that at various times one Pueblo village has borrowed certain of its performances from another village. But these acquisitions are seldom believed to be as important as ceremonies considered original and intrinsic to the adapting village. By intrinsic, I speak now of ceremonies known to have been practiced for at least 600 years . . . which does not circumscribe the entire lifespan of the Anasazi-Pueblo, but is an impressively long time to maintain any practice. Moreover, if a certain ritual was in vogue at a village like Awatovi in 1350 A.D., it follows that it had been in effect for some time before that.

Typical Hopi symbols for use on ceremonial items

Famed anthropologist Jesse Walter Fewkes, who knew the Hopi more intimately than any other professional, stated as he considered the beautiful Walpi village Flute Ritual:

It is demonstrable that in a complicated ceremoniology there is much mythological lore intimately connected with the ritual. This lore is known to the thinking or devout member of the priesthoods, and it is referred to by them as explanatory of ceremonials. The ritual is not to them a series of meaningless acts performed haphazardly and without unity, varying in successive performances, but is fixed by immutable, prescribed laws which allow only limited variations. Modifications are due to the death of celebrants, or other circumstances equally beyond the control of the priests; and as the ritual of peoples changes very slowly, that of the Tusayan (Hopi) Indians is one of the least modified of their customs. Throughout the Flute Ceremony there is the same rigid adherence to prescribed usages which exists in other rites, and there is the same precision year after year in the sequence of the various episodes.[1]

In another account concerning the Fire Worship of the Hopi, Fewkes says he learned that living priests often did not know why they performed certain rites, "for they are not antiquarians and no sacred books exist among them; explanations that have survived have been transmitted by memory and have lost or have been modified much in transmitting."[2] Individual priests had prescribed functions to perform in ceremonies, but while they might know the meaning of these, they were densely ignorant of other rites, and they often confessed that the rites were meaningless to those who performed them. "We sing our songs, say our prayers, because they have been transmitted to us by our ancestors, and they knew more than we what is good." Fewkes concludes that rites practiced for a long time are looked upon as efficacious, and that, to the Hopi, is sufficient evidence that they are given by the deities and are best for the purpose.

Like other researchers, Fewkes was concerned about lost meanings. He wanted to know why each ritual was done and the meaning of its parts. Non-Indians always have a passion to understand. They want and even demand of God reasons for everything. But the Indians do not presume to interrogate the Spirits as to why they instruct the created world to perform as it must. It is

---

[1] Fewkes, Jesse Walter, 1892a, A Few Summer Ceremonials at the Tusayan Pueblos. *A Journal of American Ethnology and Archaeology.* Vol. 1, pp. 99-133. Houghton Mifflin Company, Riverside Press, Cambridge, Mass.

[2] Fewkes, Jesse Walter, 1922a, *Fire Worship of the Hopi Indians.* Smithsonian Institution, Bureau of American Ethnology, Annual Report, 1920, pp. 589-610, Washington, D.C.

accepted that the Spirits always know what is best, and if man wishes to receive their blessings, he will do what is required without insisting upon proofs and explanations. He will not distress his benefactors by impeding the process with questions about things his finite nature cannot fully understand anyway. "The wind blows where it wills." Indians accept that many things are simply beyond human comprehension and that human joy is found in knowing that greater powers than one's own are doing for him what must be done. The Indian finds no shame or diminishment in admitting that he is dependent upon higher powers. It is the Way of the Above Beings, and he does not allow pride or preoccupation to cut him off from a cornucopia of surpassing blessings. In his mind, only the foolish do that . . . perforce the silly and bawdy Hopi ceremonial clown serves in some instances as a reminder of what man will become if he ever forgets or ignores who he is and what his responsibilities are.

The Native American's attitude of acceptance may distress our inquisitive nature, but the sobering truth is that the Indians are not concerned about what we think of their religion. They do not ask us to investigate them, they do not perform for us, and it would trouble them little if we all agreed forevermore to keep our questions to ourselves.

It should, however, be pointed out that Indians are not entirely bereft of understanding where ritual practices are concerned. Centuries of use have brought comprehension. Certain things done correctly make certain things happen, and the doing and the happening are linked together. But even these enlightenments are given reluctantly to outsiders for one reason above all others: Most scientists reject any possibility that a prehistoric people could possess a true relationship with a real and living God, who through prayer and nature has imparted truth and tangible blessings to those who have entrusted themselves wholly to Him. Virtually every missionary has applauded this scientific view — at least until recent times when a few churches who serve Native Americans are including some traditional practices and thoughts in their worship services.

The traditional Indians know full well the opinions of scientists and missionaries in this regard, and they wonder why we still expect them

to be utterly open in revealing and explaining their religious life. Would we not feel the same if circumstances were reversed? So long as non-Indians treat the Indian religions as false, the Indians will remain silent. Consequently, we can assume that as most books, articles, and films are produced, Indians will, as always, be projected to audiences as less intelligent and less worthwhile than white people, hence never to be listened to, always to be pitied, and certainly needing to be converted to non-Indian ways and religions. It is a situation that at the very least is counterproductive, for as this book will show, it cuts the non-Indian world off from information about life and survival that it sorely needs.

A Summary of Hopi Pathways

The Hopi Pathways are more complex than those of the other tribes in this book, so perhaps a summary of them would be useful at this point.

The Hopi believe that their pathways are given by the Above Beings, who place blessings and events along the Ways. As we walk along the Ways, we can pick up the blessings and apply them to our lives.

The pathways are designed to prepare the people for what may come, and to go hand in hand with one's daily tasks. You will find that all of the pathways of the other tribes considered in this book are also preparatory.

The Hopi people are confident that their deities watch over the whole of life and provide all of the information they need to obtain supernatural help at proper times and in proper seasons.

Most ritual acts are carried out in a subterranean kiva that is believed to represent the womb of the Earth Mother, giver of life and renewal. The place where one worships and petitions is extremely important. Closeness to the deities, the very warmth and power of their beings, must be felt. When this is so, people hear the powers speak, motivation comes, and amazing things happen. The dead return, magic and miracles occur, and believers are simultaneously transported back into ancient time and forward into the future. Consciousness is expanded. The present becomes more intense. Emotions and senses are sharpened. Mood is deepened. People are elevated. Bodies tingle. There is expectation and excitement. Wondrous things happen.

Life is a cycle. It has no beginning and no end. Belief in life after death is accepted, but this does not include reincarnation. One dies, only to be born again in the Underworld where life on earth is continuously duplicated. Death holds no fear, for each person has a firm grip on an always-fulfilling existence. There are ongoing contributions to make.

Life is best when things are never easy — it fixes minds on the things that matter and on one's dependent status.

The welfare of the entire village comes first, individual welfare last. This view gives the individual the benefit of the whole, and the whole the benefit of the individual. Cooperation in all things is guaranteed. And, the welfare of the tribe is seen as depending upon the responsible and wholehearted fulfillment of each person's role.

Nature (of which humans are only one strand) and the Above Beings are one in the sense of unity, spirit, outlook, and purpose.

Success in the life-way requires a person to act out and think through every role that a human being is required to assume in the life cycle from birth to death. It also requires the acceptance of, and gratitude for, one's ongoing role in the Underworld.

Appreciating the need for the place of elders and the ancient ways remains essential. Neither of these can ever be dispensed with if an individual hopes for balance and success.

The rules for effective ritual observance are balanced and include both the physical and the psychical . . . performing the proper acts, observing tabus, exercising control over one's emotions and heart, and exulting only when appropriate. The ability for such control grows with practice. If either side of ritual observance is neglected, balance is lost, and failure results.

Prayer is a form of willing something into being. The formula is: **prayer + ritual acts + Katcinas = limited control of nature**.

If humankind fails to carry out its responsibilities, the universe might cease to function properly. Accepting this is an ego builder offering self-esteem, a sense of place, and a feeling that personal contributions matter.

The Katcina is synonymous with blessings. When masks are donned, the spirits represented by the masks take possession of the wearer.

The wearer becomes more than finite man. He is man plus spirit, doubled in strength or tripled when associated with the original Katcina deities.

The dead add their strength and counsel to the living.

The original Katcina deities keep the living Hopi connected to the source of life, the center that must never be neglected, taken for granted or abandoned.

Rituals must be performed with good and pure hearts.

Effective time has less to do with clocks than it does with one's mental state and psychological realities. The use of time and one's awareness of time on the person and the life scales is what matters and is in all ways productive.

Crises of identity — having to maintain a knowledge of who one is when something or someone is attempting to take that away — lead to balanced perspectives. Depression is avoided. Life is never an endless, bleak present with no hope of change. One gains a sense of self, a place in society, a belief in what one is, and a sense of continuity with the past, present, and future — an immutable identity.

The tiponi is the mother and heart of one's ritual, the symbol of identity and accomplishment.

Observances are to be performed at proper times, and the sequence is geared to winter and summer solstices.

The Central Pathway:
Rituals are nine days in length.

Day One, Entering:
Image of Dawn Woman placed on kiva hatch. Two small fires built, and pine-needle offerings sacrificed to the fires. Prayers for blessings offered in acknowledgment that they will be granted.

Days Two Through Four, Positive Preparation:
Tiponis refurbished with new appendages. Smoking, singing, and

praying, accompanied by music. Altar constructed — designs consisting of core things essential to life. Sand paintings are made. Construction of pahos and other gifts. Placing of tiponis and pahos on altar and sand painting, dead called back, conversations with the dead. Medicine water made, crystal used to reflect light into bowl, smoke and whistle blown into bowl, water sprinkled for purification using spruce or field-grass switches.

Day Five:
Distribution of pahos at shrines.

Day Six:
Nothing left to chance, making certain that all things needful to success of ceremony are included. Continued sprinkling and drinking of medicine water.

Day Seven:
Preparation of traditional food using corn — for feast of celebration.

Day Eight:
Preparation of supplementary foods — for feast of celebration.

Day Nine:
Public dance and feast of celebration; giving away of pahos and other gifts. Acknowledgment of belief that Sun has taken spirits of pahos from shrines and given them to deities; belief that requests will be honored.

Days Ten Through Thirteen:
Abstinence from salt, fat, and sexual indulgence. Last day, purify self and mask with ashes.

The Peripheral Pathways:

Superstition: Witches. Whenever failure assumes the proportions of a crisis, such as a drought or an epidemic, the Hopi believes that one or more individuals who are witches have allied themselves with ants, owls, crows and the like. These witches have both an animal heart and a human heart. They are members of a secret society, and they seek to recruit sleeping children. They are greatly feared and difficult to identify. But certain charms and colors, such as turquoise, can turn witches away, and these are commonly found in the home and on the person.

Such superstition is usually scorned by modern society as useless and untrue, yet it has kept the Hopi ever mindful of the perils of life and of their constant need for the Above Beings to watch over them. It has also caused them to fear illness more than death. While the latter is only a transition from life on the surface of the world to life in the Underworld, illness can reduce a victim to a state of utter dependency. Even worse, illness can result in a failure to fulfill one's role, which might disrupt the functioning of the organized household group and even of the universe.

Healing: All Hopi learned how to use herbs for medicines, and there were medicine men and medicine women. In curing, the adage was followed that "like cured like." If the cause could be found, so could the remedy. Therefore, hairy seeds would make hair grow. Even today, two plants growing close together are believed to be related, and one is spoken of as the child of the other. Plants are also known as male and female, and each is associated with a cardinal direction. Many plants play a role in religious ceremonies; some are placed on altars, and others are tied to prayer sticks. Crystals are employed to locate an affliction. To do this, the medicine person looks at the patient through the crystal for four or five minutes, swaying back and forth and moving his free arm toward and away from him. Suddenly then, the crystal is laid gently on the body at a place that is certain to elicit severe pain.

Among the varieties of treatment practiced in ancient times were those of eye-seekers who moved around, peering and gazing everywhere, until at last they determined the direction in which the malign influence lay. For headache or some minor ailment, the treatment was massage, with eyebrows, forehead, temples, and root of the nose rubbed with straight strokes or passes, and with acupressure applied at certain points on the neck and shoulders. Certain non-Katcina dancers used a "lightning frame" constructed of pine or spruce that had been struck by lightning. These frames were used for exorcising, and Flint Doctors, who cured lightning-sent disease, struck initiates over the heart and on the back with them to impart the power of lightning. In one reported instance of severe illness among children, medicine men made an altar in their kiva and placed prayer sticks on top of it at sunset. A nightlong vigil of parents and children followed in the kiva.

Despite the demise of medicine societies, individual healers are still present in Hopi villages. In their approach to healing, if time permits, four days are taken to prepare for the actual healing. During this period, they ritually purify their persons so as to become a fit channel through which the spirit powers will perform the actual cure. This view closely parallels that of Sioux and Apache healers, and more is said about this under those headings.

Work and games were of kinds that contributed to the ongoing health of the Hopi. Women's work has already been described, and the ancient women were thin and lean. Men often raced for miles across the broiling desert without water or resting. Even now, when pickup trucks are in vogue, some farmers still run long distances from their homes to their fields, making the round trip there and back in a single day. A trader at Canyon Diablo and Oraibi once hired a number of the best Hopi runners to round up wild horses for him. They gathered in the horses, plus several deer and antelope.

~ ~ ~

The combination of the foregoing beliefs and practices has brought the Hopi a remarkable inner peace. If you ever have an opportunity to meet them, you will see it in their faces, demeanor, and unharried pace of life. Thos who still live in the older villages have, compared to the living standards of the average American, virtually nothing, and yet they have everything. What remains for us is to apply their thoroughly learned pathways to our lives, and we will do that in Part Three of this book.

CHAPTER SEVEN

Cherokee Pathways

Central Pathways

I have pointed out that the central pathways of the Native Americans were preparatory in nature, and the central pathway of the ancient Cherokee is a wonderful example of this truth. Preparation was the essence of their annual cycles of festivals that had its origin in the annual cycles of the seasons. Nature taught the Native Americans no end of things.

Preparing in Advance

Since the complex ritual details of the Cherokee festivals are for the most part not something we can put to use in walking the pathways today, we will concentrate on their thrust, for that will be a precious commodity in all that we do.

In their Great New Moon Feast of Autumn, which they called The Commencement, we encounter an unusual twist — the beginning of a cycle at the end of nature's productive year. As the fruits of their crops were harvested and feasted upon, the people acknowledged that the Above Beings were blessing them as promised. The Cherokee expressed in ritual their thanksgiving and their awareness of the source of the blessings — that they were being watched over according to the ancient promise. Thus the cycle opened on a resounding positive note. Everyone acknowledged that all was well between man and God and that they were convinced the relationship would continue.

To drive this point home, immediately thereafter they held the Cementation and Propitiation Festival. In this unique ceremony, the union of the Above Beings and mankind was symbolized by two men who performed the cementation rite, done publicly by two fully clothed and armed men who stood facing one another as they exchanged their garments and weapons until each was fully clothed in the other's attire. They were then inseparable brothers and were expected to fully support one another for life. This symbolized for the people the higher fact that the Above Beings, by blessing the people so abundantly with crops and in other ways, had proven that nothing stood between themselves and the Cherokee. They too had exchanged garments — prayer and faith for produce and protection — and they too were inseparable brothers. Then, in the intense purification rites that followed the cementation rite — when the people fully immersed themselves seven times in running water — any unforeseen barriers or hindrances humans might have placed between the Beings and themselves either deliberately or unknowingly were put aside and done away with. The gates of heaven were thrown fully open and confidence abounded.

Next came the Bounding Bush Festival, the natural climax for the assurance just celebrated. In this rite, the Cherokee expressed unrestrained joy in acknowledging the source of their blessings, and thanksgiving was offered as everyone threw Sacred Tobacco into the Sacred Fire.

However, the Cherokee learned by trial and error that overconfidence could become a serious problem. They might begin to think they had accomplished their blessings on their own or that they had received them from the Beings simply because they deserved them. So, winter followed hard on the heels of the Bounding Bush Festival. In winter's frigid atmosphere and pristine bleakness, the

The Cherokee cementation rite

Cherokee were reminded over a prolonged period of time that, without the Beings, they were nearly helpless. As the leaves fell from the trees, the fields became barren, the game retreated, the snow piled up, the sleet cut at flesh and bones, and the wood stores grew ever smaller. The tribal elders found advantage in this — they sat by lodge fires and told the wide-eyed children and the edgy adults reassuring stories about how for countless centuries the winters had come and gone, and the Beings never had forgotten to provide for the people.

Sure enough, the snow melted, the winds subsided, the rains turned warmer, chunks of ice floated down the rivers, and the first blades of yellow-green grass poked their friendly heads through the surface of the soil and looked up at Sun. New creatures were born. Mother Earth was renewing and continuing creation. She had triumphed once again over Cold Maker, and in concert with all creation, the Cherokee were called to renewed celebration. As the elders had said, the Above Beings had not forgotten them. It was time to plant again and, as always, to call upon Old Woman Corn Mother to come and give life to the seed.

The next celebration in the annual cycle was the First New Moon Feast, in which some of the old fruits from the previous year — kept as testimonies to the dependability of the Above Beings — were brought out and consumed, and the New Fires, symbolizing fresh beginnings, were kindled.

Now questions were asked: Could all of this really be true? Was it not, considering the base nature of mankind, too much to hope that the Beings had so much love for the Cherokee? The priests answered:

Look out there at the fields where the fruits are showing themselves.
Old Woman Corn Mother did come when we called to her.
She did implant true life in the corn and the other plants.
There too are the evidences of the beans and the other vegetables.
Fruit is appearing on the trees.
The streams are running full.
Fish abound.
Out in the hills fawns are prancing around.
The Beings are coming down to us and they are revealing themselves in what they create anew.

There must now be total purification of the people so we will be fit vessels for the divine/human union that is taking place.

Next, the New Green Corn Feast was held. The people tasted the green corn as a tangible proof of hope and assurance fulfilled.

Finally, the end of the cycle of rituals came as the ultimate victory was proclaimed with the harvest of the mature and ripe fruit. In the midst of rich aromas, exultation and rapture were expressed with abandonment in the Mature Green Corn Feast.

But the next year lay ahead, and to assure that the blessings would continue, the annual cycle of festivals must begin again. So it would always be.

Important aspects of Cherokee religion included an extreme emphasis on purification by immersion seven times in running water during rituals and the use of the color white that symbolized purity. Also, while the festivals in the annual cycle included rites that were duplications of those performed in other festivals, each festival had rituals that were unique. While we can assume that these variations were handed down from ancient times — the Cherokee were certain they came directly from the Above Beings — we can also deduce that, in the individual festivals, priests were expected to develop approaches that were unique and appropriate and that, in each instance, would produce the desired result. Therefore, the people were called upon to be creative, and no two festivals in the annual cycle were ever exactly alike. Moreover, monotonous repetition in any religious act was to be avoided, for one was never to be careless where the Above Beings were concerned or to take for granted the relationship between the divine and the human.

The Cherokee Lifestyle

The sagacious Cherokee handled monotony uncommonly well. Knowing the problems that could result from monotony and boredom, they developed a lifestyle that counteracted dull routines at regular intervals. Some activities were unorganized and were carried out in leisurely fashion. Others were organized and carried out swiftly and with intensity.

Their philosophy regarding most daily activities was, "Put off until tomorrow or for as long as you can anything you can . . . then if something doesn't get done, it probably wasn't important in the first place." They did not think it especially prudent to get work done and behind them. Even when new houses were needed, they put off building them until late fall, while we might think it best to do the task early in the

Cherokee purification rite

year and have it over with. But they preferred to relax, fish, hunt, raid an enemy, do draft work, or play with the children . . . when and if a task couldn't be postponed any longer, everyone joined together to complete it in short order. In this wise, the house that would have taken a man working alone three months to build was up and finished in two or three days.

The Cherokee carried out their activities according to the seasons and to the position of the sun. They knew about the sundial principle and employed it for a few ritual purposes, but usually they did not use it as a clock to govern what they did. This view applied to certain portions of ceremonies as well as to daily events. At sunrise or at high noon or at dusk, things would begin. But these times were approximations, and the Cherokee were never under pressure to begin or to finish anything at precise times.

On the other hand, warfare was a highly organized matter from beginning to end and was carried out with precision and intensity. The most formidable foe was met with the maximum effort, and no detail was overlooked in the way of preparation, the order of march, the religious rites performed along the way, the manner of attack, and the victory celebration and purification upon returning home.

Accordingly, the Cherokee led a life of variation that lessened pressure by avoiding boredom. Prolonged activities were regularly interrupted to break the tension. When life became too serious, some foolish act was performed. Everything was put in proper perspective, and the general view was to make the long haul as pleasant as possible. Everything had a relief valve attached to it. Most assuredly, we can profit by applying to our own lives this extremely sensible finding from their peripheral pathways.

Crystals

In these days of spiritualism and holistic healing, rock crystals have become extremely popular. Shops in America and in Europe report that crystal sales and prices have more than tripled in the past few years. There is also a thriving market for books, seminars, and personal instruction in the crystal arts of healing and meditation. Since crystals vibrate precisely in response to electrical current, they are essential components for radios, watches, computers, and lasers. The crystal's prismatic effects and the tiny electrical charge it emits when rubbed lend credence to the idea that the stones transmit and magnify electricity. Crystal users talk about energy, vibrations, and balance, and they employ the stones for many purposes. Some believers simply

Ancient Cherokee priest and his crystal magnified with power

argue that while there is no scientific basis that crystals can heal, meditating with them is helpful since the resulting belief system induces harmony and peace.

The Hopi and Apache medicine persons used crystals, but to less an extent than the Cherokee. Indeed, it is essential to recognize that the ancient Cherokee priests centered everything in their divining crystals, which formed an essential part of their working paraphernalia and their peripheral pathways. Although the crystal was not always part of his dress — that is, he did not always carry one with him — it was essential to the priest's vocation.

Translated, the Cherokee name for the divining crystal means "Light That Pierces Through." The light referred to is both a light piercing through what it falls upon and a light conveying, through the substance of which the object is composed, instructions to the observer.

If anyone who was not sanctified and initiated touched a divining crystal, it was believed that he or she would die. The ordinary priest would sometimes wear his crystal suspended on his chest by a neck thong, but it was always hidden from public view by his clothing. Exceptions were the Chief Priest at the Propitiation Festival and the Great War Chief who wore theirs openly. All others who carried divining crystals kept to themselves even the knowledge of the place where they were worn or carried, and those crystals were not being carried were either stored as treasures in a holy box called an "ark" or carefully wrapped in seven deerskins.

There were five different sizes of divining crystals, each one of which was in the shape of a hexagon and composed of crystalline quartz. Some early informants said that in ancient times the stones were diamonds, but archaeologists doubt this. Researchers have not learned what the Cherokee believed about how the crystals received their power, although my friend Archie Sam (of whom I tell more at the end of this chapter) gave me some information about this. On tape, he denied that he knew anything of consequence about the stones, but privately he told me he learned from his father, White Tobacco Sam, that crystals are special "stones of God," which, as they form, gather their powers from the entire universe. Every crystal displays these powers in its facets; the purpose of the many facets is to impress upon the users that there are many facets or shades to whatever is seen and that each of these facets must be meditated upon to arrive at a true and useful answer.

For the ancients, however, it is only known that each priest possessed a crystal and that all sizes of crystals were consulted with equal confidence and held in equal honor.

The largest of the crystals was used by the Chief War Priest for divining the outcome of a forthcoming battle. A little after sunrise, he folded and placed seven deerskins on a small table and laid his crystal on top of the skins. He then moved back a few steps and prayed to each of the seven heavens. While he did this, he first touched the ground with his hands and slowly raised them, stopping a moment at each heaven until he reached the seventh and highest one. Between each thumb and forefinger the priest held a large stone bead, and if the Cherokee were to conquer the enemy, the bead in his right hand would seem to move and be alive. If they were to lose the battle, the movement and life would be in the bead in his left hand. If they were to win, blood would flow down the right side of his crystal or, if they were to lose, down the left side.

The four crystals used by the White Priests were smaller than the war crystals and varied in size according to their use. The first was employed to ascertain whether sickness would come to an individual, a family, or a town. A sacrifice was offered by the priest, and in one of three manners the crystal was set to catch the first rays of the morning sun — either on top of seven folded deerskins, on top of a post covered with fawn skin, or in a crevice of a house. If the resulting omen was favorable, a bright and unclouded blaze of light would appear in the stone. But if the omen was unfavorable, the crystal would appear blue and smoky, and as many persons would die as appeared lying down on its right side.

"As he prayed, the crystal would shine brighter and brighter, until finally a dazzling brightness would be reflected from deep within the stone . . ."

This same crystal was, on certain occasions, consulted for an identical purpose by large bodies of people. One of these instances was at the appearance of the Great Autumnal Moon, when the Cherokee began their lunar year. Before sunrise on the appointed day, the priest of each town would gather the entire populace into the Town Council House and seat them in rows with their faces turned toward the east. Then he would open a crack in the east wall of the house and set his divining crystal in the crack to catch the first rays of the rising sun. He backed up until he was four feet from the crystal, and with his eyes riveted upon the crystal and his face turned toward the sun, he offered a prayer. As he prayed, the crystal would shine brighter and brighter, until finally a dazzling brightness would be reflected from deep within the stone to the ceiling of the house, where the light first moved back and forth, back and forth, and then descended lower and lower until at last it would glance like a thunderbolt toward the seated people.

Without illuminating their persons, the light would pass over those who it was believed would die before the return of the next new moon. During this ritual the priest never touched the crystal. He simply remained where he was and repeated his prayers.

Credible participants in this amazing rite in the late eighteenth century adamantly declared that they had known of actual instances where Cherokee the light failed to rest on as it passed by — while they did not die within the first month — did die within three months.

The next smaller sized crystal was used for recovering lost or stolen objects. To do this, the priest set the crystal out in the sun and prayed for it to relay information. When a theft had occurred, he would see in the crystal the stolen object as well as the thief.

The hunting crystal was smaller still. The hunter began with an appropriate prayer and placed the stone where it would catch the morning sunlight. If a buck deer was going to be killed, he would be seen in the stone; if a doe, a tinge of blood would appear; if nothing would be killed, nothing would be seen, and the hunter might as well forget hunting for the day. Tomorrow he could try again. Crystals used during an actual chase were set on a wooden stool that was placed on a riverbank, then covered with seven folded deerskins. Great success was indicated when the cover was raised and a multitude of deer horns could be seen in the crystal. Failure was foretold when only a few deer horns or none appeared.

Individuals used the smallest divining crystal to discern how long they would live. If the inquirer was to attain old age, a figure with gray hair and a long white beard would appear in the crystal.

Sometimes a jealous or suspicious husband would go to a priest and ask him to determine whether or not the man's wife was faithful to him. In such instances, the priest would set out his crystal and pray for information. If she was faithful, the appearance of the crystal did not change. But if she was unfaithful, she and her lover would appear in the stone. It is said that the priest would then pick up a handful of flies he had killed for the purpose and solemnly pronounce the evil that would descend upon the wife . . . if he opened his hand and one of the flies came to life again, it would instantly fly to her, settle on her body, and burrow its way into her . . . in seven days, with bitter tortures, she would feel it gnawing its way into her heart, and she would die. It is reported that such women invariably died on the seventh day. The sources did not say whether or not a wife could go to a priest and work this same justice on her husband.

So dearly did each Cherokee priest prize his stone and its powers that when he knew he was going to die, if he had no favorite disciple to bequeath the crystal to, he would go alone to the woods and locate a tree into the side of which a woodpecker had pecked a hole. He would bury the crystal there, stopping up the hole with clay and bark in such a way as to render its discovery impossible. If he did not take these precautions and the stone was found lying about after his death with no properly authorized person commissioned to take charge of it, every person in the priest's family would die.

". . . a major use of crystals was that of prophesying life or death."

No doubt you have noticed that a major use of crystals was that of prophesying life or death. This becomes understandable when we realize that the Cherokee lived in circumstances where longevity was always threatened by one means or another — not the least of which was warfare with neighboring tribes. But the first point of divining was to discover what was going to happen so they could get ready for it and not be caught unprepared. Seemingly gloomy predictions were not taken as being final. In the usual instance, additional rituals were held in an attempt to receive — after proper purification, prayer, and sacrifice — a favorable prediction. The Cherokee believed that conditions could be altered and that circumstances could be changed. Even the presence and proper use of the crystals were taken as harbingers of good health and well-being. Crystals were believed to provide enlightenment and to have an intrinsic protective quality. This fits in quite well with the current opinions regarding them. The Cherokee did not, however, find so many uses for crystals as we do. Times, insights, and needs have changed somewhat, and the Cherokee priests would probably be the first to say they do not disagree with what is being done today with the Sacred Stones of God.

CHEROKEE HEALING

Healing was another peripheral pathway walked by the Cherokee. Again, the principal value for us is found in the direction that the

Cherokee healing took. We are not likely to employ many of their practices — other than the use of herbs — or to reject modern medicine in their favor. But, as will be seen, some of what they did was fully modern, and we have at last come to recognize its value as much as they did.

It is essential that Cherokee healing consisted of a combination of act and prayer on the part of the healer. The two were inseparable, and the Cherokee believed absolutely that one would not heal without the other. Faith was vital on the part of both healer and patient. Both must have believed either that the illness would be cured or that there was some good and spiritual reason why it would not be.

Present-day physicians and psychiatrists acknowledge the importance of faith in the healing process. They have determined that the mind can influence chemical mechanisms in the body which may be either beneficial or detrimental. Remarkable cures have been effected by optimism alone. In contemporary holistic healing patients are given hope and a sense of control. The patient/healer relationship is all important. Cherokee healers and their patients recognized this truth hundreds of years ago, long before Anglo doctors did.

St. Mary's Hospital and Health Center in Tucson, Arizona, currently sponsors what have been extremely successful conferences in various cities in the United States in which Native American medicine men and women are the featured lecturers. They offer in-depth experience in "didactic and experiential learning, the utilization of meditation as an avenue toward personal and professional growth, and show how to relieve distress, and offer self-actualization through an expanded spiritual consciousness." Edgar Monetathchi, Jr., a Comanche medicine man, is Executive Director of Traditional Indian Medicine at St. Mary's Hospital and Health Center. There are eleven lecturers on the regular faculty, including a brilliant Oneida, David Powless, and equally talented Mescalero Apache medicine man, Paul Ortega.

"They believed that their own best good was served when the Above Beings . . . had ultimate control."

It is not surprising that the priests, hence religion as a whole, played the dominant role in Cherokee life and that religion was inseparable from any part of life. When calamities of any sort befell the people, they turned to the priests, as intermediaries, for solutions. Thus it is clear that the ancient Cherokee were willingly a dependent people, and personal satisfaction was subordinated in matters where credit for achievement was concerned. They believed that their own best good was served when the Above Beings, who were not limited as humans were, had ultimate control. Priests were turned to, but only because the priests themselves turned full time to the higher powers. The respect of the people for their priests came from the priests' knowing how to fulfill their intercessory role in accordance with the ancient teachings.

Even during alien and overpowering tribulations, such as a smallpox epidemic, the priests were depended upon, and while there was a natural disappointment in failure, any unfortunate consequence was attributed either to the divine will, to a lack of knowledge as to how to prepare, to a miscalculation in determining the cause or the manner of treatment, or to the abuse or misuse of persons or holy property. Impending death or other loss did not cause panic and, in fact, was accepted with stoicism. The Cherokee prepared in advance, because they wanted to know insofar as was possible, what was ahead so they would be ready for it when it came in and not be irretrievably broken. The preparation was the reason behind that constant divining with the crystals and with beads.

To use beads for divining, the priest would take a large white bead between the thumb and forefinger on the right hand and a large black bead between the thumb and forefinger of the left hand. While he prayed he would hold his hand high above his head, and whichever bead moved first or most noticeably would give him the answer he sought. The white bead gave favorable replies, and the black bead unfavorable.

Thus the priests and the people had various ways — and more of these are set forth in the pages ahead — to combat disease, other adversities, and death before any of these reached out to claim their victims. The people believed in a vast pantheon of higher and mostly beneficial powers who could be called upon as needed. A combination of act and faith were essential elements in obtaining assistance, and prayer was an inseparable part of faith that was practiced constantly. Prayer formulas were evolved for special needs and for obtaining spiritual direction. They also blocked out, or covered over to render helpless, enemies of any kind. Both priest and people expected that prayers would be answered. The people began with a positive attitude, and prayers contained no expressions of doubt.

As shown in their seeking of inner balance in healing, the Cherokee employed good sense in their way of life. People were given minds, and the Cherokee knew that the Above Beings intended these minds to be used. They also knew that a moral life was pleasing to the Beings and important to personal and national survival, and they considered abstinence to be sometimes both necessary and positive. Fasting and other acts of denial were regularly practiced. Personal dignity, honor, and shared responsibility were looked upon as valuable assets. People cared about these things, and they cared enough about one another to wish not to become someone else's burden.

In the manner of all ancient peoples, the Cherokee believed in many things that whites would call superstition, for there were no other means of explaining certain mysterious happenings and counteracting those events and portents that were detrimental and fearful to man. Witchcraft was accepted and addressed by both the people and priests.

The Cherokee were practical people; they made practical approaches to religion and to ordinary life. Their villages were organized carefully, their civic/religious buildings were functional, and they made practical economic and military choices. They carefully observed and imitated nature and her creatures to find many of their proper medicines and effective ways to apply them.

"… the healer proceeded by questioning the patient about whether he had infringed upon a tabu and about his dreams and omens."

In the practice of healing, the healer began by learning the location of the patient's pain, for the healer did not so much aim to cure the disease as he did to remove its cause. He proceeded by questioning the patient about whether he had infringed upon a tabu and about his dreams and omens. Investigation of these might cause the patient to mentally travel back in time for months or years before the healer would feel he had learned the proper cause. Even then if the healer made a mistake in treating the cause it was really not considered a mistake, but simply a wrong diagnosis based on erroneous or insufficient information. Only if the real culprit was not hit upon could a healer be forced to surrender his patient to someone else. Once the cause was found, the proper roots or herbs could be determined and obtained. In doubtful cases a healer could use beads to determine whether or not his guesses were correct. If, in seven days after treatment, the patient was not showing improvement, it was accepted that he was afflicted by more than one cause, so either further treatment was undertake or a change of healers was in order.

The intrinsic properties of the remedies used and the careful observation of rules and regulations for the rites and prayers were equally important in achieving a cure. Paraphernalia used by the healers included objects for divining, scratching instruments to cause bleeding, the blowing tube made of trumpet weed, gourd dippers, a gourd rattle (never a tortoise shell rattle), and a persimmon-wood stamper used for massaging and acupressure.

Methods of application included administering the medicine in chewed or liquid form, blowing the medicine by spraying it over the patient with a blowing tube, blowing the healer's breath on the patient, sprinkling the medicine on the patient with a small pine branch, exposing the patient to the vapors of the medicine, using a sweat bath followed by a plunge into a cold stream, massaging with warmed hands that had been empowered by a Sacred Fire, vomiting into the river to get rid of the disease, scratching and sucking on the patient and then burying the extracted cause of the disease, and walking around the patient in a prescribed manner.

The Cherokee priests and physicians did not do surgery as we know it. They believed that they could heal without it and that it was better for a man to die than to undergo an amputation that would render him unable to care for himself or to be less than a functioning part of the greater community.

The powers to which the ancient healers prayed involved a countless number of fascinating creatures: earthly, spiritual, and celestial. Basically, these beings were prevailed upon to remove the illness or its cause and carry the affliction away. It was a mental exercise that had substantial value where faith in recovery was concerned. These creatures are far too numerous to report here but, for those who are interested, more comprehensive coverage of them can be found in my book, *Cherokee People,* and in the works of anthropologists and ethnologists such as James Mooney and Frans Olbrechts, who have broadly researched Cherokee healing lore.

There are medicine persons who are active as healers among the Cherokee today, but their patients consist of only the most traditional of the peoples and of some non-Indians who believe in their power. Some of the healers work cures, while others serve as counselors, answerers of questions, and as finders of lost objects. A few manufacture protective charms. J. T. Garrett, Ed.D., a Cherokee medicine teacher, is Deputy Director of the Office of Program Operations, Indian Health Service, and is one of the lecturers at the Traditional Indian Medicine conferences mentioned earlier. He was formerly a member of the hospital staff at the Cherokee Reservation, Cherokee, North Carolina.

Superstitions

The Cherokee lacked the scientific means we have to investigate and deal with the unknown, so they embraced superstition as their method of addressing it. Notice that I do not say they were "prey" to superstition, as is so often said of primitive peoples. They were "innocent," but I do not believe they were unwilling victims of it. Instead, they found superstition to be a useful tool for explaining and excusing what they otherwise could not. In so doing, they were very much like the rest of the world prior to the twentieth century, and if we are honest we will admit that a fair amount of superstition is still practiced by people who claim to be enlightened. Many of us have a few phobias and good luck charms in our arsenal of defenses.

The Cherokee people and their healers believed there were both natural and supernatural causes for disease, misfortune, and death. They also believed that good fortune could be influenced by natural and supernatural causes.

They knew some things were the result of common accidents or carelessness — a man cut himself, a running child fell and broke a leg or arm — but the vast majority of problems came from supernatural causes. If anything at all strange attended the onset of a problem, it meant someone or something with special powers was upset with the individual and was taking vengeance. Human or animal spirits could be the cause of any mysterious, unexplainable, or insidious diseases. Usually these spirits did not act on their own. They might be prevailed upon by a witch or some other human agency. Rarely, Sun might send disease, but more often was called upon to cure it. Fire might become angry and retaliate if someone threw waste into it, but like Sun, Fire was more often invoked against the causes of disease. The Moon might be responsible for blindness, but never caused diseases. A polluted river might strike back at those who insulted it. Thunder was another being who was more likely to help. Animal spirits were invisible, but their presence could be sensed. Their motive for sending disease was mainly that of self-defense against wrongs done to them. Human ghosts felt lonesome and wanted human companionship. They caused sickness so that people might die and come to be with them. Animal ghosts caused most diseases. There were the reincarnations of animals that had been killed by hunters, and the same animal might have as many as seven reincarnations before going finally to the Night Land.

Witches were men and women who could steal the life or vital principle and power of an individual, then add what they stole to their own power. They preferred to attack the weak, so hovered around the sick and feeble. Witches were indoctrinated into the profession by fasting and at the same time drinking, over a prescribed period of days, a certain sour brew made from a beetle-shaped plant. Those who drank it for four consecutive days could change themselves into any person or animal living on the surface of the ground. If they drank it for seven days, they could take on the shapes and powers of birds or animals that lived under the ground or flew above it. Witches loved to work at night, so this is when the people most often guarded against them with Remade Tobacco.

MAN-KILLERS

Human beings known as "man-killers" were witches who had the power to cause distress by altering food in a victim's stomach, to change or twist peoples' minds, and to change a minor ailment into a serious one. Above all, they might shoot an invisible arrow into a person's body and kill him.

There were a number of dreaded diseases that were thought to be caused by the trickery of a human agent who deluded both the patient and the healer by sending a disease that looked or seemed like one that it was not. Thus the healer might make a wrong diagnosis and not realize his mistake until it was too late. Menstruating women could spread disease to whatever they had touched or to those who touched them. Even such a woman's presence in a group could cause frightful problems. Pregnant women were only slightly less dangerous.

Dreams, signs, and omens also caused diseases. Neglected tabus and disregarded injunctions worked in insidious ways to cause physical defects such as toothaches and abdominal pains.

Last of all, yet the most dreaded, were contagious diseases and epidemics, caused by immorality and the evil influences or activities of intruding white people. The white people were thought to let loose epidemics to ravage the Cherokee towns and villages so that they could possess Cherokee land.

To explain and to combat the foregoing, the Cherokee created a complex realm of beliefs that scholars have since summed up under the headings of Spirit People, Superstitious Practices, Signs and Portents, Dreams, Uncleanness, Prayer formulas, and Myths. We will not examine these beliefs in detail here, since our concern is more with the concept than with the lore.

SPIRIT PEOPLE

There were two kinds of Spirit People — the Immortals and the Little People. Both lived in secret places in Cherokee country, and their manners of life were very much like that of the Cherokee. Other than when they wanted to be seen, the Immortals were invisible, yet they looked and spoke just like Cherokee. The Immortals were very friendly, and they often located lost Cherokee, cared for them until they were ready to travel, then returned them to their homes. More than once, the Immortals aided the Cherokee warriors against the enemy and saved them from defeat. They were invisible when they did this, but from the miraculous things that happened on the battlefields, the Cherokee knew that the Immortals had been present.

Full-grown Little People hardly reached up to a man's knee, but they were well shaped and handsome, with long hair falling almost to the ground. They were great wonder-workers and were very fond of music and dancing. They were helpful and kindhearted, and finding and returning lost Cherokee children was a specialty of theirs. They also came secretly at night to help people plant or harvest their crops. Only those Cherokee whom the Little People wished to could see them; these people were able to describe them to others.

Belief in the Immortals and the Little People did not end with the Cherokee's conversion to white ways and religion. Cherokee continued to see them as well as the evidences of their presence. This is true today among both the eastern and western Cherokee — mainly among the full bloods.

Beyond the Spirit People there were fairies — tiny people who were good-natured and tricky. They caused the strange things that happened in people's homes and to hunters — such as when a hunter shot an arrow into a perfectly clear space and then couldn't find it.

One spirit was not so friendly. He prowled around at night carrying a lighted torch. No one knew what he looked like, because they were afraid to get near him.

PURIFICATION AT DAWN

Superstitions did not explain or take care of every problem, but, together with the solutions offered by other aspects of life, they went a long way toward bringing the inner peace the people needed to cope with the unfriendly supernatural powers and adversities that might otherwise have destroyed them. For example, women always threw a small piece of the fattest part of the meat into the fire while they were eating or before they began to eat. This act assured that good things would happen, and it turned away those things that were evil. A piece was cut from the thigh of every deer a hunter killed and was thrown away; unless this was done, sickness and other misfortunes — such as spoiling the hunter's aim — would surely follow. Newly killed venison was waved several times through the smoke and flame of the fire as a sacrifice that released the creature's spirit, which must never be eaten. It was supposed and feared that certain uncleannesses might be unknowingly contracted during the night while asleep, either from witches or some other unknown cause. Therefore, upon awakening before dawn, people turned onto their faces and sang a repetitious chant. They then devoted some time to meditation, sang the chant again, and repeated this ritual

Cherokee priest using face mask for control to lure rain clouds closer

until sunrise. After this, they arose, went to a nearby river or creek, and, while standing on the bank, sang the same chant again. They plunged into the stream and continued to remain under water for as long as they could hold their breath. They then stood up and again plunged in as before, doing this seven times, after which they considered themselves to be cleansed from the impurities of the night and ready for the day.

Certain signs usually indicated that death or some other form of tragedy was about to strike. Should someone see the apparition or appearance of a friend come and then quickly vanish, that friend would soon die. Should a whippoorwill make its sound in the daytime, it was supposed that a witch has assumed the appearance of the bird. If it sang repeatedly near a house, one of the family in that house would soon die. If an owl landed in a peach tree in a town and hooted, enemies would approach that town within a few days. When a certain bluebird sang, there would soon be a storm. Some signs smack of Cherokee humor, for we can reasonably assume they seldom happened: should a hen crow, someone in the family would soon die; or if a dog talked like a person, there would soon be a catastrophe. If a hominy pestle moved about a house unassisted, all in the family would soon die.

If a person dreamed of going toward the west, that was a sign that he would soon die. Other dreams that signified death included seeing an eagle or crane on the ground or flying low, seeing anyone floating down a stream of high water, seeing a house burning, and seeing a person wearing exceptionally clean clothing. Some dreams foretold illnesses or were signs that witchcraft was being practiced. To dream of flying was a sign that the dreamer would live to a great age. A woman who dreamed of her son becoming an eagle was being told that he would become one of the great warriors.

Uncleanness was in large part associated with post-childbirth and menstruation, and purification rituals were performed to counteract both. If, during the wife's menstrual period, the husband lay with her, he too became unclean and must immerse himself seven times and put on clean clothing. Prior to bathing, he drank an emetic tea for inner purification. After a man and his wife had sexual intercourse, they were both unclean and must immerse themselves seven times in running water. Their garments must also be washed. All who touched a dead body, a human bone, or a grave contracted uncleanness and must remain alone until the uncleanness was removed by purification. Warriors who killed enemies in battle must also, upon their return home, undergo purification by water immersion.

CHEROKEE PRAYER FORMULAS

The Above Beings provided the Cherokee with several ways to make predictions and to cope with their losses and disasters. Chief among these was the annual cycle of festivals, both major and minor. But there were also the peripheral pathways to walk. These included divining with crystals and beads — which has already been described — prayer formulas, sacrificial offerings, purification, and a few other practices that will be useful to us.

Prayer formulas were formalized statements repeated by rote. There were two main types: those for love and those for curing disease. Love formulas were employed for attracting and retaining a wife, winning a woman away from a rival, achieving popularity with someone, and working revenge when betrayed. Disease formulas were recited for the removal of the causes of disease, for protection, and for long life.

Formulas with lesser strength were employed by hunters and healers. Hunting formulas were designed to lure the game closer so that it could be more easily killed and to make the traps more effective. The gathering of medicinal herbs also called for attraction formulas, and there were ritual prayers for the finding of lost people, animals, and objects. In conjunction with the latter, the priest might suspend a pebble, straw, bread ball, or brown stone from a string held between thumb and forefinger; the direction of its swing indicated the position of the lost object. Weather-control formulas were applied to stop bad storms, to induce rain during a drought, and to stop rain when there was too much of it. There were also formulas for warfare and for ball play.

Generally speaking, the main thrust of prayer formulas was to throw a cover over — thus to block out and bring in — an evil or negative aspect or thing. In effect, the petitioner would enter a prayer process of putting the adversary out of sight and then out of mind. Once free of the adversary and unburdened, the petitioner could proceed with his life or particular pursuit. The secondary thrust of prayer formulas was to draw in or draw closer things that were desired or desirable. We will make contemporary applications of these two uses in Part Three.

SACRIFICIAL OFFERINGS

Corn

Sacrificial offerings consisted primarily of corn, venison, and tobacco. Corn was the food staple of the Cherokee, and they treated it accordingly. Among all vegetables, corn held the first and highest place in the household economy and ceremonial observance. In its prayer formula, it was invoked as the Mother of the Corn, an allusion to its origin from the blood of an old woman who was killed by her disobedient sons. The first and foremost event of spring was the preparation of the fields and the planting of the crops. The Great High Priest and his seven counselors determined the beginning time for the planting so that the fruits of every field in the nation would ripen at the same time. In order to obtain good crops, seven ears from the last year's crop were put carefully aside by the Great High Priest, and these were believed to draw the new corn closer and closer until it had ripened, and the harvest ceremony, when the old ears were mixed with and eaten with the new ears, was performed.

The annual thanksgiving ceremony of the Green Corn Dance, celebrated before the eating of the first new corn, was the most solemn tribal function, for it included propitiation and expiation for the errors of the past year, an amnesty for criminals, and prayers for happiness and prosperity for the year to come. Only those who had properly prepared themselves by prayer, fasting, and purification were allowed to take part in this ceremony, and no one dared to eat the cooked new corn until after the ceremony was performed. In eating the latter, care was taken not to blow upon it to cool it, for if someone did this, it would cause a windstorm to beat down upon the corn still in the fields and destroy it.

In planting the corn, seven grains (seven is a sacred number) were placed in each dirt hill within a row, and these were not afterward thinned out. After the last tending of the newly planted crop, the owner of each field built a small enclosure in the center of the field. Then he and the Chief Priest of his town sat within it upon the ground, their heads bent down. While the owner kept perfect silence, the priest smoked his sacred pipe filled with sacred tobacco, shook his medicine rattle, scattered grains of corn on the ground, and sang invocations to the Mother of the Corn. Soon thereafter, a loud, rustling sound would be heard from outside that both men knew was caused by the Old Woman as she brought the True Corn with its spiritual power into the field and inserted it into the corn they had planted. Neither man, however, was allowed to raise his head and look for her until the priest's songs were ended, and by that time, she had always done her work and disappeared. This ritual was repeated on four successive nights, after which no one entered the field until seven more nights had passed. Then the priest entered, and if all of the sacred regulations had been observed correctly, he would find young stalks. If the owner of a field was willing to pay a sufficient fee to the priest in return for being taught the proper songs and rituals, he could perform the corn prayer ceremonies himself.

Tobacco

Tobacco was used as a sacred incense, as an ingredient in purification rites, as a conveyer of prayers to the Above Beings, as a love potion and as the guarantee of a solemn oath in nearly every important function. It bound a warrior to go to war against the enemy, it ratified a treaty of peace, it confirmed sales or other agreements, it sought omens for the hunter, it drove away witches and evil spirits, and it was used in healing. For use, it was either smoked in a pipe or crushed and sprinkled upon a Sacred Fire. It was never rolled into cigarettes or smoked for pleasure. The variety was the *Nicotiana rustica* (wild tobacco), which was called Old Tobacco by the Cherokee.

Tobacco had no true power of its own until it was remade through a ritual that began with its planting. In the spring, in a secret place where no one would see the growing tobacco and accidentally damage its power, lightning-struck wood was placed by a priest on a small patch of ground and burned. Then the tobacco seeds were planted in that location, and if it thundered while this was being done, that was an especially good omen — the crop would be an excellent one. In the fall, the tobacco was harvested at sunrise and was immediately taken to the bank of a stream, where a sacred prayer formula was said over it either four or seven times. By this act, power was infused into the tobacco, which was considered remade. For additional power, the tobacco was held up to absorb the rays of the rising sun, and since one's saliva and breath were believed to contain the essence of a person's life force and personality, chewing the tobacco and blowing on it invested the tobacco with even more strength.

There were four main ways to use Remade Tobacco for healing and dealing with witches: It could be smoked in close proximity to patients so that the smoke touched them, the fumes could be blown around to pervade a general area, the smoke could be blown toward where an individual was likely to be, or the tobacco could be placed where the desired individual would come into contact with it.

Venison

Venison was the other main sacrificial item because the deer was nearly equal in value with corn as a staple food. As such, the procreation of the deer population was of prime concern to the Cherokee, and special power was associated with the deer. For every festival, the first task carried out was that of sending out seven ritually trained hunters to procure the first seven deer needed for the feasting. The tip of the tongue of each of these deer was cut off, put in a sacred container, and brought back to the Great High Priest to use for divining purposes in the Heptagon rituals. During the ceremony, the priest would take the tips of the tongues and throw them upon the Sacred Fire. Everyone would then watch intently, for the direction in which the pieces of meat popped off as the tongue tip burned would be an omen. If none at all popped or if they flew east, all would be well with the people. If they popped off and flew west, misfortune would come. Sometimes the number of people to die in a certain circumstance would be indicated by the number of pieces flying off, and the Chief War Priest often used this device to make predictions concerning battles.

ARCHIE SAM

"... he would tell me things he considered so secret I was not to reveal them until after his death."

During our many discussions, Archie Sam told me in general terms about ancient Cherokee customs that either were no longer performed or were close to being extinct. Sometimes, after asking me to turn off the tape recorder and not make notes, he would tell me things he considered so secret I was not to reveal them until after his death. While he did not say so, I knew that his reason for this caution was fear of retaliation by living medicine people or by the spirits of deceased medicine people. He was a well-educated man, but he believed profoundly in the ancient ways. Actually, I didn't think some of the information he gave me in confidence was that sacrosanct, but the fact that he did was what mattered. Native Americans put great store in the keeping of unwritten laws of conduct, and they firmly believe that violations will lead to terrible consequences. I, on the other hand, am not Indian, not a medicine man, and to make certain no ritual will be harmed when I do reveal secrets, I do not reveal enough of any ritual to enable a non-Indian to perform it exactly as did the medicine person. In any event, our need where pathways are concerned is not to duplicate or perform any ritual. We want to understand its thrust or essence and use what we can of this for our modern-day purposes. I will provide assistance and guidance for that in Part Three, "Following the Pathways."

Regarding the Sacred Fire that burned in the National Heptagon, Archie stated that the last Fire had gone out in 1729 in Natchez, Mississippi. The people were accepting too many white ways and just let it happen. Later they regretted it, so the priests went into the mountains to ask for forgiveness and guidance. They were taught to use ashes instead of live coals, but the ashes must always be those of the Fire that had been kept since the beginning. These ashes were carried over the Trail of Tears. Subsequent Fires at the grounds were kindled from, or on top of, these ashes. Secret information about these ashes involves the knowledge of what must be done to properly move them from one location to the next — as must be done when a new dance ground is begun — to avoid the loss of power in the ashes during transit. Specific prayers must be used, and any ground over which the ashes will pass must be exorcised.

"This water . . . has power, and the power is released when you apply it to your body in connection with prayer."

Going to water for purification was becoming a lost ritual, Archie said. He felt this was very sad because it helped tremendously to live by the water and to use water in ceremonial functions. The secrets of its use are that running water, as opposed to a stagnant pond or even a lake with no outflow, is empowered by the Above Beings to carry away the effects of error and any bodily impurities. Therefore, to be effective, water used for ritual purposes should be that of, or that taken from, a flowing source. This water, even though taken from a natural source and placed in a bowl, has power, and the power is released when you apply it to your body in connection with prayer.

The use of divining crystals, Archie said, was also coming to an end among Cherokee medicine persons. In an instance familiar to him, a medicine man used a crystal to identify two men who had raped and killed a young woman. He looked into the crystal and saw who they were. Later, the medicine man reported this to the police, and the criminals were caught, tried, and convicted. Once, a medicine man who owned a crystal was asked by White Tobacco Sam to use it to predict the future. He put it in running water, and while it was there, he saw a picture on its surface showing that the traditional life of the Cherokee would decline until a day came when the Cherokee youth would raise it up again. Secretly, Archie informed me that crystals were used for determining the cause of an illness, and they could also determine what course the healing should take. For this purpose, the crystal was first warmed over a fire, then laid at different points on the patient's body until, while looking through the crystal, the healer could see the main point or center of the illness. Then the crystal, still holding this picture, would be placed in the sunlight, and the cause or nature of the illness would be revealed. By turning the crystal to its different faces, the steps that should be taken to accomplish a cure would be revealed, and the type of medicine or acupressure to be used might also be shown.

Healing with Crystals

Archie also said that medicine men rubbed their warmed crystals rapidly between the palms of their hands. When they did this, the stone gave off strong vibrations that, when placed on the patient's body at the point where pain existed, would remove the pain. Often, the vibrations were so powerful the patient's entire body would shake violently; afterward, the patient would be completely relaxed and at peace.

Gazing deeply into a crystal would bring clarity to one's thoughts, and when placed against the forehead, a crystal would focus and magnify perceptions so that the users became far wiser. They could see straight to the heart of a problem or into whatever was going on elsewhere. They could travel back into the past and forward into the future.

In obtaining herbs and roots for medicines, some of the medicine men of the old times — and this includes a few who lived during Archie's lifetime — were able to go out into the woods alone and, using certain chants, call to them the spirits of deceased medicine persons. The latter would speak in harsh gasps that were hard to understand as they explained the values of the medicines they were about to reveal, and they would lead the living medicine person to the places where the right herbs or roots were located. Off-the-cuff information Archie gave was that the deceased came in frightening, wretched forms, sometimes as partial skeletons. It took a brave person to stand there and meet them, and knowing this, they reward that person accordingly. White Tobacco Sam was one person who had done this.

Calling Back the Dead

There was also the eerie practice of calling the dead back to talk with you, to give you advice and better understandings. The dead would float in the air as they came into a room, and they would hover close to the ceiling. When White Tobacco Sam wanted to call someone back, he used an ancient dialect that only trained people would understand. When the dead did return, he could see them and hear them talk, but a person who lacked his medicine training could not. The dead returned in ghostly representations of the age they were at the moment in life that the one who called them back wanted to discuss with them. For instance, if the caller was remembering a moment in his life that the other person had been associated with, the deceased would return at the age he had been at that time. Then the two of them could talk about the problem or issue, and in this way, the deceased could offer advice and enlightenment.

Archie had never told anyone else this, but he said that when he was a child, one night when he and his father were home alone, White Tobacco Sam went by himself into the room he used when people came to see him for healing. About midnight, Archie heard several Cherokee voices coming from the room. Even though he knew he shouldn't, he crept to the door and peeked in. It was pretty dark in there, for only a single candle on a table was lighted. His father reclined in a rocker and was actively engaged in conversation with several people, none of whom Archie could see, but all of whom he could distinctly hear. The conversation was about healing a man Archie's father was treating. Archie was frightened and didn't stay to hear much of it. He thought that the next morning his father looked at him in a way that indicated he knew Archie had eavesdropped. But White Tobacco said nothing to him about it.

White Tobacco also had a secret prayer formula he chanted when he wanted to ask the spirits to guard his house while he was away. In particular, they were to watch his medicine items. Certain things were required to properly ask for this help: some medicine, a pipe, and Remade Tobacco were placed outside by the front door at the same time the call was made. If the spirits didn't come right away, the Little People might wander by, take the medicine, and give it to the sick. Then the house was left unprotected.

Taking Animal Forms

At one time, certain Cherokee medicine persons in Oklahoma could change themselves into animals. Archie was positive his father could do this, but he never saw him do it. In one instance, an old man with medicine power who lived near the Sam family was very ill, and Archie and his father went to visit the man and took him some food. The old man looked awful and was delirious, and Archie's father believed he was near death. When they left, the old man's hound dog followed them, growling and mean. Finally, White Tobacco threw a rock at the dog to frighten it off. He didn't intend to hit it, but he did, right between the eyes, making a big gash that bled instantly. The dog howled and ran away. Two days later, they went back to see how the old man was doing. He was lying on the floor dead, with the same stone embedded in a huge gash between his eyes. The dog was nowhere to be found and was never seen again. White Tobacco told Archie that the old man had been a witch.

"There are strange powers at work," Archie said, "and no one knows when they are after you."

Life After Death

I asked him where the medicine people believed the dead go. He answered that we live on four levels of planets, with this planet being the first level. At death, we first spend some time in ghostly form at this level and then we go to the next level. It is from that level and the next two that the dead are called back when living medicine persons need help and advice. The deceased individual is in a state of being where there is no time. He or she moves slowly through the levels, quietly ascending from one to the next. Ultimately, they reach the highest level, where the Above Beings live. This is where they stay; no one can be called back from that level.

Puzzled by the latter statement, I pointed out that if people at the highest level could not be called back, then available help was restricted to those who were at the lowest and intermediate levels.

Archie admitted that was so and said he assumed that some people who were called back would not come. In that case, the appeal would be directed to others. "But," he went on, "the journey to the highest level takes ages according to our time measurements, although the deceased do not know this or care, they are not conscious of or circumscribed by time. In any event, the living medicine persons usually called upon someone they had known, so the deceased had not been gone that long."

Sometimes, though, one of the great Cherokee of the past might on his own see something taking place here on earth that he wished to talk about to a medicine person. He would come in the night and make strange noises to get the person's attention. Once the person was awake, the two of them would hold a conversation, and the deceased person would tell the medicine person what he wanted him to know.

The Seven Heavens

I then asked why there was a difference between four planets and the seven heavens and what the relationship was. Archie, off the tape recorder again, said that the seven heavens were the working places of the Above Beings, and as such were not the same as the planets to which one ascended after death — although the fourth planet and the seventh heaven were one and the same. When a person concentrated on making a mental journey through the seven heavens, he would not want to be thinking about death and the life after, even though these things are not to be feared by those people who have healthy attitudes about death.

The Power of Unity

Regarding dancing at the medicine grounds, Archie told me that the key to a powerful dance is beginning with people who are united in body and mind, people who are going through the rituals as one person, totally united. If this is so, then the Sacred Fire picks up and sends out waves like a radio station. If everyone is emitting the same waves, then the outpouring through the Fire and smoke is sure to reach God. "Unity possesses a fantastic power. Nothing needs to be spoken when this is so. God feels it and responds. No audible prayer can be as strong!"

Archie Sam's Death and Reappearance

Archie died suddenly of unknown causes in Oklahoma City on May 23, 1986. He was not quite sixty-two years of age. On the second night after he died, two of his closest friends, who lived in Tulsa, Oklahoma, and who slept in separate rooms in the same house, were awakened about two a.m. by the lights of their rooms, which they had turned off when they went to bed. The lights were now turned on and blazing much more brightly than they ever had before. Without calling out or otherwise contacting one another, they emerged simultaneously from their bedrooms and entered the living room, where the lights, which they had also turned off earlier, were again on and blazing. Amazed, they looked around, and there stood Archie. He announced he had come to visit them, and when they had calmed down, the three of them visited for several hours about the days and events they had shared before his death. Then, just before dawn, he announced he had to return to his casket and took his leave. When he had passed ghost-like through the front door and was outside, there was a loud, thundering sound. The house shook like an earthquake had hit it so strongly that both of the people were nearly thrown off their feet. In a few moments, the shaking stopped; the lights dimmed and went out. The awesome experience was over. Archie had said nothing to them about why he had come or what death was like, and he did not suggest that he would come again. They were astonished and had no explanations. They related the story to me somewhat reluctantly, and I doubt they've told many others besides me . . . perhaps a few of their close traditional Cherokee friends who knew Archie and had danced as they had at his Medicine Spring Ground. He has not paid me a similar visit.

CHAPTER EIGHT

Apache Pathways

The central pathway of the Western, Chiricahua, and Mescalero Apache finds its focus in the annual Sunrise or Coming Out Ceremony for a pubescent girl who becomes Changing Woman, the Apaches' greatest culture hero. Changing Woman is also referred to as White Painted Woman or White Shell Woman. According to Edgar Perry, during the rite at White Mountain the girl is called *Saan Nabidegishe*. *Saan* means "an old woman," and *Nabidegishe* means "making motion(s) by hand." Taken together, the words mean Old-Woman-Making-Motions-With-Her-Hands. In the course of the ceremony, the pubescent girl changes from a girl to a woman of marriageable age, and during a particular portion of the rite, she makes certain significant hand motions.

The information I include here is based upon Sunrise Ceremonies I personally witnessed at White Mountain and San Carlos in the 1970s and upon comprehensive and unparalleled information given to me by the White Mountain Head Singer and medicine man, Renzie Gordon, who — at the time we talked and tape-recorded on October 8, 1974, in the home of our mutual friend Edgar Perry — was sixty-two years old and had led the dances at White Mountain and Cibecue for forty-six years. A special man, Renzie Gordon — with his smooth brown skin and close-cropped gray hair. He smiled often, now and then breaking into hearty laughter. Yet he was serene, dignified, and keenly intelligent. His brow wrinkled often when he was puzzled by a question and was attempting to answer as honestly and completely as possible — a factor that led to prolonged discourses in Apache that Edgar struggled to translate for me.

As a little boy, he lived in a wickiup, and he chuckled when I asked him what it was like to live in one. "Cold in the winter, good shade in the summer. In winter, we dug a pit in the wickiup floor, put a cowhide in it, and slept in that." Renzie had limited formal education in the white man's mission schools. He had three married daughters and sixteen grandchildren. He also had sons, but none were trained in medicine. "They are too green. They've got to be older. I wouldn't teach them until they were at least thirty years old." He hoped some would want to be trained in conducting the Sunrise Ceremony, since that was all Renzie did. He did not practice other kinds of medicine.

In all, Renzie had done forty-nine Sunrise Ceremonies, including four at San Carlos, and he hoped to do more to make an even fifty before he retired. Renzie began while he was still single and lived at Cedar Creek. He was sixteen years old at the time, and his own father taught him how to do the singing and the other things connected with the ritual.

Three years before we talked, Renzie had trained a young man named Ryan Burnette to lead the Sunrise Ceremony. Renzie told me he assumed that, when Ryan's son was a little older, Ryan would teach him "or another loved person" how to lead the ceremony.

Renzie said that a long time ago there had been five or six Singers, but they had all passed away. Now there were only two — he and Ryan — to do the singing. The reference was, of course, only to the White Mountain Reservation; my friend Phillip Cassadore, who lives at San Carlos, is also a renowned Singer, and at Mescalero, another friend, Paul Ortega, is the Chief Singer.

CHANGING WOMAN (SUNRISE) CEREMONY

My wife Lisa and I attended the Gift of a Changing Woman Ceremony (as it was called in the invitation) for Phillip's daughter, Jonell. It was held in a beautiful forested area on the north end of the San Carlos Reservation. There were hundreds of Apache present and perhaps a dozen non-Indians who were friends of the Cassadore family. About sunset on the first afternoon, which was a Friday (to accommodate work schedules, all Sunrise Ceremonies are held on weekends now), Phillip announced that the girl would appear for the first time in public at 9 p.m. and that the ritual would continue at sunrise the next morning if all of the paraphernalia was on hand — mentioning in particular the blue-green stone (turquoise), the white stone, and feathers. On Saturday night, the girl would dance around a bonfire for about three hours, until midnight. Then, taking pauses to rest, she would dance all night in her wickiup with her sponsor and six medicine men, each of whom had a special skill. One knew herbs, one the body, one vein circulation, one the head, one the proper food to eat, and one the heart and soul. Each man would tell the girl what she should know about these things.

Sponsor and Medicine Men Instruct the Sunrise Girl

When the medicine men had finished, her sponsor, who in this instance was Phillip's seventy-seven-year-old mother, would "admonish" the girl. She would tell her the legend of White Painted Woman and what life would be like — how to cope with hardships and depression, how to be happy, and how the ceremony would give her guidance and protection for the rest of her life. In particular, the girl would have thirty-two lightnings that would shield and surround her to protect her. "People who have faith and understand don't need guns," she would say. "Guns are an admission of a lack of faith, and they won't save anyone."

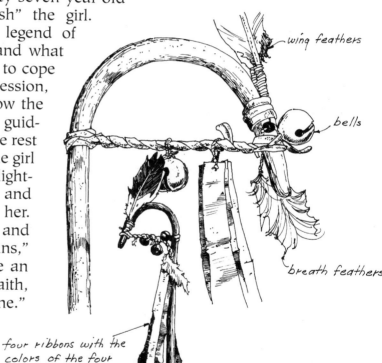

wing feathers

bells

breath feathers

four ribbons with the colors of the four directions

The Legend of White Painted Woman

Phillip then related the White Painted Woman legend as follows: She was created in the beginning by Giver of Life, who told her of a coming flash flood (here Phillip mentioned how the Apache legend was similar to that of the flood story of Noah's time). White Painted

The Apache sunrise ceremony girl's cane

Woman was directed to find a large abalone shell and to place in it a mano and metate, fresh water, corn, other food to eat, and a walking stick with a curved handle like that of a cane. Then she was to get into the shell. The flood came, and she floated around on the surface of the water. After some days, the waters receded, and the shell came to rest in a sandy area. The Apache think it was the White Sands area of New Mexico.

When White Painted Woman got out of the shell, Giver of Life told her to kneel down on the sand. She kneeled down three times, but nothing happened. She was discouraged, but Giver of Life ordered her to kneel a fourth time. She became pregnant and immediately gave birth to Son of Sun. She thought that was all there would be and that the two of them would be alone. But Giver of Life told her to kneel four times again, and after the fourth time, he told her to let water drip into her. She did and gave birth to Child of the Water.

While Phillip went no further with his description, other sources in the literature concerning Apache lore give slightly different versions of the legend and state that as the brothers matured, White Painted Woman told them how to live correctly. They then left home and, following her advice, rid the earth of most of its evil. Unlike other figures in Apache mythology, White Painted Woman never grew old. Whenever she reached a certain age, she went walking toward the east. After a while, she would see a youthful image of herself in the distance coming toward her. When she and the image came together, they merged, becoming the young one. Then she was like a young girl all over again.

The Purpose of the Sunrise Ceremony

The primary objective of the puberty ceremonial is to transform the pubescent girl into Changing Woman. At the invocation of the Singer on the first night, and continuing at sunrise when the first shaft of sunlight strikes an abalone shell disk that hangs on the girl's forehead, the power of Changing Woman enters her and remains within her for seven days. As the rite continues, the girl acquires the surpassing qualities of Changing Woman and is equipped to live a useful, bountiful, and long life. The power is implanted and transforms her; then she is like a seed that bears good fruit for the rest of her life. Vicariously, she makes these same blessings available to all who by their presence or prayers or both share with her in the ceremony.

Since the Sunrise Ceremony is so important to the Apache, I asked Renzie whether he was worried about his survival, for outside sources continue to do their best to terminate it as a heathen and deluding rite. He replied that he was not. There were supposed to be one, two, or three of the ceremonies each summer, but he would not be concerned if a summer should go by without any. "The year must come and go." But there would never be a time, he thought, when for two summers in a row some family would not have a daughter ready to become Changing Woman. The longevity of the tribe depended on that. Nevertheless, the reason he was talking to me was to make certain that the necessary things about the ritual would not be lost, although he did speculate that if things continued as they were, the ceremony might come to an end in fifty years.

Preparations for the Sunrise Ceremony

Preparations for a Sunrise Ceremony are quite involved. The girl's father must obtain a medicine man to sing, a sponsor, a site for the ceremony, firewood, water, and food for hundreds of guests. He must also prepare the structures to house the girl and the medicine man while the ceremony is in progress, storage buildings, and shady armadas for dining. Of course, family members, relatives, and friends help him with these things and also with the expenses, which today are considerable. The sacrifice is great, and it explains in part why only a few girls have the ceremony.

Things to Be Worn During the Ceremony

The effectiveness of the ceremony depends upon its being performed in the prescribed way, and any violation will be construed by one or more of the powers as signifying lack of respect. "Everything has to be done just right; there is no other way." Precautions are taken to guarantee it will be so.

During the ceremony, the girl must wear a straight drinking tube, a wooden scratching stick, feathers, and at least a buckskin dress-top of ancient style like that worn by Changing Woman. Her skirt can be cloth, but it must be ankle-length as in the early reservation style. Jonell's full-length buckskin dress was borrowed from the Heye Foundation in New York. It was a very old, spectacularly fringed, beaded garment.

The drinking tube is fashioned from the stalk of a cattail plant. It is approximately two inches long and is painted yellow. The scratching stick is a little longer, is pointed on one end and sometimes carved on the other, and is also painted yellow. Both items are tied to a long rawhide thong, which is worn like a necklace. During the ritual, and for four days thereafter, the girl is to drink only through the tube and to scratch herself only with the stick.

Renzie stated that if the girl does not use the scratching stick for the entire four days of the ceremony, her fingernails will get long and bend back. If she doesn't use the drinking tube, she will get whiskers or a beard like a man.

A small eagle-down feather is attached to both shoulders of her dress, and a single eagle-down feather is fastened to the girl's hair at the back of the head. The shoulder feathers enable her to walk, dance, and run lightly during the ceremony. Renzie explained that the head feather serves as the girl's guide. Wherever she goes for the rest of her life, the feather will take care of her and look after her. Even though her sponsor removes it on the fourth day, "it is still like that."

Singing to the Stick

Renzie always does a sweat bath before the ritual begins, and he takes all of the aforementioned items, plus a special deerskin on which the girl kneels or lies, into the lodge with him so that he can pray for them by singing four ancient prayer songs. He described this as "singing to the stick," but added that in praying for the stick, he prayed for the other things also. "The four songs you sing bless everything, not only the stick, but the feathers and the tube, and the others."

Making the Sunrise Girl's Cane

When the prayers are finished, he decorates the stick, which is made from the limb of an acorn-bearing oak tree. "We don't ever use cotton-wood trees or trees without fruit or nuts." The bark is peeled off so that the stick is "white." Then the stick is painted with a yellow mud that is obtained at a sacred site along the banks of the Salt River. No other color is added to the natural material. Four ribbons are attached to the cane — black, blue, yellow, and white. Sometimes other colors are used, but those mentioned are the proper ones for they symbolize the four cardinal directions. Wherever the girl goes after the dance is finished, Renzie said, there will be some of the different colors, which means "there is somebody to watch her, somebody hears her, somebody watches over her and guards her."

Gifts Prepared in Advance

Two golden eagle tail feathers are tied to the curved top of the stick in an upright position. Attached to one feather is a white stone bead and to the other a blue-green (turquoise) stone bead. The eagle feathers and the beads protect the girl forever against any power-caused illnesses. Oriole feathers are also tied to the eagle feathers, and since the oriole is a happy bird that minds it own business and behaves well, the feathers assure a good disposition for the girl. The protection and the assurances begin to enter and to surround the girl as soon as she starts to dance, and she is filled with them by ceremony's end.

Since one of the most important gifts bestowed upon the girl and the tribe during the ceremony is protection and long life, she holds the stick, which is the symbol of this, in her right hand while she dances. It is called by the Apache *keshe ya ha* (hook stick or curved stick). When she is old, the girl will use this stick to support her while she walks.

The Singers, the Substitute, and the Sunrise Girl

On the first evening of the ritual, the Singer tells the sponsor, also known as the "godmother," what to do as she dresses the girl in her ceremonial costume and puts the appurtenant items on her. Once the girl is dressed, the ceremony is underway, and the Singer sings four cradleboard songs, which are the first indication of the change taking place in the girl. After dark, the girl joins her guests for a social dance around a bonfire where the cradleboard songs are repeated and other songs are sung — such as harvest, deer, horse, and antelope — which herald the good things to come to the girl and to the people because the ancient ceremony is being held.

The public and spectacular portion of the ritual begins at sunrise the next morning, and for its description, I use my notes for the Sunrise Ceremony held at Whiteriver on May 24-27, 1974, for Olive Thompson, adopted daughter of Mr. and Mrs. Rupert Thompson of East Fork. There are distinct phases in the ceremony, and as I describe these, I add the explanations of their meanings provided by Renzie Gordon. Each phase includes something special that lies along the pathway and is to be picked up and made use of by the girl and the other participants.

I arrived at the ceremonial ground at 6:10 a.m. on a cool, crisp morning. It was light, but the sun had not yet broken above the eastern mountain ridges. The smell of pine trees was in the air, and mingled with it was the pungent aroma of a nearby fire tended by two men. At 6:25 a.m., pickup trucks arrived carrying the girl, her family, the godmother, a few friends, some singers, and the head Singer, who in this instance was Ryan Burnette. I was the only non-Indian present.

The group set to work immediately, arranging the items required for the ritual. In the center of a twelve-by-sixteen-foot canvas tarp — its longest dimension laid out east-west — was placed a pile of eight colorful blankets, one on top of the other, and on top of these, with its head toward the east, a tanned deerskin. According to Renzie, this could be the skin of a blacktail or a whitetail deer. The head portion of the skin was painted yellow, and close to its tip was tied a white eagle breath-feather with a turquoise bead attached to its quill. In ancient days, the hide had to be unblemished, but Renzie stated that there could be one bullet hole in it now. "We're not very particular about that; it's all right if you've got a hole." He did not know why the head was painted yellow: the important thing was that it was the way it had always been done. The turquoise and the feather were a prayer that the girl and the people would always have plenty of meat to eat.

Placed at the front edge of the tarp was a small, shallow, woven basket that was filled with cattail pollen. This is called a "stitch-basket plate," and it is especially made for and used only in this ritual. On the ground, stretching out toward the east for a distance of twenty-five feet, were first two medium-sized, traditional Apache burden baskets filled with wrapped candy, then dozens of food boxes filled with oranges, Crackerjacks, soft drinks in cans, and the like. The purpose for all of these things is explained as the ceremony progresses.

Rapidly now, the Singer and seven male assistants, four of whom held small kettle drums that were filled with water, took their places at the back edge of the tarp and faced east. Directly in front of them, also facing east, was the girl and another girl who would serve as her assistant, filling in whenever the godmother was not dancing with the girl. Accordingly, the assistant is referred to as the "substitute." She can be a sister or a friend and will probably undergo the Sunrise Ceremony herself in another two or three years. Her long, traditional dress on this occasion was cloth, although it can be made out of the traditional buckskin. In this instance, both girls were very attractive, demure and dignified as befits the occasion, and their shiny black hair hung beautifully down their backs. The substitute stood on the girl's left. Tied to the girl's forelock and hanging down on her forehead was a small, circular abalone shell, with the concave side facing out. (This can be a whole shell or a cut piece of shell.)

Phase 1

It was 6:35 a.m. Olive stood stock still as she faced east. Her eyes were tightly closed, and she concentrated intensely on what was about to happen. Everyone else watched her keenly. Suddenly, as the sun broke above the distant mountaintops, a shaft of light came toward her like a laser beam and struck the abalone shell on her forehead. The shell blazed brightly as the light continued and entered her. She was Changing Woman. She rose up on her toes and began to move vertically up and down as she danced in place. Her movements broke the spell of the spectators. The Singer, accompanied by the other singers and the drummers, began to sing, and the substitute began to dance alongside Olive. Voices rose, drums boomed, and small bells on the girls' dresses tinkled. At 7:05 a.m., guests began to arrive, and by 9:30 a.m., from 300 to 350 people were present, the air saturated by the clouds of red dust raised by their pickup trucks.

Thirty-two songs were sung during this phase. Each lasted about two-and-one-half minutes, and there were one-minute pauses in between. There were no long pauses for resting. Each time there was a pause, the girls stopped dancing. When the Singer began again, the girls joined in and danced in perfect tempo; they were active but very graceful in their movements. Olive had added to her attire the familiar Apache beaded T-necklace. It was an especially attractive one. She also wore a wine-colored beaded necklace with many strands. Traditional women's moccasins with turned-up toe pieces were on her feet. As the air warmed up, during each pause the substitute pulled back Olive's hair and gently wiped her face with a purple scarf tied to the right shoulder of her dress.

As Olive danced, she struck the ground firmly with the tip of her cane, always in time with the music. During the pauses, the Singer and his assistants quietly discussed things and seemed to be checking and confirming details. Ryan appeared confident, competent, and reverent, and he had a strong, excellent voice.

In the middle of phase one, an older man gave a five-minute lecture to the crowd in Apache. This concerned their good thoughts and behavior during the ceremony. Another man lectured about thirty minutes later, but concluded with the English expression, "Behave yourselves!" Not everyone paid close attention, and some appeared to ignore the lectures completely.

Renzie had emphasized that the power to become Changing Woman entered the girl as soon as she was dressed and admonished on the first evening. But as the sun struck the shell and she began to dance, the power was intensified and continued to grow for the remainder of the rite so that at the end she was literally filled with the power of Changing Woman, which would remain with her throughout her adult life.

Phase 2

Two hours and ten minutes had gone by, and the last of the thirty-two songs had ended. With only the briefest pause, the substitute left Olive's side, and the godmother — a middle-aged, handsome woman wearing a buckskin top and a taffeta skirt — took her place at Olive's left. At 8:45 a.m., the Singer began again, and both girl and godmother danced in place. They continued to face east, but their eyes were downcast, so as not to look directly into the strong rising sun.

At 9:15 a.m., the godmother took the cane from the girl and, assisted by the Singer, planted it in the ground at the head of the row of food. The hole for the cane had been dug by a man with an ordinary pick. While the cane was being placed firmly upright in the ground, the Singer prayed for and instructed the girl. Once the cane was set, she knelt on the deer hide and pile of blankets and began to sway gracefully back and forth with upraised hands. Four songs were sung, and the girl swayed in accompaniment to each.

I had read that the girl's kneeling and making motions with her hands recreates the impregnation of Changing Woman by Sun, but Renzie disagreed. "The sun is looking down at her," he said, "and the medicine man told that girl to look at sun while she was kneeling. After that, the sun will shine upon her wherever she goes, especially after we finish with her." The position she assumed had nothing to do with her being impregnated. "No, nothing. She is a virgin, see." What the girl did is a prayer, and her swaying back and forth was simply keeping time with the music.

The Apache sunrise ceremony girl being massaged for external and internal beauty

Phase 3

Taking only the time needed to change position, the godmother helped Olive lie face down on the deer hide — head toward the east, with arms by her side and legs straight — in preparation for being molded. The godmother first straightened Olive's hair and dress. At 9:40 a.m., the godmother began to mold her. During the molding, she rapidly circled Olive four times during each of four songs. As she circled the girl, she used her hands and her bare feet to mold Olive. She began on the right side, moved down over the buttocks and legs, then circled to the left side and repeated this. Afterward, she gently molded Olive's face. In all, she made sixteen clockwise circles. At 9:50 a.m., the godmother took hold of Olive's shoulders and helped her rise to her feet. The cane was retrieved by the godmother and returned to Olive, and when the Singer and the music began again, Olive and the godmother danced in place side by side.

Olive was already a very attractive girl, but amazingly she was taller now and more beautiful . . . radiant, in fact, and fully aware that the power was working in her. She was being completely transformed, and everyone there could see it. The spectators linked arms and began to dance, forward and back, forward and back; they passed back into time, remembering when the Apache were a great and independent people. They continued to dance this way until the public portion of the ceremony ended on Sunday.

It is said that Changing Woman's power causes the girl to become soft so she can be molded, that molding her puts her in the right shape for life. Renzie stressed that the godmother must first put the girl down, then stretch the girl with her hands and feet. This is because the girl is not supposed to use her own hands to lay herself down.

Phase 4

At 10 a.m., after a pause only for rearrangement, the godmother again took the cane and, with the help of the man with the pick, placed it upright at the eastern end of the column of food. The Singer began to sing. The godmother brushed Olive's hair back and straightened Olive's dress. Moving behind the girl, the godmother placed her hands on Olive's back, giving her a sharp shove, sending the girl off on her first run. As Olive ran, the godmother followed her. A few spectators joined in. Olive made a turn around the cane and came back to her place. As the godmother passed the cane, she retrieved it and returned it to Olive. Then both danced in place until the song ended.

The entire process, including the preparation and pushing, was repeated three times. For each run, the godmother moved the cane out in two-foot increments, so that Olive ran a little farther each time. In runs two, three, and four, so many spectators joined in they crowded out the godmother, making it difficult for her to get the cane. On run four, their enthusiasm was such that they nearly overran the cane itself!

While it is said that the running symbolizes the four stages of life — infancy/childhood, adolescence, adulthood and old age — and that as the girl circles each stage, she owns it. Renzie emphasized that the girl runs so that "she will become a strong lady by running, so that in the future . . . her legs will be strong. It is almost like doing exercises for the future. This is a symbolic action."

Phase 5

At 10:20 a.m., Olive ran to the four directions, with the cane set out for this as it was in phase four by the godmother and the man with the pick. The crowd was so closely packed around Olive that lanes had to be cleared for her to run. When she did run, she moved at a moderate speed.

As each of the four songs began, she was pushed off and she ran. She began at the east, then went to the south, the west, and finally to the north. Once again, the godmother followed, and each time picked up the cane. On returning to their positions on the tarp, the woman and the girl danced in place until the song ended. While Olive and the godmother ran, the crowd began to take food from the boxes, and this continued with great shouting and joy.

This phase served much the same purpose as that of phase four, enabling the girl to run swiftly without tiring. "It's not different," Renzie said. "Four times she runs for the same reason." It is implied, however, that in running to the four directions, the girl captured their powers, which contribute to her endurance. When the people ran with her and began to take the food from the boxes, they were acknowledging their faith that the ceremony will bless them all with food and good things during the years to come. "All that fruit and food . . . it means much for people who run around with her and follow her."

Phase 6

At 10:35 a.m., with only the briefest pause, the next phase began. The Singer picked up the first of the two baskets that were filled with wrapped candy, and as the singing and the music began, he danced back and forth, toward and away from Olive. As he ended his song, he blessed Olive by sprinkling pollen on her head and face, after which he poured the candy over her head. The children scrambled for the candy — along with a few adults who received good-natured ribbing from others for doing this.

It is said that the candy becomes holy as it is poured over the girl's head and that those who get some are assured of plenty in future years. Renzie agreed, adding that the act was a prayer for the girl to have this much in life. "So we pour it all on her. But it is a prayer for everybody too . . . the boys and all the adults that grab and take all that candy. It's all mixed — acorns and chestnuts and corn are in there mixed in with the candy. The medicine man prays first with that yellow powder. Then when they finish with that, the person standing there with the basket full of candy calls to them, 'Are you ready?' 'All right, go ahead, pour it on,' is what they answer." There was no special meaning to the man's dancing back and forth, "that's just the way it is done." Only one basket was poured, "just a small one, not a big one."

Phase 7

At 10:40 a.m., a new set of songs began, and at the end of the first song, the Singer blessed the girl and the godmother with pollen taken from the stitch-basket. Then Olive's father, a few other men, and Olive's mother blessed the two with pollen. Finally, all of the spectators lined up in single file and sprinkled pollen on the girl and godmother. They did this only while a song was being sung. As soon as the song was completed, the sprinkling stopped. When the Singer started a new song, it began again. The girl and her godmother danced in place as usual, but they stood on the deerskin at the tail end. While the Singer and his assistants sang, the crowd shouted with great enthusiasm.

The pollen was lemon-yellow in color, and it was applied first to the head, then to the shoulders and chests of both the girl and the godmother. Then a little was dropped onto the deerskin at the head end. After the sprinkling, each person streaked pollen on one or both of his or her own cheeks.

When everyone had finished, the girl and the godmother were virtually covered with pollen. In all, the sprinkling consumed about twenty minutes, and after this, men threw candy and other gifts to people from the back of a pickup truck.

Renzie explained that before the pollen was sprinkled, the Singer moved quickly among the people, singing and asking who wanted some pollen to sprinkle. When he had given some to each of those who did, he began the sprinkling. The pollen was a mixture of five different kinds. "There's a corn, grains of corn real fine, cattail, a white pollen, and a plant pollen. You've got to use all five." The father of the girl procured all of these, but the medicine man told him what they must be and where to get them. There were several different places where they could be found in Apache country. Renzie verified that this phase was the first where the girl and the godmother would step onto the deer hide. The pollen on the deer hide, he pointed out, must be dropped on the turquoise bead and the feather. "This is a sacred place, and you gotta pray for her, so nothing bad would happen to her." So when the pollen was put there, "that's a prayer for the girl; this is when they are starting to put those things on her and the godmother, and the main place is over there where the deer's head is."

" . . . after the girl has been sprinkled, those who have so blessed her have the right to ask her to invoke her Changing Woman power to grant them a request."

Of particular interest is the fact that after the girl has been sprinkled, those who have so blessed her have the right to ask her to invoke her Changing Woman power to grant them a request. This can be for any kind of help, but "sometimes a woman brings her child to that girl. That's the Apache way. If a child is sick, then the puberty girl would sort of spit into the child's mouth, because she's holy, to make the child well." The people do not know when the actual healing will take place. "The healing happens maybe that night, maybe next day. That's when they start feeling better. But it can be right there — at the moment the girl treats the child."

Edgar Perry interjected that his mother-in-law had done this to his little girls, "spit into the little baby's mouth so the baby could have a long life."

Renzie pointed out that the people who streaked their own cheeks with the pollen were supposed to do so on the right side only. "This means great things, you know . . . this will bless me, too, that I will share in this great experience." The candy and other gifts were distributed at that point to emphasize that the people will share in the blessing that come to the girl. "Then there's four more songs to sing, and that is the final act."

The rituals for this day ended with this phase. The pollen on the deerskin was collected in a basket by two women. Then, moving very swiftly, Olive stepped off the deerskin, picked it up, shook it firmly, and threw it toward the east with a rapid motion. Then she circled around the pile of blankets, seized them one by one, and quickly whipped them off toward each of the four cardinal directions. They didn't go far, for the crowd was closing in on her from all sides — so closely that some of the blankets landed on the people.

In less than two minutes, the eight blankets had been thrown, and the phase ended. It was 11:05 a.m., and the eight phases had consumed a total of four hours and thirty minutes. All of the paraphernalia and boxes were picked up and placed in trucks, and everyone dispersed. The girl, godmother, Singer and his assistants, and the girl's family and their special guests headed for the camp prepared for the occasion, and only a few other whites and I stood alone on the ceremony ground.

It was obvious that Olive was very tired, yet she had danced with vigor during every song, even though the day had been very warm and the powdery red dust from vehicles and dancing spectators had been thick and encompassing.

In discussing this phase, Renzie explained that the deerskin and the blankets must be thrown as Olive threw them, the skin first, then the blankets to the four directions as she turns clockwise. Then relatives or the godmother, whoever had loaned blankets for the occasion, would come and retrieve theirs. She threw the blankets quickly because "she's tired." The relatives would bring them back the next morning so she could use them again. The act of throwing the blankets and the hide were a further means of assuring that she and the people would have plenty of meat and blankets during the coming year.

Renzie went on to say that there would be a big feast for the main participants that afternoon. Then the girl would rest until nightfall when she would move to a tent at a specially prepared dancing ground near the place where the Sunrise Ceremony was being held.

The Big Tipi and the Ceremonial Circle

During this afternoon, the Big Tipi was prepared for use in the next morning's Sunrise Ceremony, and the dancing circle, which was on level ground and approximately two hundred feet in diameter — situated just to the east of the place where the Sunrise Ceremony proper was being performed — was readied for the Saturday evening dance. Ryan Burnette told me that the tipi poles would be prepared at 4 p.m., and the tipi would be erected by 6 p.m., "before the Crown Dancers danced."

When I arrived at the ceremonial ground at 4:10 p.m., the four tipi poles were already lying on the ground. Nearby were four spruce trees, each of which was shaped like a Christmas tree about ten or eleven feet tall.

The tipi poles were grouped in pairs and lay in an east-west direction with the trunk bases pointed toward the east. Two men were preparing one set of poles. The poles were approximately twenty-two feet long, including their branches. Two had leaves on their branches, and two did not. On Sunday, I would learn from an informant, and still later from Renzie, that four different kinds of trees were used. The two with the foliage were the cottonwood and the spruce. The other two the informant could not identify. "But," he said, "the four poles and their four colors are four kinds of prayers."

I learned that, in preparation for painting, the bark was removed from the poles with a hand axe. The families of the girl and the godmother each provided a man and a helper to furnish and prepare two poles. In keeping with these modern times, the painting was done with commercial products. The painting consisted of symbolic designs running from the base to where the branches connect to the trunk. Each pole had a different, simple design. One pole was spray-painted blue-green; the other was spray-painted white.

The next two men did their poles in black and in yellow. The black was liquid shoe polish applied with a dauber; the yellow was mixed on the spot in paint cans. It was applied with a bunched-up rag. It should be noted that the four colors were the same as those of the ribbons on the girl's cane, representing the cardinal directions.

When the painting was completed, the four poles were laid side by side and the trunks were trimmed so that the poles were all the same length. At this moment, a serious problem was discovered. One of the poles was broken where the branch portion met the trunk. There was consternation, for the broken pole could not be used. Poles must be perfect, and to use a defective one would bring harm to the person who prepared it. The pole could not be mended. A new one had to be obtained from a certain place in the mountains. Two of the men left to get the new pole. When dusk fell at 7:30 p.m., they had not yet returned. With no lights to work by at the ceremonial ground, I wondered whether the tipi would be ready for the morning ritual, and what would happen if it was not.

About 6:30 p.m., a pickup truck arrived with a small canvas tent and some refreshments that would be used by the girl, her attendants and family. Other trucks brought heaps of wood for the bonfire. The wood was piled on the east side of a circular ceremonial area, which was marked off by a small ridge of dirt that circled the perimeter. The tent was set up just outside the northeastern edge of the ridge.

Ryan Burnette had arrived, and with the help of the men who prepared the poles, he set the four spruce trees on the outer edge of the ceremonial area — one at each of the cardinal points. The east tree was put up first, and the movement for erecting the others went clockwise. A brief prayer was said as the trunk of each tree was planted in the ground. When they were done, wood was taken from the large pile and stacked for the evening fire at a place just east of the center of the circle.

It was surprising to see how clearly the four spruce trees defined the ceremonial area. Later I was told by one of the men that these trees did not symbolize the four directions. "People go around these trees to be good," he said. "Not everyone can go around them." He could "because he was O.K. If a person can go around the trees, then others won't say bad things about them. The trees are not directions; they are four ways." Later still, a younger man volunteered that "the trees form a boundary across which no cars or trucks can go. Vehicles can't cross inside the circle . . ." (as they frequently did before the trees were set up).

The tent, the front of which faces the circle, was a commercial model. Its front opening was triangular, and the tent was supported by two poles that crossed at the top. The back was about eight feet square. A man told me that the tent was used to repair the costumes of the Crown Dancers and the girl, but in actuality, the girl, godmother, substitute, and the girl's family would occupy it and the areas immediately adjacent to it for the entire night. About 7 p.m., a small fire was built in front of the tent, and the crowd arrived.

About 7:45 p.m., the large bonfire was kindled. Before 8 p.m., Olive and her family, her godmother, and the assistants had arrived and were seated in front of and inside of the tent. Ryan Burnette, his assistants, and the drummers took a position on the west side of the circle and began the music. Four attendants gathered with Olive; they were about her own age and were splendidly dressed in buckskin tops with T-necklaces and long, full, taffeta skirts that shined in the light. The crowd was very large now, and it completely surrounded the ceremonial circle.

"They cast long, frightening shadows, and they were awesome in appearance, wearing their knee-high buckskin moccasins and fantastic . . . high wooden crowns."

At 8:15 p.m., the Crown Dancers, who in Apache are called *Gans*, entered the ceremonial area at a point next to the east spruce tree. They came quietly, only the bells on their buckskin shirts jingling. No special sounds from the spectators accompanied their arrival. A person asked, "I wonder when they are coming," and suddenly there they were, five of them in all, walking in single file with the clown last. They cast long, frightening shadows, and they were awesome in appearance, wearing their knee-high buckskin moccasins and fantastic three-or-more feet high wooden crowns. They carried painted wands in each hand, their faces were hidden by black masks, and spruce branches were inserted under their belts at the back and sides. Their bodies were painted with bold symbolic designs; the body paint was gray over which black spots and other designs were neatly applied. The clown had black stripes around his legs at four-inch intervals. The awed crowd backed away as ever so slowly the Gans circled the area, going around the outside of the spruce trees, then entering the ceremonial circle again by the east spruce, at which time they approached the Singer and his assistants.

The first dance of the Gans was only mildly active. The clown did several things, such as drawing lines on the ground with his wands, pausing occasionally to whirl his bullroarer. Now and then he chased the children, who scattered like frightened birds, but actually were delighted. At one point, the clown lay on his back on the ground and kicked his striped legs frantically in the air while the crowd laughed. What did it mean? Only that human beings often do foolish things at the most serious of moments, that we don't always show proper respect.

Whenever the music was going, some of the spectators linked arms and danced the social dance back and forth. At regular intervals, the Gans left the area in single file and were soon swallowed up by the darkness. Before long, they returned and danced again, often more actively than before. During the time I was present — I did not stay the entire night — at intervals, Olive and her four attendants entered the ceremonial area in single file and circled the bonfire while doing their vertical motion Sunrise Ceremony dance. Then they formed a side-by-side line at the northeast side of the circle, and while the Gans danced on the west side, they danced there, doing the linked-arm, back-and-forth social dance. Olive was fresh again, demurely radiant.

During those times when the Gans were away taking their tight masks off and catching a breath of fresh air, Olive obtained her cane and led her attendants single file in a circle around the bonfire, striking the ground with the cane in time with the music. I could hardly help noting that she always seemed to do her part with slightly more vigor than the other girls. I assumed this was not accidental. It was her moment, and no doubt the others suppressed their efforts somewhat to allow her to live it to the fullest.

I did not learn that night how long the pattern repeated itself. I left at 10 p.m. and went to my motel to get some rest. Earlier though, some of the people said, "She has to dance all night; she can't stop." Probably, I thought, that was why the tent and the food were there, as a place for her to rest and refresh herself at certain intervals.

I needed to turn to Renzie for the information I lacked about the duration of her dancing. He confirmed that the girl, her godmother, and the attendants remained at the ceremonial dance area all night. But in all, the girl would only dance for about two hours "because there's going to be another one coming up Sunday morning. She needs a good rest. Her mother or her father don't let her dance all night because she needs a good rest. Sunday, it all starts over again. Sunday morning, early before the sun comes up."

Renzie did not support the previous information I had received about the spruce trees. He said they were there for the Crown Dancers and had nothing to do with the puberty ritual itself. However, he said that the north tree must be piñon; the east, chestnut; the south, cedar; and the west, oak. Moreover, all four should have leaves on them. "See, because all four produce seeds, you know, the piñons and chestnuts . . . seed trees, and she's like that, too, that girl. When she gets married, she makes seed . . . she gets children. It's the same with that hook stick; that's oak. We don't use trees that bear no fruits or nuts." Each tree must be painted with its proper color after the bark has been peeled. "To make them white. It's just the way it was done a long time ago, and I still do it the same way."

The Big Tipi had a lengthy Apache name that Renzie translated as "The four poles, all four of them that go together, all pointing in one direction and in one place." Although he had not been present to see the damaged pole, he knew about it and said that the men preparing it had made yet another mistake. They should have left the leaves on all four of the poles, and since two poles didn't have them, they must have cut them off.

He said the tent used on Saturday night could be any kind of tent and either old or new. It received no special blessing from the Singer. He also stated that the Gans were not a necessary part of the Sunrise Ceremony, but their appearance was traditional. "It's been done that way all through the ages, but they aren't directly connected with Changing Woman."

When I arrived at the ceremonial area at 6:20 a.m. on Sunday morning, I was surprised to find that the ritual was already underway and that the Big Tipi was up. I never found out when the new pole arrived or when the poles were set up. I did notice that the new pole — the white one — was not as neatly prepared as the others, and the paint was barely visible. The four spruce trees that marked the previous night's dance circle were gone.

Olive and a new substitute were already dancing in place on the west end of the tarp. Behind her were the Singer and his assistants. In front of her was the pile of blankets; their numbers were doubled, making the pile twice as high as it had been on Saturday. Accordingly, the head and tail of the deer hide hung down over the front and back. The deer head still retained some of the pollen that had been sprinkled on it Saturday.

" . . . the yellow pole at the northwest, the white pole at the northeast, the blue pole at the southeast, and the black pole at the southwest."

Two men sat on the ground just in front of the tarp facing Olive. On the north side was a medicine man, and on the south side was another man, whose place would be taken by several other men in turn as the ritual progressed. Just behind the medicine man and off to his right was a second medicine man who was mixing pollen with water in a shallow basket. Behind this man, and ten feet to the east of the front edge of the tarp, was the Big Tipi. Its four poles were set up tipi fashion, crossed at the top, with the trunk ends forming the corners of a square — the yellow pole at the northwest, the white pole at the northeast, the blue pole at the southeast, and the black pole at the southwest. About six feet up from the ground, a rope stretched in clothesline fashion from the black pole to the white pole. A six-inch-long golden eagle feather was tied at the rope level to the white pole, and a similar one was tied to the blue pole. To the butt-end of the quill of these feathers were tied several small tufts of yellow feathers.

Ryan Burnette had been singing as usual, but now several other medicine men were participating. One was identified to me as the head medicine man; he spent most of his time squatting down and stirring the liquid, orange-yellow mixture of pollen and water. He did this whenever a song was sung, stopping during the pauses. At intervals, another man would take his place to allow him to rest. The mixing basket was placed directly on the ground at the base of the yellow pole, and a ten-inch-long hand-carved, flat stick with a rounded point was used as a stirring paddle.

A large crowd was present when I arrived, and even though they had danced throughout the night, they showed few signs of exhaustion — their enthusiasm for the ceremony and its benefits was too great.

"Her hair was still covered with a sheen of pollen; the lemon-yellow grains stood out clearly against the deep black in the early morning light."

I was curious to see how Olive had fared. The strain of the long ritual was apparent, and she appeared drawn and tired. Her costume had been cleaned. Her hair was still covered with a sheen of pollen; the lemon-yellow grains stood out clearly against the deep black in the early morning light. The feather at the back of her head was grayed with dust by now, and so were the feathers on her shoulders and on the deerskin. As each song began, I marveled at how she immediately picked up the beat with her cane and danced with vigor — drawing, no doubt, upon the deep well of energy that came from the ecstasy of the incredible changes taking place inside her.

The medicine man on the north side held an eagle tail-feather in each hand, and to the quill of each of these was tied a buckskin thong that was in turn looped around his hand. I was told that the two feathers had been taken from the cottonwood and spruce poles — thus explaining why only two of the poles still had feathers attached to them. The man standing to the medicine man's left held in his left hand an eagle tail-feather that had tied to it a long sheaf of dry, stiff field grass shaped to form a tubular bundle, perhaps one-and-one-half inches in diameter, which I later discovered was the brush used to paint the girl with the liquid pollen mixture and also to cast pollen onto the crowd.

Throughout phase nine, Olive and her substitute danced in place as the girls had done on the previous day. The two men who faced them also danced in place in accompaniment to each song. Different men occupied the left position on different occasions, including the girl's father, Rupert. Each of these men held the grass brush in his left hand while he danced. Olive's mother danced in a line of women to Olive's right, some eight to ten feet away. Since she remained so near, it was obvious that she was deeply concerned for her daughter and was watching her closely. As the temperature rose, at 7:35 a.m., she stepped forward with a soft drink can and held it for Olive while the girl drank from it with her drinking tube. Later, the substitute would also do this for Olive.

During every pause, the substitute brushed Olive's hair back and wiped the perspiration from her face with a scarf that was attached to Olive's dress. Then she wiped her own face as well

Phase 10

At 8:05 a.m., the Singer moved directly behind Olive and, holding his hands about two inches away from her body, he spoke an audible prayer. Without ever touching her, he passed his hands gracefully alongside her head, shoulders, and arms. He also seemed to be giving her instructions. At this point, the substitute left Olive's side, and the godmother, in a blue traditional dress, moved into position on Olive's left, but not at her side. Olive gave her cane to her father, who stood to the left of the medicine man, and he danced with it, striking the ground with it just as Olive had.

Olive knelt on the deerskin and blankets, and as the song began, she raised her arms at her sides with her elbows bent and her hands open. She swayed gracefully back and forth, back and forth. History was alive! Changing Woman, the Old-Woman-Making-Motions-With-Her-Hands, was dancing again, and the spectators were nearly overwhelmed with emotion. In all, four songs would be sung, and Olive would sway and make motions for as long as each song lasted.

It was at this juncture that both the tempo and attitudes of those present began to rise noticeably. Eyes sparkled. Breath came faster. The drums were louder, the Singer's volume increased, and the two men facing Olive, her father and the medicine man, began to dance energetically in unison toward and away from her. Sounds of expectation began to bounce around the spectators. It was exciting, and it was apparent that the climactic moment was approaching.

Phase 11

At approximately 8:15 a.m., Olive, with guidance from the Singer, assumed a seated and supplicatory position on the deerskin, her feet stretched out in front of her and her hands upturned in her lap. Three songs were sung, during which the men danced forward and back. The man who stood to the left of the medicine man and held the tray filled with the liquid pollen mixture now stepped forward. When the fourth song began, he dipped the brush in the mixture and, like an artist daubing a canvas with an oversized brush, began to paint Olive with it.

He started on her head and face, applying the mixture liberally. Then he drew the brush down the length of her left arm and continued on to her feet, circled around her, and did the same on her right side. After he had done this, I learned the penalty for moving up close to take photographs, for he now dipped his brush in the liquid and, turning swiftly, began with devastating effectiveness to spray the crowd. Considering the small quantity of liquid available, it was remarkable to see how thoroughly the happy bystanders were doused. Although I moved quickly, my camera and I were splattered from head to toe . . . yet I in no way minded, for it made me part of this great and blessed event.

Four songs were sung, and four times the sprinkling procedure was repeated. When it was over, Olive was yellow from head to foot.

Sometimes, the loaded brush was drawn over her face and body. Other times the paint was flicked on, causing her to blink to avoid getting it in her eyes.

Phase 12

At 8:30 a.m., Olive stood up, and women quickly removed the deerskin and pile of blankets. When the medicine man extended the tips of his two eagle feathers toward her, she seized one with each hand. Her father, holding the cane, was now standing at the medicine man's left and facing her. As the next song began, everyone became amazingly enthusiastic. Squeals of delight came from the women, and the men made happy grunts of approval. Even Olive, who by tradition was expected to remain demure and unsmiling during the ceremony, began to smile as the main group, accompanied on all sides by family and friends, started to move in unison toward the Big Tipi, with Olive stepping rapidly forward and the two men who faced her moving backward at the same pace. The effect was as though the men were drawing her through the four stages of life that were now hers to claim.

The first song carried the group to the center of the Big Tipi. As they moved, the arms and feathers were pulled back and forth alternately — like engine pistons working horizontally — and Olive seemed to be enjoying the moment immensely. She was openly ecstatic, and her fatigue seemed to melt away as she fully became Changing Woman, an adult with a long, rich life guaranteed.

In all, four moves were made with only brief pauses between chants. The first move was to the center of the Tipi. The following moves were each about thirty feet in length; the crowd of well-wishers packed around the central group so tightly they made observation of exactly what was happening impossible. While the procession advanced, the crowd shouted with glee and acclamation. As the fourth and final song began, the men who had prepared and assembled the Big Tipi, and who had been standing ready, lifted the poles vertically into the air and began to lay them together. Just as the last

Apache sunrise ceremony girl

song ended, the poles were swiftly lowered to the ground — but not dropped — their tops pointing northeast.

The Sunrise Ceremony was over, and as the happy crowd departed and moved toward their vehicles, I could not see exactly what was happening to Olive. One of my friends who had been a Gan dancer on Saturday night came by dragging behind him two of the spruce trees. He stopped long enough to tell me goodbye and informed me that he had to dance at the girl's camp with the other Gans very shortly. For Olive Thompson, the most trying parts of the ordeal were over. For twenty-seven unrelenting hours, without significant rest, she had been undergoing the most rigorous ritual I have ever seen any young person experience, and she had carried it off with superb grace. Ryan Burnette had done the same, and I could only marvel at his endurance and skill.

" . . . the ceremony had been well worth doing, and . . . it would work its marvels in the lives of Olive and the Apache people — just as the Sunrise Ceremonies had always done."

Just before the painting with the pollen, Rupert Thompson — handsome in his cowboy hat, red velvet shirt, jeans, and cowboy boots — turned and looked at me. It was a gentle, welcoming look from another culture, and not knowing what to say, I asked a foolish question, "Are you tired, Rupert?" He smiled and nodded in affirmation. But if ever I've seen pride and dignity, it was precisely then, in the midst of that dusty, hectic, and crowded place. He knew and I knew the ceremony had been well worth doing, and both of us believed it would work its marvels in the lives of Olive and the Apache people — just as the Sunrise Ceremonies had always done.

For a final time, I turned to Renzie to make certain my understanding of phases nine through twelve was correct. He confirmed that only water is mixed with the pollen, and he said there was no special name for the mixing process. The blankets are doubled because the girl has to use them for a seat while she is being painted. "And that eagle feather and that turquoise that are hanging, that man is going to stand her up when he dances with that eagle feather. That means the same things like he did to her on Saturday morning at that Sunrise Dance." His dancing forward and back is to invite her to get up, and she will grab the feather and rise. "Just almost like a baptism" she is accepting the new life that she has been given during the ceremony, a new life in which she has all of the powers of Changing Woman that can be given to a human being.

The group advances four times because it takes four songs to do this part of the rite properly. Everyone is excited and happy because "it's about through with her; it's close to the end. Everybody is yelling, you know. Like a victory, almost literally a victory. They know what she has." It is correct to say that the four moves are like going through the four stages of life. The arms are pumped back and forth because that is the way the people want her life to be — strong and energetic — to help her dance, to help her move. It is like saying, "Now I've done all this, it's mine. I'm going to have all these good things, and the people will be blessed."

The girl's swaying back and forth means the same as it did the previous day, but Renzie explained, "It's kind of a little different there." There are added meanings for the Apache. The songs are the same also. I was not correct in assuming that the two feathers held by the medicine man had come from the poles. Renzie said that each of the poles must always have a little feather tied to it and that the big ones held by the medicine man had hung throughout the night on the rope that was strung between the poles. The Singer puts the two feathers there when the poles are first set up. Then he takes them down in the morning and gives them to the medicine man, telling him what to do with them.

Renzie gave me a few final details about the ceremony: The paintbrush is made with nothing other than an eagle feather and grass. No stone beads are attached to it.

The girl's father has the right to dance with her, but he doesn't have to if he doesn't want to.

The paint is drawn down the length of the girl's body and onto the ground as "a protection or a shield that no harm will come to her . . . that she'll have good health and a long life."

I wanted to know if the girls who have gone through the Sunrise Ceremony always lived to be old and if they have been stronger and healthier than women who have not undergone the rite. "Yeah, there's a lot of old women here among us who have been passers through that. They do have longer lives."

" . . . it means that all these people could be like the puberty girl . . . they share it."

I loved the way Renzie described the purpose for the girl sitting with her hands upturned: "That person that dances here," he said, "they [Changing Woman and the other deities] let her fill her purse, and then they give that man that feather and that's where he's gonna set her up." As for spraying the crowd with pollen: "Well, it means that all these people could be like the puberty girl, you know, to have long life . . . they share it."

The blankets are removed so that no one will step on them or walk over them. As for the four poles, they must be laid down "facing towards the north." The owners of the poles must take them away and put them somewhere, and they cannot be used for firewood or for anything else. There is no further ritual on Sunday afternoon, and it is up to the Crown Dancers' medicine man to decide whether or not they will dance.

On Monday morning, the fourth day, the godmother removes from the girl her costume and paraphernalia, and any borrowed things are returned to their owners. "You see, they have to take off all those feathers and all those things on that girl — all the buckskins, dresses — take all the things off on Monday morning. This would be final. The godmother takes everything off from the puberty girl . . . when we started on Friday evening, the godmother, she puts all those things on her. Then on Monday, she has to wash her hair and dress her up. After this, the girl could put her school dress on again because it's finished with her. The dance is ended."

While this act of undressing ends the Sunrise Ceremony, the girl remains holy for four more days, and there are specific rules of conduct she must follow. "The godmother is the most important one, and she's the one that has to tell that girl what to do after we're finished with her. On Monday, that's the last day, the godmother is going to tell her to stay out of mischief, and she gives her good advice on how to behave and how to be the best kind of woman." Then the girl's Changing Woman power enables her to do these things. "One of these days, see, the girl gets married, and she will bring love and children. That's the way. We pray for that. She is just like a seed. You plant something, and it will grow up. That's the way the girl's gonna be too."

APACHE PERIPHERAL PATHWAYS

Foremost among the peripheral pathways of the Apache has been the matter of understanding power and it's important uses. As power sources, invisible supernatural beings and ghosts are believed to be just as real as nature's visible forces. The supernaturals become involved with human affairs, are addressed as though they were human and alive, and are expected to answer in a detectable way. In particular, certain classes of celestial bodies, mythological figures, animals, plants, and minerals are believed to possess holy powers, and some small part of these powers may be acquired by human beings and put to use. The balance of the power remains with its source, which is free to help or to harm as the supernatural being wishes — depending upon whether it is pleased or offended by human conduct.

The view, then, is that power pervades the entire universe, but human beings cannot approach it directly. It must come to them through something such as the sun, moon, lightning, bear, eagle, owl, lizard, or snake. Nevertheless, it is the human who, through contact with the power itself, learns how to apply the power in a beneficial way.

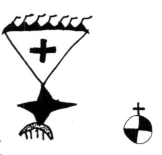

Power

A power and the ability to apply it are acquired by purchase; by taking lessons from a person who has already obtained it; by fasting, prayer and ablutions; or through a strange event. These are the steps toward visions or dreams in which the power presents itself and gives itself to the individual. In the people's eyes, those who obtain it the latter way are favored over those who purchase power, for the power came to them voluntarily. Only a few Apache seek power today, since its acquisition requires more time, energy, expense and responsibility than most people wish to expend. Power has its rewards, but also its costs, not the least of which may be the jealousy of envious people. People who haven't a power are dependent in any crisis upon those who have, and assistance is expensive.

It is important to understand that, in the Apache mind, the medicine person is only a vehicle employed by the supernaturals in order to cure. The persons in and out of themselves have no healing ability. The custom has been for the medicine person to request that his patient offer him four gifts, such as eagle-down feathers, bits of certain stones or shells, and small bags of pollen. These are presented to the medicine person, but are considered to be payment to the supernatural power. The act of making the offering is what invokes the presence of the power, and it is taken for granted that the power will comply. Whenever the power is present, every ritual act performed by the medicine person — such as brushing pain away with feathers or sucking an object of some kind from the patient — is simply a visible sign of the true healing being effected at the same time by the power.

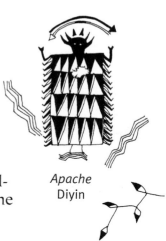

Apache Diyin

Typical Apache symbols used on ceremonial items

Once a power has given some part of itself to its seeker, the person must determine by trial and error what the power is capable of doing through him. Over a long period of time, he learns what the power can accomplish when correctly used. Although they may have the same type of power, no two people will exercise it in the same way. Some

powers can be called upon to diagnose, cure, and protect against illness. Those who have this gift are commonly known as medicine men or women. The Apache term for this is *diyin*. Aside from medicine persons, other men and women have what are considered lesser powers to prophesy and to find lost objects.

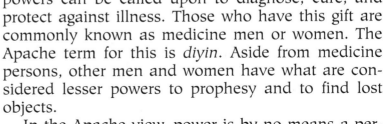

In the Apache view, power is by no means a permanent possession or quality — the privilege of being a channel for power can be withdrawn by its dispenser any time he is displeased or when he feels an appropriate time has come in the possessor's life. Power's presence is in large measure dependent upon the respect accorded it by its holder, who should be concerned about the power and keep its welfare foremost at all times. He must never take it for granted. Should he lose it, there is virtually no way to get it back; the loss of power brings an understandable fear and insecurity, for the person who had it is now defenseless and, moreover, may have forfeited it in such a way as to merit retaliation by the Being who gave it.

In most instances, power is most effective for Apache men and women in their early thirties, a fact that reveals an association with physical health and prime activity. As this period passes, the ability to use the power is thought to weaken. For many, it never passes away entirely. Others are made to understand through dreams, ghosts, or the like that the investor wishes the power to be transferred by traditional means to a more fit recipient.

Since the dawn of time, each power has been so closely associated with a multitude of chants and prayers that these concomitants are considered to be an integral part of it. Therefore, the ability to dispense the power is directly dependent upon the capacity of the person to learn and retain the power's chants and prayers. These are a part of Apache tradition, and months must be spent in private sessions with medicine men or women who are able to pass on the chants and prayers. Payment depends upon the amount of work and time involved, but the learning is always expensive. In the old days, payment was made in goods; now money is preferred. In truth, cost has become one of the prime reasons for the declining interest in the pursuit of medicine power today. In addition, there is the incredible complexity of the medicine language and ceremonial structure to be mastered, plus the retentive abilities needed and the sheer physical strength required to sing the exhausting chants for hours on end at a ceremony.

Even considering all this, the rewards of gaining power outweigh the costs. An individual with power has a prime opportunity for status, social contacts, and respect. He has a sense of personal security and a source of income. Moreover, if the medicine person is prudent and successful in the use of power and can avoid charges of witchcraft, the entire community benefits.

Protection from Witchcraft

Just as it did with the American colonists and with the people of England, the subject of witchcraft appears to have emerged as the Apache sought to explain and to deal with misfortune. Since the supernatural powers had the qualities of both benevolence and revenge, it was accepted that some of them had chosen to follow almost exclusively the latter course. Power was involved in the witchcraft question; in order to practice witchcraft, a person had to have a power. This meant that the medicine men and women would be the prime suspects, along with private individuals who had, for some reason only they knew, acquired their witchcraft trade from someone who already practiced it.

There are two classes of witches. The most dangerous of these possess sorcery or voodoo power, usually practiced at night by various mysterious means. This power can inflict an individual or his possessions with a "poison" or sickness that has sudden and calamitous results. The other power has to do with sexual practices and is referred to as love magic. It is bad only when applied in full strength; that is, at a time when the normal physical attractions are heightened to the point of lust.

The commonly employed protections against witchcraft are turquoise beads and eagle feathers — attached to objects and carried on the person — and cattail pollen. In the event an individual is stricken anyway, he can resort to a curing ceremonial; lightning, bear, and snake rituals are favored in such instances. In the old days, the Gan impersonators were often called in to do battle with the witches, but nowadays their cost has become prohibitive. In performing a ceremony, the medicine persons pit their power against that of the witch. If they are successful, the witch will die or suffer a tragedy, and the patient will recover.

The survival of the belief in witchcraft is due in large part to the fact that it explains antagonism and adversity, and validates the need for continuing the culture and the traditional ceremonies. Further, it serves as an excuse or explanation for excesses in sexual and social activity. It's a variation of "The Devil made me do it." Because those who are blessed economically may be particularly suspect, the belief in witchcraft encourages them to avoid reactions by sharing what they have with others. In the same way, since offending or arrogant persons are also liable to suspicion, witchcraft provides strong motivation for living in harmony with one's family and others. In substance, then, the presence of witchcraft beliefs has both its negative and positive sides. It can be grievous for those accused of it, but at the same time, it provides a regulating force in daily life.

Reservation life and Anglo contact may have brought a sweeping decrease in Apache ceremonial activity. Most of the gender rituals that at one time accompanied the vital pre-reservation lifestyle (and which are described in my book, The People Called Apache) have passed out of mind and existence. Some rituals were stamped out by Agency authorities; others were abandoned because they were no longer needed; and some ceased to be practiced because of the complexities and costs involved. Only the Sunrise Ceremony, a few minor personal rites, and a few curing ceremonials are still performed; even these occur less frequently than before. Nevertheless, medicine men are active on every reservation today. Despite the objections of, and the questions raised by, Christians, the Apache people are reluctant to entirely abandon the ancient rites.

Their faith in the rites is reinforced by diagnoses of ills, by cures, and by effective protections against harm. Furthermore, the people understand the ceremonials for what they are, not a replacement for Anglo medical services, but a complement to them. They use the medical facilities of the Agencies, but find that the rituals help them to determine the causes of disease and bring protection against recurrences in a way that puts the Apache mind at ease. While Apache medicine persons have often admitted they cannot posit the exact nature of an illness as well as can a competent physician, the point of the ceremonies is to discover the original cause of the problem; that is\, what the person thought or did to bring it about. And they might also find the physical or spiritual location of the illness. Even where trained physicians have failed, a cure might be performed by an Apache healer. Also, having recognized where an illness came from — the violation of a tabu or the disrespectful treatment of a power — the medicine persons can show their patient how to avoid the same difficulty in the future.

By and large, the Apache view illness as the result of violating a power. As mentioned earlier, the powers are free to act as they wish, and they are not always benevolent. When offended, they sometimes retaliate, causing illness. Their act is not evil, because men have been forewarned and given instructions in how to maintain good relationships with the powers. Hundreds of tabus exist, and so long as a person doesn't break one, he is safe. For example, one should avoid stepping on a trail made by a snake, and one must not kill a snake, for the snake is a power source. If this sounds simple enough to do at first, it is not actually so. While some tabus are practical and can be associated with common sense, most are not, and as such are neither easy to learn nor to remember. Thus, the probability of violating through carelessness or error an unknown or forgotten tabu is increased. In substance, the power idea serves as a governor for Apache life, since it encourages people to live respectfully and in harmony with their environment. The violated power enters the offender the moment he breaks the tabu. After this, it chooses its own time to make him ill. He may then do nothing and take his chances, go to the hospital, or seek the aid of a medicine man.

As mentioned, in earlier times, a profusion of wondrous and mysterious ceremonies was enacted for every aspect of life, and somehow the Apache found the time to carry these out. But while many of these were recorded by Captain John G. Bourke and Albert B. Reagan, neither of these men was able to plumb the deeper meanings of the events. Nearly all of the ceremonies they observed began about 9 p.m. and continued until dawn. Other rituals began at dusk, and the Medicine Disk Ceremony — one of several in which a huge and complicated sand painting was made — was begun and completed in daylight.

Some ceremonies continued for several nights while a progression of different rituals was carried out.

Curing Ceremonies

Today two types of curing ceremonials are performed. One is a short ceremony to determine what caused an illness and what to do about it — these usually begin at dusk and end by midnight or shortly thereafter. The other is a long ceremony to cure or remove the problem — these begin at dusk and continue until dawn. Some of the latter will go on for more than one night, the length determined by the gravity of the problem, the success of the medicine man, and the ability of the patient or his family to pay.

As late as 1940, a typical custom for engaging the services of medicine man or woman was to make a cross with pollen on the toe of his or her moccasin or shoe, then place a down payment of money, turquoise, or eagle feathers on top of the cross. If the medicine person picked up the offering, it indicated a willingness to perform the curing ceremony. Depending upon the amount of work involved, it was also customary to give more than the initial payment. There was also a practice of drawing a half moon with pollen on the palm of the medicine person's hand when services were needed. Such customs varied in different parts of the reservations and depended upon the nature of the illness. They are not always practiced today.

Once the arrangements are made for a curing rite, the age-old traditions come into play. Shortly before the actual ceremony is given, the medicine person or an informed elder meets with the family and friends and describes the mythical origin, the purposes, and the many successes of the rite. The stories are filled with drama and provide an enthralling setting for the actual event.

Apache curing crosses

The ceremony begins with an exhortation to the people attending to maintain pure and harmonious thoughts. The ritual includes a succession of things that must be done in proper order and the paraphernalia to be employed at specific points. Although chanting is the main device employed, a number of traditional objects are used.

The modern medicine men have only a small white feather pinned to their shirt as a badge of office. In the old days, they wore painted medicine hats and shirts, plus other intriguing items such as four-strand cords, medicine necklaces, and crosses.

While some ceremonies continue without interruption through the entire night, others reach a midpoint when everyone rests and eats. The children sleep, adults talk quietly, and for a few hours little is done. Then the fire is stoked up, and the ceremony resumes, continuing until dawn. The singers who are employed to assist the medicine persons are not medicine persons themselves, and they may or may not possess powers.

Many ceremonials employ specific equipment such as mysterious charms, certain plants, or parts of animals. These contain exorcising power and are applied to the patient to draw out sickness, either being held against the patient's body and drawn away, or used as a brush to sweep the sickness off. Pollen is the most important ceremonial offering, although ears of corn are used in some ceremonies. White shell, turquoise, black jet, and catlinite embody power and are of equal importance, each having directional associations. Eagle feathers, particularly those of the golden eagle, also form an important part of the religious equipment.

Ceremonial Hoops

At one time, ceremonial wooden hoops were commonly used. Known as *penseh*, they were made in two sizes: small ones only a few inches in diameter and large ones over two feet in diameter. To fashion the hoops, the ends were overlapped and tied with buckskin thongs. They were used in sets of four, each painted with the color of the direction it represented: green or black for the east, blue for the south, yellow for the west, and white for the north. When placed over a patient, they removed sickness. White sage, eagle's feathers, stones, and shells were tied to the hoops to give them additional power. Cross-shaped ceremonial staffs, four or five feet long, with a short, straight or curved crosspiece near the top also were made; these were painted with symbolic lines and figures such as deities, animals, cosmos symbols, and lightning lines. Laid on a patient and lifted off, they, too, removed the sickness. Usually, curing ceremonies have been held for only one person at a time, but there are rites that can be given to groups to fend off epidemics. Some ceremonies are of a protective nature and take place in the spring and summer when lightning and snakes, scorpions and other poisonous forms of life are present. The Lightning Ceremony is held for the community when an evil influence is thought to be at work; it can also bring rain.

When circumstances warrant it, and when the patient can afford it, the awesome Gan Dancers are called upon to perform. They are prepared for their role in the curing rituals by a medicine man with the power to do so. The stories told today by Western Apache informants regarding the origin of the Gans vary somewhat in minor details, but are similar to the following one:

In the beginning, the Supreme Being, known as Giver of Life, took the Apache from the center or bowels of the earth and brought them up to the country where they were to live. Having been placed there, they were instructed to conduct themselves reverently as a part of nature, preserving the land and, in particular, caring for all living things. But the Apache were finite and vulnerable like all humans, and they gave in to the corruption and crudeness with which the evil powers tempted them.

At this point, the concerned Giver of Life sent the Gans as his emissaries to teach the Apache how to live a better way. The people learned in plain terms how to live decently and honorably, how to cure the sick, how to govern fairly, how to hunt effectively and responsibly, how to plant and harvest, and how to discipline those who failed as Giver of Life wished them to live.

Apache curing hoop used to remove sickness

The Gans also revealed that they had the power to assist or to harm the Apache, and the awed people responded by seeking to live as they were instructed to, at least for a time. Then once again they gave in to temptations and backslid into wicked ways. The Gans were most unhappy with the Apache and decided to abandon them, letting them reap the bitter harvest they justly deserved. Shades of Eden, the Flood, and Romans 1:18-2:11! But the Gans were kind spirits who still had hope for the people, so before they went away they drew pictures of themselves on rock surfaces in and near the sacred caves. These drawings can still be seen today. When they were finished, the Gans entered the sacred caves and went deep into the sacred mountains to the place where the sun shines even when the earth is darkened by man's ignorance, to the place where there is always pleasantness and serenity.

The crestfallen and contrite Apache studied the drawings for a long time, giving much thought to the wicked nature of man and its unhappy fruits. Finally, they decided to impersonate the Gan Dancers in an attempt to live as Giver of Life wished. They copied the splendid headdresses, skirts, and moccasins depicted on the rocks and used them in performing the power-filled dances the Gans had taught them. In this way, the Gan Dances came into being, and in this way, they continue today.

Gan Dancers

The Gan, or Crown, Dance is performed just as it always has been. There are four dancers in a set, plus the clown. The identity of the performers is kept secret, and those who violate the no-recognition rule "make trouble" and are severely rebuked. Each dancer chooses his own headdress and costume style, but the medicine man tells him what materials to use and how to make the headdress. Mask styles differ; the Western Apache model is made of broader boards and is more varied in concept than the styles of the Chiricahua and Mescalero.

For color and symbols, black, blue, yellow, and white represent the four directions. On every mask there is one character that indicates the dancer's clan. While one informant claimed that all the decorations are painted on the costume with an eagle feather, which is then washed clean and attached to the face of the mask, others say that regular paintbrushes are often used. A blue-green stone is always attached to the butt of the eagle feather or brush that is used for painting. Black or turquoise stones are sewed inside the cloth portion of the mask. In curing, each dancer sometimes carries a stone in his mouth, which he spits onto the sick person. Yellow butterflies painted on the wooden part of a dancer's headdress, called the "horns," are said to remind the people that butterflies were among their ancestors. The stars, sun, and moon painted on the back of the mask and on the dancer's chest are "light" to frighten away angry powers. A cross with a red line around it represents Giver of Life and the sun that shines through him. The white dots painted on the headdress frame and on the dancer's body indicate a pure heart. White triangles on the body represent the sacred mountains or a dancer's teeth. A red sun painted on the headdress designates dancer number four, and a cross on top of the sun represents the victory of ceremonially employed animal horns over the evil powers. A green sun painted on each side of a headdress tells the dancer "which way to go." Inverted triangles on a mask represent the rock that only the medicine man is allowed to sit on. The clown's entire body is painted with black dots. A snake is sometimes painted down the middle of his mask. On occasion, he is the only dancer to have evergreen boughs tied to his waist and wrists. However, the other dancers do wear evergreen while curing some illness and during the Sunrise Ceremony. Any harmful spirits enter the boughs, and after the dance, the clown carries the boughs away and burns them. Clown paint symbolizes the deer, which is the clown's symbolic horse.

The Gan (Crown) Dance

Western Apache Gan wands are more ornate than those of the Chiricahua and Mescalero. They are either painted in various ways or left unpainted. They are made of sotol stalk or yucca, varying in length from two to four feet, with a slight curve. While the headdresses were once made of sotol stalk, modern versions are often fashioned of thin lumberyard slats or of plywood painted with commercial enamel paints. Also, they are seldom as elaborate, delicate, and subtle in design as the stupendous headdresses of early times.

The Gan Dancers of today continue the practice of removing their costumes in a secret place after dancing and then hiding them away in a sacred cave. Prayers are said over the costumes, and sometimes the knots of the thongs used to assemble them are untied to prevent their being worn if discovered. This is because the Western Apache believe that if anyone other than a dancer puts on a Gan headdress, he will go mad.

Apache Curing Way — How It Works

It is important that we end our consideration of Apache pathways by emphasizing the value of their curing ceremonials as they see them. When an outsider thinks about Apache curing ceremonials, he tends to avoid dealing directly with actual and surprising cures that have taken place in favor of emphasizing the psychological benefits. Since we can't offer plausible explanations in conventional medical terms for the former, we let that portion lie and deal only with the mental aspects.

This is not to suggest that the psychological aspect is of lesser importance. On the contrary, the medical profession has realized for a long time that many physical disabilities are the by-products of psychic disorders.

The Apache learned this too, and they also recognized that when psychic disorders are breached or replaced by hope — by the conviction that the ceremony will make the patient well — a significant step has been taken toward recovery. The nature of the Apache ceremonial is such that it accomplishes this positive step. It occupies the patient's mind in positive ways, bringing about peace of mind, imparting strength by undergirding the will to get well, and assuring that family and friends truly care.

Tradition and personal experience have always been the touch-stones of Apache healing. Everyone learned from childhood on about the firm roots of the Apache beliefs. They grew up participating in numerous ceremonials, and they witnessed many cures. The medicine person was fixed in the life-way as an integral part of the curing process, and his powers were known to everyone. The entire emphasis, once the decision to proceed had been made, was on positive results.

Involvement

Having procured the medicine person, the patient and all who would join in the rite became intensely involved with the traditional details. They knew that if these were properly carried out, success was assured. Everyone was doing something about the illness, and all activities were carefully coordinated.

Positive Thoughts

Long before the actual ceremony began, the medicine person lectured about the ancient teachings regarding the ceremony and its benefits, impressing upon the patient the need to think positive thoughts. Then, as the time for the event drew near, the place to hold the ceremony had to be selected; women cooked, men went for firewood, invitations to guests went out, and the ceremonial paraphernalia was gathered and made ready.

Those who attended were those who cared. Everyone important to the patient would be present, and everyone who came participated in some way. The food preparation went on, and many speeches were made about proper conduct and thinking good thoughts. The men were expected to join in the singing and drumming. Everyone shared in the pollen blessings and in the important social dances. Through this activity, the children were taught important lessons about faith and prayer.

Music

The stress was on involvement, and this brought about the healthiest possible results. Holding the ritual at night offered the advantage of a time period when people would not be distracted by the usual things they could do and see in the daytime. The darkness formed an aura of wonder and provoked spiritual thoughts. Even the length of time given over to the ceremony was an important factor. The ceremony went on all night, lasting long enough for everyone and every aspect of the rite to phase gradually and progressively into and then out of what was happening.

Happiness

The Apache believe that the powers work best in a positive atmosphere of happiness. The opposite attitude conveys an impression of doubt and defeat. So there was little restraint among the guests, and an outside observer without understanding would often criticize their expressions of joy. As the curing ritual wore on, the adults not directly involved socialized, laughed, and joked; some men and women searched for the drink tulapai (which the Apache make from cacti) and consumed what they could. The children ran and shouted freely in the midst of it all.

Results of the Curing Way

The curing way is still performed like this today. It has much to recommend itself to those who ponder the question of determining how a religious ceremony is likely to bear its best fruits. An Apache curing ceremony was often the beginning of a close and lifelong friendship between the medicine person and the patient. Furthermore, when a ceremony failed to effect a cure, the medicine person suffered irreparable injury to his reputation only when he or she had been too confident of success in the beginning. Failures could usually be smoothed over by the suggestion that the medicine person had not been retained soon enough or that witchcraft was involved. Also, as Renzie noted in discussing the cures worked by the Sunrise Ceremony girl, the cure might be taking place, yet not show its ultimate effect for some time to come. Therefore, the patient must guard against carelessness by wearing the protective amulets given him by the medicine person and observing the ever-present tabus.

The people realized that a medicine person might not succeed in every case, so excuses were actually built into the traditional process. In some instances, the services of several medicine persons were sought before relief was obtained, and sometimes it never came. However, even allowing for the fact that desperation drives people to seek aid, it appears that the curing ceremonies would not have persisted into the present had they not been in some measure effective for the patients and for the people as a whole.

In Part Three of this book, you will have an opportunity to test for yourself some of the Apache pathways for healing and for changing your life in a splendid way. I am certain that the results will more than surprise you. You will find that when ancient things are picked up, pondered, and put to use, they have a power-filled way of coming startlingly to life.

Sioux
Pathways

The central pathway of the Sioux nation was and still is the Sun Dance. No one, including the Sioux themselves, knows how old the ceremony is or what its earliest form was, but it was being practiced when the first white explorers entered Sioux country in the eighteenth century.

THE SIOUX SUN DANCE

It has been my special privilege to count as close friends the two men who, during this century, have been the most prominent and best informed leaders of the Sun Dances at Pine Ridge and Rosebud: Fools Crow and Eagle Feather, whose English name was Bill Schweigman. Since they wanted the information preserved for posterity, both of these men decided without persuasion to tell me about and show me the innermost details of the dance. This material is published in full in my book, *Sundancing at Rose Bud and Pine Ridge*.

According to these men, and as substantiated by more ancient authorities, the Sun Dance is a rite of rebirth, renewal, procreation, and thanksgiving. While it is held in midsummer, when Sun is at full strength, plans for each year's celebration are begun in the spring — at the same time as, and in concert with, Mother Earth as she and Sun join forces to drive off Cold Maker, then give birth and nourishment to the new growth and to life as a whole.

The Sun Dance is held in a large open circle whose perimeter is marked by a shade bower with seats for spectators and at whose center is set up a tall cottonwood sacred Sun Dance tree, also called the Sun Pole. While the site is selected early in the year and certain other details are attended to in the spring, the actual ceremony is held during four days in summer; another eight days of concentrated preparation precedes it. Certain restrictions must also be observed by the dancers for four days after the ritual ends, so in all, sixteen days are consumed.

Piercing

When the Sun Dance is done properly, on the last day — and sometimes on one or more of the other days — each of the men called "pledgers" is pierced by having two wooden skewers (or sometimes eagle claws) inserted under the skin of their chests. These skewers are then attached to a strong rope and the other end tied to the Sun Pole. Then the men form a circle around the Sun Pole and, after going forward four times to lay their hands on it and pray, pull back as hard as they are able until the skewers are at last torn free. An alternate method is to have two of the skewers inserted under the skin of the back at shoulder blade height. Heavy buffalo skulls are hung by thongs from these and then dragged around by the bearer until their weight tears the skewers loose.

As the uninitiated outsider can easily imagine, early missionaries were horrified by this torture aspect of the Sun Dance and, without the least effort to understand its full significance to the Sioux, began immediately to do everything they could to put an end to the ceremony. By 1890, they thought they had accomplished it, but they hadn't really, because the Sioux consider the Sun Dance too vital to their well-being and survival to permit it to end. The Sioux secretly continued to practice it in remote places on the reservations.

Their reasons for continuing the Sun Dance are already implicit in what I have said about the purposes, or goals, of the dance — annual rebirth, renewal, procreation, and thanksgiving. The fact that the missionaries made no attempt to understand these purposes did not change Sioux needs and beliefs. The torture aspect of the dance was not nearly so terrible as the missionaries imagined. It was purposefully painful, but surprisingly little blood was shed. No one died from it or even suffered long from the wounds after the dance was over.

The point of this segment of the dance was to have a means whereby a representative few men, along with a few women who had flesh-offerings taken from the skin of their arms, could vicariously thank the Above Beings on behalf of the entire tribe — in a manner whose sincerity could not be challenged and was plain for all to see.

No simple spoken "thank you" was enough for the Sioux. Someone had to say it in a way in which heartfelt sincerity was obvious. But even Roman Catholic priests, whose orders once practiced flagellation and other forms of self-punishment, made no attempt to understand this. They saw the sacrificial act as heathen and barbaric, and immediately determined that it could in nowise be given by God or acceptable to him. The worst part of this summary judgment was that it also self-blinded them to the virtues of the rest of the ceremony — and there are many.

Interestingly enough, after a century of sharing life with the Sioux, Roman Catholic and some Protestant missionaries have finally come to realize that the traditional religious practices of the natives have much to recommend them, and on the reservations many of these are now incorporated into church rituals and teachings.

Sioux fertility symbols used on sun dance sacred tree

In case you are wondering, I do not suggest that you practice piercing as the Sioux do, or that in following the pathways you undergo any other form of self-torture or punishment. Nor do I recommend that you dance for hours under the broiling sun as the Sun Dancers do when they are not piercing. These practices are for the Sioux alone, and for the other Plains tribes that also do the dance in one of several variations. What will be beneficial for you are some of the other aspects of the dance and the positive actions and thought patterns that accompany these. I will describe them now, and in Part Three.

The Sioux idea of annual renewal was similar in its thrust to that of the ancient Cherokee ceremonial life. After the long and bitterly cold Midwestern winters, the people always longed anxiously for the first signs that new life and growth were returning. Since the people had been taught to think of themselves as part of nature, they saw spring as a time when they, too, could join in celebration and call down into themselves the power for rebirth, renewal, and procreation that was being made available by the Above Beings. Thanksgiving was also in order for having survived the winter.

Thanksgiving

In the days before reservation strictures hemmed in the Sioux and suppressed ceremonial life, the Sun Dance addressed itself openly and joyfully to each of these: to renew power by considering themselves reborn so that all of life and its opportunities were free of past problems and unreservedly open to them; to renew power by becoming new, fresh, and strong again through restoration, recreation, and revival; to renew procreation power by continued reproduction, begetting, and bringing forth both children and creative ideas that assured the longevity of the family and the nation; to renew thanksgiving power by expressing proper gratitude to the benevolent and protective Beings who answered the people's prayers by granting them the power to accomplish their rebirth, renewal, and procreation.

In considering the Sioux pathways, never forget that the enthusiasm and devotion of the people came from their belief that they were celebrating in concert with the whole of creation. As they danced, the idea was fixed in their minds that the entire world and the heavens danced with them and that an orgy of mutual blessing was going on. In addition to receiving their personal rewards, this made the people feel important and needed. They were contributing and felt worthwhile. Their thoughts and love were appreciated. Their wisdom had worth. Quite naturally, they felt good as they danced. They were happy, and they were secure.

In essence, the entire dance was a prayer made up of requests, acknowledgments, and thanksgiving. Each segment of the dance addressed itself to one or another of these.

Rebirth

Rebirth was considered and treated as the dancers danced barefooted to unite with Mother Earth as she gave new birth to all of nature: soil, vegetation, rivers, streams, fish, and the bird and animal worlds. Since the dancers were barefooted, there was no barrier to keep her from imparting rebirth power to them. Around the dancers' ankles, wrists, and heads were woven bands made of sacred sage that kept evil spirits from entering them and affecting the power of the dance. Sometimes, buffalo-hide wristbands were worn as a prayer for the continuation of the animal herds. The drumming that attended the dancing was Mother Earth's voice sending to the people her words of encouragement, approval, and love. The Tree itself, having been ritually cut down for the occasion, represented a transition period as it now died — the death of the old was occurring, and after the four days of dancing were over, the new would begin for the Sioux nation.

Renewal and Healing

Renewal was considered and treated as the dancers danced in the sun and absorbed its beneficent power and strength into their minds, bodies, hearts, and souls. Those who danced — and through them, all members of the nation — were filled with the light and enlightenment needed to grow, flourish, be beautiful, and survive. The process was the same as that for the beings in the plant world. Power and assistance were also called in from the four cardinal directions whose positions for the Sun Dance were marked by pairs of flags placed at the perimeter of the circle: red for the north, yellow for the east, white for the south, and black for the west. Sun also imparted a healing power to the dancers, and at least once during each dance, healings were performed for all of the spectators who requested it.

Prayers

Individual and group prayers were offered during the dance in several ways. The first was through songs sung by the singers who accompanied the dancers. The second was by the blowing of whistles made from the wing bone of the golden eagle. The third was by the use of each dancer's sacred pipe, whose bowl represented the earth, whose stem represented all that grows upon the earth, whose stem carvings represented all of the four-legged creatures, whose pendant feathers represented all flying creatures, whose tobacco grains represented all of the Sioux people, and whose sweet-smelling smoke — and even the pipe's mere presence — carried prayers up to Wakan Tanka. The fourth means was for the Intercessor, the person who led the dance, to offer up prayers at specified intervals. The fifth means was to attach long strips of colored cloth to the base of the Tree. Each color was a prayer in itself, and those who were knowledgeable understood their meanings. Nowadays, there is always a color to represent a prayer for the well-being and cooperation of all of the races of the world: black, white, yellow, and red. Two banner-like red cloths, representing the bloodline of the Sioux nation, are tied to the uppermost Tree branches and flown in the wind. As with Hopi pahos, once a cloth is attached to the Tree, it begins to offer its prayer, and it continues to do so for the four days of the dance. The flesh offerings given by male and female dancers are put in small cloth packets tied to long strings and also secured to the Tree as individual prayers.

Procreation

Procreation was considered and treated by attaching two symbols made of rawhide to the leafed boughs of the Tree top. Dancers focused on each of these at certain stages of the dance. Not always, but in most instances, these symbols had large phallic appendages to represent procreation. One was of a man, and it was painted red or black. The other was of a buffalo, and it was painted black. Sometimes, the figure of a bird, representing Thunder, was substituted for the buffalo. Tied crossways just below the lowest branches was a long, hide-wrapped bundle of cherry tree branches with the buds left on. This, too, symbolized continuing life through procreation.

Provision

As the dancers and the accompanying musicians centered their minds and prayers upon the symbols, they thought through and sang about matters associated with the continuation of life, especially about how the Above Beings blessed humankind and how they provided everything in season that was needed — particularly the buffalo and the rain upon which the Sioux depended heavily for existence. In addition to the rawhide symbols, the Intercessor made a small symbolic altar at the west end of the dancing circle that included a painted buffalo skull placed on a bed of sacred sage, two black flags, and a pipe rack to hold the male dancers' sacred pipes when they were not in use.

Authors who write about the Sun Dance frequently note that in the early days the men and women who pledged to do the dance and to undergo the piercing and flesh offerings were those who had made vows to do so during a time of crisis. For example, a man whose life was in peril during a battle with the enemy might vow to Wakan Tanka that if he survived he would do the Sun Dance the following year. But dancers in this century often do it year after year simply as an expression of their faith in the traditional beliefs. I suspect that was also true for some pledgers in earlier times.

Purification

In preparation for the present-day Sun Dance, the Intercessor, his assistants, and often the pledgers, gather in sweatlodges to purify themselves and to pray for Wakan Tanka's blessings. Once the dance is underway, a pre-sunrise purification ritual is held each day in a sweatlodge that is set up outside the west side of the Sun Dance circle. Later, more is said about the sweatlodge and its important role in Sioux religious life.

After having been done in secret for more than half a century, the public celebrations of the Sun Dance with piercing resumed at Rosebud and Pine Ridge in the 1950s, and have continued there and at other reservations without interference ever since. Most dances are held either the first week of July or the last two days of July and the first two days of August. Non-Indian visitors are welcome at these dances, but the Sioux expect them to be as reverent as they would be at a church service. With few exceptions, photography is not permitted, although I was allowed to take still photographs of the entire ceremony and its preparations, as well as to make a motion picture of the same. The latter film is now in the archives in the Center for Western Studies at Augustana College in Sioux Falls, South Dakota, where it is available to researchers.

A special note: When you consider Sioux pathways, remember that they, perhaps more than any other tribe, employ diversity in their rituals, adapting them to meet the changing circumstances of the times.

FEAST OF THE VIRGINS

One of the most impressive of the early ceremonies that served as peripheral pathways was the sacred Feast of the Virgins. When given for the first time, it served as the public announcement of a pubescent girl's arrival at marriageable age, as does the Apache Sunrise Ceremony.

In its most ancient form, it was also called the Bull Buffalo Ceremony. One of the Buffalo Women taught this ceremony to the Lakota so they could purify their daughters at their first menstruation, drive from them evil influences, induce them to become industrious and hospitable and live such exemplary lives that husbands would never cut off the tips of their noses for infidelity. There was no fixed ritual governing the ceremony, but each performance was similar to others in the rites and songs and in their sequence.

When a girl's first flow came, she was placed alone in a tipi, and her mother and female friends taught her how to care for herself and dispose of the waste products, as well as how to purify her body after the flow ceased by bathing or by using the sweat bath. They also instructed her as to the part she was to play in the ceremony. Items needed for the ceremony were a new tipi, a new dress, and a breechclout for the girl; a wooden bowl; chokecherries, either fresh or dried; an eagle plume feather with the quill wrapped with the head-skin of a mallard drake; sagebrush; dried wood, either box elder or cottonwood; a drum; a pipe with dried willow bark to smoke; sweetgrass; food for the feast; and presents for the guests. The medicine man who would conduct the ritual would first seek a vision that he would relate during the ceremony. He would also provide a buffalo skull with the horns on it, a staff made of cherry wood, a holy fire stick, and the ceremonial pipe. Guests were invited by means of invitation wands, and a dried bone was sent to anyone whose presence was not desired. One day was appointed for the ceremony, which would last from dawn to sunset. Guests could arrive prior to the day and were welcome to stay after it to prolong the festival.

An eagle plume was tied to the girl's hair; its spirit would bring her many children. She was given a staff of cherry wood to help her find plums and chokecherries so she could make plenty of pemmican. When the ceremony was finished, she was given the name Buffalo Woman, and she became part of a class distinct from women who had not gone through the ceremony.[3]

Prayer for Buffalo Woman

Since our purpose is to make use of the essence of ritual pathways and not to duplicate them, I will not go further into the Bull Buffalo Ceremony details. But the prayers offered for the girl were significant . . . that during her life she would not be a lazy woman; that she would not do foolish or shameful things; that she would not have trouble; and that she would have a good and brave husband, bear many children, and be very happy.

A Nineteenth Century Puberty Ceremony

The coming-of-age ritual that Charles Alexander Eastman, whose Sioux name was Ohiyesa, was familiar with in the late nineteenth century is quite different from the one just described, and it illustrates the Sioux tendency to adapt their rituals to the times. The village herald would announce the event by proclaiming that the daughter of a certain family would kindle her first "maiden's fire" on the next day, and that all other girls who had neither yielded to the pleadings of men nor destroyed their innocence were invited to join with her to proclaim anew their chastity and purity before their companions and in plain sight of Sun, Earth, and Wakan Tanka.

Since this event was next to the Sun Dance and the Grand Medicine Dance in importance, it also took place at the time of tribal gatherings for the summer festivities. So that everyone could attend, it was held in

---

[3] Walter, James R., 1980, *Lakota Belief and Ritual*, pp. 241-263. University of Nebraska Press, Lincoln and London.

the great circle around which the lodges of the great encampment were placed. Here, two large circles were inscribed on the ground, one within the other. A crudely heart-shaped and red-painted rock was placed in the precise center of the innermost circle. Thrust into the ground on its east side was a sharp knife, and on its left side were two barbed arrows. The girls stood within the inner circle and faced the rock. Their female sponsors, who had already undergone the rite, stood within the outer circle. Outside this were the spectators, and one of the warrior societies was responsible for keeping order.

A medicine woman directed the ritual, and once it was underway, any man among the spectators was free to approach and challenge any woman whom he knew to be unworthy. But, if he could not prove his accusation, he would be severely punished by the warrior society in charge.

To perform the rite, each girl in turn approached the sacred rock and solemnly laid her right hand upon it. This was her declaration of virginity and served as her vow to remain so until she married. She also agreed by this act that if ever she should violate this vow, she deserved to be punished with the knife or the arrows.

In ancient times, girls were eager to attend one or more of these feasts, and, on occasion, a girl was compelled to give one to put an end to gossip about her conduct. At such times, the rite served as a challenge to others to prove their accusations.

Sometimes, a similar ritual was performed by young men, and their rules were stricter still, for no young man could participate in the ceremony who had so much as spoken of love to a maiden. It was considered a high honor among the Sioux to have won distinction in warfare and in the buffalo chase, and, above all, to have been invited to a seat in the tribal council before speaking to any mature woman save one's own sister.[4]

A Contemporary Puberty Ceremony

Although the puberty ceremony is rarely held today, it was my good fortune to have a dear friend at Rosebud attend a puberty rite for her granddaughter in 1977, then send me an account of it. I suspect it is the only such account that has been released to an outsider. For obvious reasons, I will omit names, but these are available to qualified specialists.

---

[4] Eastman, Charles Alexander, 1911, *The Soul of the Indian*, pp. 95-99. Houghton Mifflin Company, Boston and New York.

On July 1, a cottonwood shade bower was set up at a certain site at Rosebud to form the perimeter of a thirty-foot circle. At 10 a.m., a tipi was erected in the center of the bower, and the rest of the day was spent collecting sage with which to cover the entire floor of the tipi. The job was not finished until 9 p.m.

On July 2, several women arrived at the ceremonial ground about 8 a.m. and proceeded to cut enough cloth pieces to make a quilt. The girl joined the women, and she was taught how to sew the pieces together. With the women's help, the quilt was completed by 8 p.m. A small fire was kindled in the tipi, and the girl remained there for that night. Relatives stayed nearby in tents to look out for her.

Activities resumed at 8 a.m. on July 3. A female relative arrived with hide and beads. When the girl had finished breakfast, the relative spent the rest of the day teaching her how to fashion moccasins in the ancient way. My informant noted in her letter that after the ceremony was completed, the girl was continuing to fashion moccasins and had made several very good pairs.

On July 4, the day began with the girl and the women participating in a sweatlodge ceremony. Over the course of that morning, a woman taught the girl how to make Indian fried bread. In the afternoon, another woman taught the girl how to do quillwork on moccasins.

On July 5, the ritual began early, since that night there was to be a special rite, a feast, and a giveaway. After a sweat bath for the women, men began to prepare the meat for the feast. Lunch was eaten about 11 a.m. At noon, my informant took *wasna* (dried meat or pemmican) to the sweatlodge, and another woman brought wild chokecherry juice. Male singers brought a golden eagle feather, sage, and sweetgrass. When all was ready, my informant took the girl into the sweatlodge, lighted the sweetgrass as a prayer, tied the eagle feather to her hair, and wiped her entire naked body with the sage so that she would be purified to face her people. After this, the girl dressed in her traditional buckskin and beaded costume, and my informant combed the girl's hair, letting it fall loose over her shoulders and down her back. This was the way hair was worn for mourning, and, in this instance, the girl was mourning for the loss of her girlhood.

With the singers leading the way, the entire party then proceeded to the ceremonial tipi, where a medicine man took the girl inside and gave her instructions as to how to treat her people: "how to be nice, kind and helpful to all, to treat them as she would her own brothers and sisters."

Then he led the way out of the tipi and to the south edge of the ceremonial circle. As they walked, they paused four times to pray. The singing, which had begun when the pair first entered the tipi, continued for about three hours. Next, the medicine man had the girl stand upright on a small square of buffalo hide that was fully beaded with red beads and was placed just in front of the tipi entrance. Since the plum tree was a fruit-bearing tree, he tied a plum tree bud to her hair and prayed to the four directions. Then he introduced her to her father and mother, her brothers and sisters, and to the rest of the people as a mature and marriageable woman. A song was sung for her, and she was given the name Buffalo Woman. Everyone danced around the lodge to the accompaniment of singing and drum music. The feast was held, and a giveaway concluded the ritual. About 9 p.m., most of the people gave the girl gifts of money, and the very happy group dispersed and went home. The next morning, the tipi and bower were taken down. In ending her account, my friend reported that "everything was done in a very pretty way."

GRAND MEDICINE DANCE

The Sioux had a secret Medicine Lodge Society, said to have originated among the Algonquin tribe, whose members must observe the highest moral standards. This society practiced and taught the use of curative roots and herbs, and held a yearly medicine feast during which all of the medicine bundles and totems of the various lodges were displayed and their medicine songs were sung. When candidates for membership to the society were accepted, a Grand Medicine Dance was held for which invitations were sent out in the form of small bundles of tobacco. Two very large tipis were pitched facing one another, a hundred feet apart, half open and connected by a roofless hall or colonnade of fresh-cut boughs. One of these lodges was for the society giving the dance and its novices; the other was occupied by the soldiers whose duty it was to distribute the refreshments and to keep order among the spectators. The soldiers were selected from among the best and bravest warriors of the tribe.

After the preparations were complete, the members of each lodge dressed and painted themselves according to their rituals, then entered the hall separately, in single file, led by their oldest man or chief. Standing before the Soldier Lodge and facing west, their chief addressed Wakan Tanka directly in a few words, after which everyone extended his right arm horizontally from the shoulder with open palm and sang a short invocation in unison, ending with a deep "E-ho-ho-ho!" The chief repeated this impressive performance in front of the headquarters while facing east. Then the members of each lodge took their assigned places and the songs and dances followed in regular order.

The closing ceremony, intensely dramatic, was the initiation of the novices who had received their final preparation on the night before. They were led out in front of the headquarters lodge and placed in a kneeling position upon a rich carpet of robes and furs: the men upon the right hand, stripped and painted black with a round spot of red just over the heart; the women, dressed in their best clothing, arranged upon the left. Both sexes wore the hair loose, which was the custom for ceremonial performances. An equal number of grand medicine men, each of whom was appointed to one of the novices, faced them at a distance of half the length of the hall, perhaps fifty feet.

After silent prayer, each medicine man in turn addressed his charge, exhorting him in his duty toward his fellow man and toward the Ruler of Life. All of the medicine men assumed then an attitude of superb power and dignity, crouching slightly as if about to spring forward to begin a footrace, grasping their decorated medicine bags firmly in both hands. Swinging their arms forward in unison, they uttered a guttural *"Yo-ho-ho-ho!"* with startling effect. In the midst of the breathless silence that followed, they took a step forward, then another and another, until they were only a yard or so from the row of kneeling novices. Here they gave a mighty swing of the medicine bags that seemed to project all their mystic powers into the bodies of the quivering initiates, who instantly all fell forward on their faces, apparently lifeless.

With this thrilling climax, the drums were vigorously pounded, and the dance began again with energy. After a few turns had been taken about the prostrate bodies of the new members, covering them with fine robes and other garments which were later to be distributed as gifts, they were permitted to come to life and to join in the final dance . . . the totality of the performance being clearly symbolic of death and resurrection.[5]

THE SWEATLODGE

Numerous references to the sweatlodge make it clear that it has played a major role in the peripheral pathways of the Sioux. It is a dome-shaped structure made with bent and lashed-together willow saplings. It is about four feet high at its peak, and the usual diameter is nine or ten feet. Originally, hides were used to cover it; today, blankets and canvas are most commonly used. The entrance for the Sioux Sun Dance Sweatlodge faces west toward the setting sun, which in this instance serves as a symbol of renewal and rebirth. Participants sit on

---

[5] Eastman, pp. 63-73.

a bed of sage. Rocks are heated in a symbolically shaped firepit that is dug twelve feet to the west of the entrance. Twelve rocks are passed into the lodge and placed in a small firepit in its center. After singing a traditional number of prayer chants while holding his pipe, a medicine man pours water over the hot stones; steam fills the lodge, and the heat rises to an almost unbearable level. The test of a person's will is determined by the amount of heat he can withstand. Strange things happen during medicine ceremonies in sweatlodges — objects fly around, voices and other sounds are heard, rattles and sparks may float in the air, and the rocks themselves are heard to speak as they pass on messages from the spirits. When we turn to the sweatlodge experiences of Fools Crow, I will say more about these wondrous things.

The sweatlodge is used for praying, for purification, for divining and for healing. Medicine persons make continual use of it, and most traditional laypersons use it often during the year.

YUWIPI

The *Yuwipi* ceremony is another Sioux pathway. It is used for healing, divining, and for finding lost persons or objects. A medicine man who performs this nighttime ritual builds a special altar on the floor of a house and allows the spectators to tie his hands securely behind his back, then wrap him head and foot in a thick blanket so that he is entirely covered like a mummy. Ropes are tied around the blanket to hold it in place. He is then laid out full length on the altar, while the other participants sit in a tightly packed circle around him and hold hands so they will know if anyone moves. The lights are extinguished, and the medicine man prays audibly so that everyone can hear him. After a specified period of time, the lights are turned on, and without anyone having helped him, the Yuwipi man will be sitting there free of his bindings with the blanket neatly folded beside him and his hands folded in his lap. He never reveals how he does this, and when asked always claims that the spirits come and release him.

During the time he remains wrapped and in the dark, the medicine man may pray for help in determining the cause of an illness he has been asked to cure, and in learning the roots or herbs that will heal it. Or, if he has been asked to find a lost object or person, he will pray for guidance regarding that. Surprising results are common, and there are many testimonies to the truth of this, including those given by non-Indians who have participated and been helped in amazing ways. In my personal experiences, these affirmations include those of white nurses and other white professional people.

VISION QUEST

The *vision quest* is another peripheral pathway finding — an extremely important one. In ancient times, all young men underwent this experience, in some instances at an age as young as eleven — never later than their early teens. Adult males quested when they were in need of spirit helpers to assure their success in war, raiding, and leadership. Some women vision-quested, too, but not as many as men. Medicine persons depended heavily upon the quests and frequently accompanied and guided other questors. This is still the case at Pine Ridge and Rosebud today.

One of the favored questing places has been majestic Bear Butte, which is situated west of Rapid City, South Dakota. In ancient times, any isolated and rugged site that would stimulate spiritual thoughts served as an acceptable questing place. After counseling by the medicine man and undergoing purification in a sweatlodge, the white-painted questor would go, either with a medicine man or alone, to a questing place. There he would spend as many as four days and nights fasting and praying as he sought a vision from the Above Beings and the spirits, in which one or more helpers — in the form of supernatural objects,

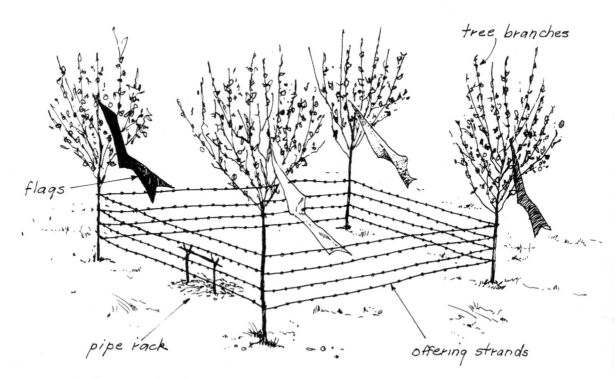

The Sioux questing place

animals, birds or the like — would appear to him and bring him instructions from the deities.

The questor's first act was to build a proper questing place. This consisted of a four- to six-foot-wide by seven- or eight-foot-long cleared rectangle, called a "bed," which he sometimes covered with flat rocks and other times with sage. Its four corners were marked by cloth flags in the colors of the four cardinal directions tied to small saplings. One or more strings with numerous small tobacco offerings tied to them were suspended between the flags to delineate the sides and ends of the bed — somewhat like ropes around a prize-fight ring. During his waking hours, the questor either stood and followed the path of Sun as he prayed or sat facing east and meditated intensely. His sacred pipe was placed at the west end of the bed for him to focus his thoughts on. Visions did not always come, but once one was received, the questor, if alone, would return to his village and consult with the medicine man about what he had seen and how he was to make proper use of it. Otherwise, he would talk with the medicine man while they were there together. Usually some physical part of the animal, bird, rock or other object whose spirit-image had come to him in the vision would be obtained and placed in his medicine bundle. This act assured the person that the power of the vision would enter into him, and thereafter remain with him to remind, protect and guide him. Visions were, and are, most often kept secret, but some that were reported long after they occurred are amazing and spectacular.

HUNKA CEREMONY

The Sioux had a *Hunka Rite* (Making of Brothers) whose nature was similar to that of the Cherokee Cementation Ceremony already reported. However, while the Cherokee ritual was for the making of brothers only, in the Sioux rite, any person could adopt another and, by carrying out the proper details of the ceremony, could become the lifelong companion of that person. The ceremony was exceedingly complex, and except for the essence of the idea, it is not easily adaptable to a pathway that can be walked — other than by Indians — in the modern world.

SPIRIT KEEPING

Spirit Keeping is a Sioux pathway finding of particular interest, for it centers itself in the beautiful thoughts and love inspired in the persons involved. In ancient times, it was widely practiced. But early missionaries considered the rite to be heathen and, as they so commonly did with other rites, sought to eliminate the practice. Today, it is rarely held, but I had the privilege of seeing it enacted at a Sun Dance at Rosebud on July 3, 1975. In this instance, a young woman who had been given a special healing ceremony in 1974 had died shortly before the 1975 Sun Dance was held. Since she had vowed that she would be in the dance if she was alive in July of 1975, a Spirit Keeping Ceremony was held to help her keep her vow.

The Spirit Keeping Ceremony was one of the seven rituals given to the Sioux by White Buffalo Maiden who brought the Sacred Pipe. It was performed for a deceased loved one, usually a child or youth, and it served a double purpose: comforting broken hearts by keeping at earth level the spirit of the dead person for a specified period of time — sometimes as long as a full year — after which the spirit was ceremonially released; and promoting good thoughts, love, and unity throughout the nations.

The Spirit Keeper's role demanded considerable sacrifice. Those who agreed to accept it must have been of good repute and willing to separate themselves from worldly concerns and involvements as long as the ceremony lasted so they could concentrate intently upon the central purpose of the ritual — to prolong through constant prayer the mourning period. This kept the spirit of the loved one close by and made the parting more bearable for family and friends.

After the traditional purification rites had been conducted in the sweatlodge, a lock of the deceased's hair and several other small possessions that had been his or hers were fashioned into an exotic spirit bundle and put in a place of honor in the Keeper's lodge. A Spirit Post was also carved from cottonwood, painted with a face that represented the deceased, and placed upright in the ground at the entrance to the Keeper's lodge for the duration of the rite. In the releasing ceremony, the bundle and the post were held up to Sun while prayers were said, then the spirit was sent off with further prayers to Wakan Tanka.

THE GIVEAWAY

Another Sioux peripheral pathway finding was learning that the love of possessions was a weakness to be overcome. They believed that such love appeals to the material side of man and, if allowed to have its own way, would quickly, perhaps even permanently, disturb the spiritual balance of the person. Therefore, one of the first lessons taught to the child was generosity. Children were encouraged to give away whatever they prized the most. So that they might know the happiness of giving, at an early age they were made the managers of some of the family goods. If a child was inclined to be greedy or to cling to any of these goods or his own possessions, he was told legends that revealed the contempt and disgrace that always befell stingy and mean people.

Public giving, or *giveaways*, were part of every important ceremony, especially those which celebrated birth, puberty, marriage, or death, and they were observed whenever someone desired to pay special honor to any person or event. Upon such occasions, it was common to give to the point of utter impoverishment. Fools Crow has done this several times. Sometimes, everything a family had was given away to relatives and friends — especially to the poor and the elderly, from whom one could ask no return. (Jesus made the same request of his followers.) Finally, there were frequent gifts to the Above Beings that might or might not have great value in themselves, but which in the giver's own mind always carried the meaning and reward of true sacrifice.

Another peripheral pathway related to the giveaway was that orphans, the widowed, and the aged were watched over and cared for not only by their own kin, but also by the entire village and tribe. In this respect, the generosity of any individual was only limited by his strength, ability, and good fortune or the lack of it. It was an honor to be chosen for special service to others, and it was considered shameful for anyone to expect a reward for it.

FOOLS CROW

Fools Crow's formal education in spiritual matters began in 1901 at age eleven, when a medicine man named Stirrup took him on his first vision quest, then gave him his basic training. Over the years, he has become the ultimate living authority among the Teton Sioux and is recognized as their Ceremonial Chief and a holy man who ranks above all medicine men and women. As such, and because he has revealed so many things to me for the express purpose of making them known to the world, I use his information to describe the rest of the peripheral pathways of the Sioux. If some of it sounds like Christian theology, please accept that while I believe that he worships and was taught by the same God as Christians, and therefore would know and teach similar things, I do not credit much of what he knows to Christian sources. Fools Crow is a baptized Roman Catholic, and he attends mass on a sporadic basis. But his knowledge of the Bible is scant, and that is true also of what he knows about the Roman Catholic Church. He has remained throughout his life a traditional Sioux who has never departed from his calling.

We will begin with Fools Crow's explanation of the Sioux concept of *power*, and how it is obtained and dispensed.

"The third person of the Christian Godhead functions like the Sioux *Spirits* who dwell in the four Cardinal Directions."

The supreme repository of *power* is Wakan Tanka. Next to him in power and authority is *Tunkashila*, whose place and role is similar to that of Jesus Christ in Christian theology. The third person of the Christian Godhead functions like the Sioux *Spirits* who dwell in the four Cardinal Directions. They send or bring spiritual enlightenment to the world, and they empower individuals to teach and to spread among the people proper understandings. Therefore, when referring to the Sioux Godhead hereafter, I will speak of them as the Above Beings. As I follow this approach, it will differ from that of some authorities who base their positions upon certain informants, some of whom preceded Fools Crow by not too long a time, and others of whom were contemporaries of his and shared in rituals with him. All of them are dead now.

What I tell you is what Fools Crow told me, and the positions he holds today are consistent with those Stirrup and others passed on to him. Therefore, they are very old, and certainly very valid. Most of them are in agreement with what the famed Sioux medicine man, Black Elk, had to say, and no other medicine man or woman has dared to question Fools Crow's authority, capabilities and power. Instead, they pay homage to him whenever he appears at a public gathering.

All power was held originally by the Creator, Wakan Tanka, but he gave portions of it to each of the other Above Beings to bestow as they see fit. Humankind may petition the Above Beings collectively or individually. In addition, Wakan Tanka created other lesser spirits to serve him as intermediaries, and humankind may also call upon these for assistance.

When Fools Crow speaks of power, he understands it as the enlightenment needed for properly understanding a given thing or teaching. It is also the spiritual and physical energy to perform what is required — whether that be common or extraordinary. Power is not limited to human beings. It is dispensed in some degree to all in the universe, and in about the same way it is to human beings, since the spirits of other things live much as humans do.

This power is dispensed by the Above Beings in two ways: either directly from them or through intermediaries — or indirectly through a basic core of teachings given by the Above Beings in the beginning of time to the first Sioux.

It is very important to understand both how the core teachings work and the place they hold in Sioux life. The Above Beings taught the first people how they should live and how they should ask for power. These teachings became for the people a kind of living core that throbbed with life and transmitted its life to people who believed in it and used it precisely as they were told. Some of the power was purely empowerment for daily living. Some of it was offered in ritual form, so that whenever a ritual was performed, its power was released by the core and came to those who participated. The illustration on this page shows how this works. At the very center is a small circle representing the original teachings, which exist today in the form of orally transmitted legends and ritual detail. The lines radiating from this circle represent succeeding generations of Sioux. As long as the original teachings are passed on and followed, these generations maintain their connection with the life-giving core, and they can call upon it and will receive

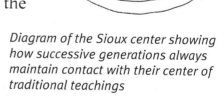

its power. If someone cuts himself off from, or allows himself to be cut off from, the power core, he will receive no power from it. Accordingly, the core teachings are described as the nation's center or heart.

Because their lives keep them closest to the Above Beings, the holy men have the greatest power and knowledge regarding power, and they are the principal teachers where the center is concerned. Medicine men and women are the next best sources. The common people also have knowledge about the center, and recognize its importance to their well-being, but in a more limited sense than the holy and medicine people.

Diagram of the Sioux center showing how successive generations always maintain contact with their center of traditional teachings

When they participate in a ritual such as the Sun Dance, they too can be filled with power and can offer that power to others. They can receive special insights, do unusual things, possess exceptional endurance, and can also heal and prophesy.

As stated, holy and medicine people receive their personal power directly from the Above Beings, and Fools Crow explains that they do this through prayer — either offered in the ritual number of four or seven chants in some private places, such as I described in the Introduction, or in a prayer ceremony in a sweatlodge, a vision quest, or a Yuwipi rite.

Purification

In the same manner as the Hopi medicine man, the Sioux holy or medicine person must first of all purify himself in order to become a fit vessel, tube, or channel whom the Above Beings will consider worthy. Of primary importance in this process is the necessary removal of one's self from the Above Beings' path, so that no doubt, human will, or willfulness will hinder the Beings as they work.

The Tube

This power is called down, not primarily for the service or benefit of the holy or medicine person, but for the benefit of others. It may be for one or for several of the following — the ability to heal, to instruct, to locate lost objects or persons, or to prophesy. It follows that all credit for what is accomplished must be given to the Above Beings. See the illustration below for help in understanding the tube idea.

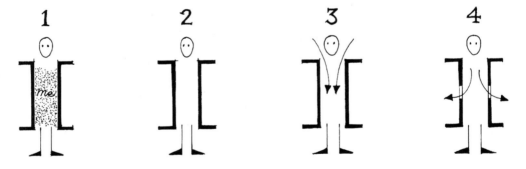

Becoming a tube:
1. Filled with "me" or "self"
2. The "me" removed by purification
3. A cleansed vessel being filled with power
4. A cleansed vessel dispensing power to others

In stating this, Fools Crow's position is in complete accord with that of Black Elk, who says, in *Black Elk Speaks*, "Of course it was not I who cured, it was the power from the outer world, and the visions and ceremonies had only made me like a hole through which the power could come to the two-leggeds. If I thought that I was doing it myself, the hole would close up and no power could come through."

The Four Directions

The Sioux obtain things from the Cardinal Directions when they pray to them. In their minds, South, West, North, and East hold fixed positions on the great circle or hoop around which life moves in a clockwise direction.

The East is the abode of the Sun and the Morning Star, both of whom are sources of wisdom and understanding. The stone that marks this direction is yellow, which is also the color of its animal, the elk, and of its bird, the golden eagle. Yellow is the color of love — which the elk represents in Sioux lore — and the wisdom and understanding which comes from the East centers in true love, both physical and spiritual.

The South is the source of knowledge and power regarding life and destiny. Questions and prayers regarding these issues are addressed to the South. Its stone is white; it is the home of the Animal Spirit Peoples; and its totem and symbol is the white crane.

The West is associated with purifying water. It is the home of the Thunder Beings. Its stone is black. The Horse People also reside there, and their spirits are called upon to empower the participants in the Horse Dance. Its totem and symbol is the black or immature golden eagle.

The North is the source of knowledge regarding health and control, both of self and of other things. Its stone is red. Calf Pipe Woman, who

Great Circle of the Sioux

Source of health and control
Sacred stone is red
Home of the Buffalo Spirit People
Messenger is the bald eagle

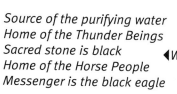

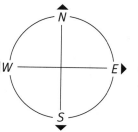

Source of the purifying water
Home of the Thunder Beings
Sacred stone is black
Home of the Horse People
Messenger is the black eagle

Source of wisdom and understanding
Sacred stone is yellow
Abode of the Sun and Morning Star
Messenger is the brown eagle

Source of life and destiny
Sacred stone is white
Home of the Animal Spirit Peoples
Messenger is the white crane

in ancient times brought the first Sacred Pipe to the people and taught them how to use it properly, lives in the North. So, too, do the Buffalo Spirit People. Their totem and symbol is the bald eagle.

Sun Dance pledgers who hold a sage- or fur-wrapped hoop in their hands as they dance are praying to the Four Directions. When the medicine people and the tribal elders want to teach adults, youth, or children about traditional life and how they should live so as to be pleasing to the Above Beings, they use a circle upon which the Four Directions are marked with their colors. As they move clockwise from one direction to the next, they talk about the things associated with each direction. Part of the education is learning how to call or draw in the power from each direction.

The circle is also used when a person wishes to reflect and meditate upon the four stages of life: birth at the South; youth at the West; middle age at the North; and old age, death, and the life-after at the East. As the person pauses in his thoughts at each of these Directions, he asks them to help him think wisely about how life should best be lived, and the Directions give him guidance. The Sioux say that those who diligently practice this ritual become the wisest of their people.

Cheyenne Medicine Wheel

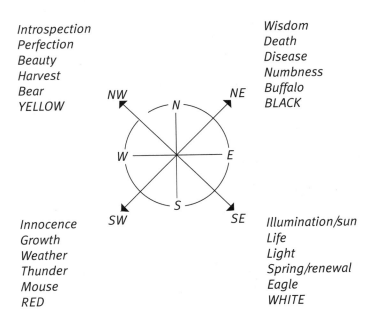

Introspection
Perfection
Beauty
Harvest
Bear
YELLOW

Wisdom
Death
Disease
Numbness
Buffalo
BLACK

Innocence
Growth
Weather
Thunder
Mouse
RED

Illumination/sun
Life
Light
Spring/renewal
Eagle
WHITE

The Cheyenne Medicine Wheel

The Cheyenne Indians also used the sacred circle and the Cardinal Directions as an educational tool and refer to it as the Medicine Wheel. In their lore, the southwest is the place of innocence and growth. Its color is red, and its totems are weather and the little mouse spirit. The northwest is the place of introspection, perfection, beauty, and harvest. Its color is yellow, and its totem is the bear spirit. The northeast is the location of wisdom, death, and disease. Its color is black, which is associated with purification, and its totem is the buffalo spirit. The southeast is the source of illumination, life, and renewal. Its color is white, and its totem is the golden eagle, who — because it flies so high and is so powerful and sharp-eyed — is considered a principal intermediary between the Above Beings and humans.

In using the Medicine Wheel for teaching and meditative purposes, the Cheyenne seek to discover themselves, to perceive things and themselves, to find relationships with the world around them, and to "turn the wheel." They explain the latter by saying that all of life takes place in a continuous circle, whose center and source of power are the Above Beings. Life flows from them into the hoop and keeps it turning. The life lived by any person is represented by marking a small place on the hoop. Using this as a focal point, the person's life is thought of as being the result of what has been inserted into the hoop by prior generations,

Sioux holy man using circle to instruct child

including grandparents and parents, all of whom have transmitted themselves into that person either literally or figuratively. While the person lives, he or she benefits from the ancestors' contributions, builds upon them, reshapes them, and, hopefully, adds to them in a positive way. When people leave this world for the next, their own contributions, including their children, are left behind as additions to the hoop that will continue to do its part in nourishing future generations. Thus the hoop turns and continues, unbroken and unending.

THE 405 STONE WHITE MEN HELPERS

The Above Beings have 405 Stone White Men Helpers. These are good spirits or powers who operate in the created world and who perform great things through medicine persons. In other words, the Stone White Men Helpers are the ones who convey the power when it comes to a person. Fools Crow thinks these spirits may be a gift to the whole of mankind, but believes Wakan Tanka has chosen the Sioux medicine men to be the intercessors through whom they dispense their blessings. Most medicine persons are permitted to use only a small portion of the Stone White Men Helpers. As an indication of the position he would achieve in life, Fools Crow was told at his first vision quest that he would have the use of all 405.

The 405 powers are divided into four groups, each of which renders service in a given area. One group is involved with nature's medicines. These are the herb and root medicines that are used to cure people. Another group deals with nature's power to understand what is important about a given matter. These spirits work through plant herbs that are taken into the body as medicines to help one think and perceive. A third group helps with dreams. These spirits use medicines to make a person dream, then they help that person understand what the dream means. The last group works in the area of inner self. They help the medicine persons look within themselves to see the things that cannot otherwise be seen. To call upon the good spirits, Fools Crow always places a string of 405 tiny tobacco bags on top of a black cloth. This serves as a prayer of invitation to them.

Mind Expansion

Fools Crow knows the 405 spirits are not subdivided into four equal groups, but he doesn't know how many spirits there are in each division. The fourth group does not work through medicines; it deals with mind expansion and is especially interesting. He says, "When you want to look deep within yourself, to probe into a realm of consciousness that goes beyond the ordinary, you paint the stem of your pipe black. Then you take it with you to a lonely place where you meditate intensely. While you do this, you must be brave, because you are asking for a response that the human mind cannot at first absorb or comprehend. When the answer begins to come, it does so in a startling way. Bright red lights that gleam like red fires often appear close by and around you at the four cardinal points. Then you will be given the message. You will either see it or hear it, and you are often given a great deal of knowledge in a brief period of time. It is a powerful experience that almost overwhelms you. Your mind expands and contracts rapidly, as though you had been holding your breath for a long time. When it is over, you are exhausted."

Guidance from the Spirits

This fourth division of the good spirits is also called upon when a person comes to Fools Crow and wants to know something about his innermost self, when he wishes to understand himself so that he can find peace and live in a more secure way. Fools Crow takes him out to a remote place and leaves him there to pray while he goes to another location and meditates with his pipe. After a while, he gets the man, and they go into a sweatlodge together. While they pray there, the spirits bring the answers to Fools Crow "in a powerful way." As the answers come, they pass through Fools Crow to the man. "Without our speaking, he will learn exactly what I have learned."

These are not, Fools Crow says, things only he can do. "Anyone who is sincere with the pipe can do it and gain the insight he wishes. If this person takes his pipe and goes out by himself, if he takes plenty of time, as long as is needed to get the message, he will learn what he wants to know. These ceremonies do not belong to Indians alone. They can be done by all who have the right attitude and who are honest and sincere about their belief in Wakan Tanka and in following his rules."

Thought Transference

In dealing with the idea of thought transference that was first touched upon in the Introduction, we now see who Fools Crow's conveyors of power for this are — the 405 Stone White Men. Fools Crow makes frequent use of transference power, especially when he takes someone on a vision quest. I experienced it once again on a summer day in South Dakota. I was giving a series of lectures to doctors and nurses at a government hospital near Bear Butte when word came to me that Fools Crow was at the sacred mountain. Later that day, I went there to see him and found him encamped in a lush meadow that lies way up the side of the mountain. He was lost in prayer when I arrived, but he heard me coming and looked up to see who it was. By the time I reached him, he was smiling broadly, his eyes sparkled, and his arms were outstretched to embrace me. We visited for a while, and then he told me he had been there several days, keeping a vigil for a Sioux man he had brought to vision quest on the top of the mountain. They had build a sweatlodge, and I observed that just inside the entrance was a black cloth on a bed of sage; on top of this was a long string of tobacco offerings — the good spirits had been called.

Then he proceeded to tell me precisely what the man had been doing during his quest, going into minutest detail, and what the man had seen in his vision. At one point, Fools Crow said he had used thought transference to instruct the man to break several small branches into pieces and to fashion four crosses with them. Then he was to set the crosses in a row and focus his thoughts upon them while he prayed. This was not a common thing to do in a vision quest.

"He will be down soon," he said. "Stay and meet him, for the vision has come to him."

About fifteen minutes later, we saw him coming down the trail. He was perhaps forty years old, dressed in the traditional Sioux breechclout and moccasins. He carried in his hands a sage hoop and a portion of a buffalo skull. He looked tired, but strangely serene. He smiled slightly when we were introduced and sat heavily down by the small fire Fools Crow had built.

"Grandfather," he said, "I have had my vision."

"I know," Fools Crow replied, "And I have told my friend here what it was, so that he can see once again that I have the power from Wakan Tanka and Tunkashila to do this. Now you must tell us both. Start at the beginning of your quest and leave nothing out."

I knew what the man would say, and yet it was incredible to find how closely his account matched that of Fools Crow — especially the part about his having been strangely moved to fashion four crosses out of sticks and to pray with them. Fools Crow smiled in a satisfied way, nodding several times as the questor proceeded. When the man was done, Fools Crow clapped his hands in approval as gleefully as a little child.

"Was it not just as I told you?" he asked me.

"Indeed it was," I answered, "indeed it was!"

I left a short while later, knowing that Fools Crow wanted to be alone with the man to discuss the meaning of his vision. Later that night, they would do a sweatlodge ceremony together.

I did not see Fools Crow for some months after that, but it was not the last time I saw him engage in thought transference. It happened often enough when we were together to convince me that he could do it whenever he wished to — as long as the person he did it with understood and believed in the power available to him to accomplish it.

One thing more must be said here regarding thought transference. What Fools Crow sees is not always imagined. More often than not, what happens is real. A surprising mixture of real birds and animals do come as a group and talk to him while he is out praying. Just as the spirit animals do, they, too, bring him messages concerning the welfare of the Sioux. With my own eyes, I have seen real birds and animals come and sit down at his feet. And when he heals, there is no imagining to it at all. It happens, and with my own eyes, I have seen that as well.

One day, while Dallas Chief Eagle was with us, we discussed the difference between imagining, or envisioning, and reality.

"Since the creatures sometimes actually come to you," I asked Fools Crow," why is the thought transference necessary?"

"Because in thought transference, the spirit people of the birds and the animals come. They are higher than the earth creatures. They live in the four directions. What they know is superior to that of the earth's creatures. It comes more directly from Wakan Tanka, Tunkashila and the Four Directions."

"What about what happens to you, the change in costume, the paint, the other things? Do those really happen, too?" I asked.

"No. I only see them happening as in my mind I slip back into the ancient past and reach for our center. They help me concentrate on what I am and what I hope to do for our people."

"But the colored smoke and the feathers? What about those you handed me as we walked back to your house?"

"I can make any part of what I see real. That is a power Wakan Tanka gave to me when I was once at Bear Butte. One night, he called me to climb up the side of its rock cliff. I told you about that, how he put a door there, and I walked through it into the cliff, how he talked with me in there. I made the feathers real and gave them to you so you would know I could do that kind of thing."

"Do you," I asked, "always tell people whether what they see is real or imagined?"

"No!"

"Can you do thought transference with a group?"

"If everyone in the group believes, yes."

"Is there a way observers can tell which is the case in a given instance?"

"When I am not doing thought transference, my clothing does not change from regular clothing to buckskins."

"What would you say to people who call what you do magic?"

"I can do many things that most white people would call magic. But they aren't really magic. I do not conceal things in my clothing or on my person. I do not set anything up like magicians do on television."

". . . word of his ability to heat rocks without the aid of fire reached his uncle Black Elk."

I had cause to remember that statement on several occasions when I saw Fools Crow do amazing things. One instance dealt with the rocks he used in the sweatlodge. Most of the time, he heats them in an outside firepit just as everyone else does. But one day, he told me about a time when word of his ability to heat rocks without the aid of fire reached his uncle Black Elk. Black Elk came to Fools Crow and asked him if this was true. Fools Crow told him it was and said he would do it for him. Black Elk asked several questions about the process, and Fools Crow described to him what items he used, what they meant, and how the rocks were placed.

Then Fools Crow arranged for some singers to join them. When all were present, they went into the sweatlodge. After chanting, Fools Crow placed cold rocks in the firepit. Then he "did his ceremony," chewed his medicine, and spewed it on the rocks. The heat came. The singers sang the required special songs, and by the time Fools Crow poured the water on the rocks, they were red hot. Black Elk held his hands out toward them and said the rocks might be even hotter than they were when heated in the usual way. When they finished, everyone was perspiring as though they were in a regular sweat bath. Afterward, Black Elk shook Fools Crow's hand and said he believed in him and in the power of his prayers. He returned to his home thoroughly convinced.

After hearing the story, I asked Fools Crow if he would heat the rocks for me. One day when we were alone, he did it. Incredibly, the rocks heated without the aid of fire just as he said they would. There was no thought transference that day. I held a branch to the rocks, and it burned to a cinder!

Then there was the time when Fools Crow was guest of honor at a powwow. It was Sunday, and he was dressed in his traditional costume. Brown ermine skins were tied in the long braids of the black wig he wore. Everyone who was there saw these and knew they were just skins. As the dances finished for the afternoon, he received word that a Sioux friend who lived in the town was very ill and wanted to see him. Fools Crow went to the man's house, along with a party of twenty-three others — three of whom were whites.

The man was in his bedroom, a small room perhaps eleven by twelve feet in size. He was in bed with a patch quilt pulled up around his chin. His face was gaunt, and his sunken black eyes darted around as people entered. He had not expected so many visitors. His look was that of one in an advanced stage of cancer. The only furnishings besides the bed were a small table and a chair. While everyone else crowded into the room around the bed, Fools Crow spoke quietly with the man, who said he had a tumor just under his forehead and that he was scheduled for surgery in the local public health hospital on the following Wednesday. He complained about the intense pain and said he was afraid to go through with the operation, that he would not survive it.

"'Would you heal me, Grandfather?' he begged."

"Would you heal me, Grandfather?" he begged. "There is tobacco on the table."

Fools Crow studied the man's face for a few moments, then went to the table and sat down. Every eye was fixed on him as he unhurriedly took out some tobacco, rolled a cigarette with it, and smoked it. Then he began to chant, and as he did so, he unwound the brown ermine skin from his right braid and placed it flat on the tabletop. He stroked it as he continued to sing, and it turned into a live ermine! Everyone else watched in disbelief and sheer fascination as the ermine leaped to the floor and then climbed onto the foot of the bed. It began to sniff as it made its way slowly up the man's body. When it came to his face, it sniffed all over it until it reached the spot on the forehead directly above where the tumor was said to be. The ermine stopped there and sucked vigorously on the skin for several minutes. When it was done, the animal left the man and returned to the table. Fools Crow sang as he stroked it. It became an ermine pelt again, and Fools Crow rewound it in his braid. While the people in the room murmured in amazement, Fools Crow told the man he was healed and said good-bye. Everyone, except the patient, followed him back to the powwow.

Was what was seen only thought transference where a group was concerned? Certainly, none of those who were there thought so. And there is this concluding note. The man went to the hospital on Tuesday to be readied for the surgery. But he insisted that the doctor x-ray him again, claiming that the pain was entirely gone. The doctor was upset and said another x-ray was a waste of time, that the tumor was there and the operation had to be done. But the man insisted until at last the doctor gave in and did the x-ray. The tumor was gone, and the doctor was absolutely baffled. The man was sent home, and the surgery was never performed.

At the time we were working on the book of Fools Crow's life, he told me that during his years as a holy man he had healed virtually every kind of illness save cancer of the lungs or stomach. The only reason he had not treated that was that no one had ever asked him to.

"But," he went on, "I could heal that, too, if I was asked."

He described many of his cures, and I recorded these in the book . . . they include cures for blindness, hearing, and kidney problems, gallstones, paralysis, heart problems, and spinal conditions. I personally saw him remove from a man's face a huge, purple birthmark in a four-day treatment using only a medicine herb. I also saw him stop in the midst of a Sun Dance and straighten out the grotesquely twisted leg of a nine-year-old boy, whose condition had existed since birth and was known to the hundreds of spectators who saw the healing happen. Two years later, I watched the boy play basketball with his friends.

"The power is there, and it simply cannot be doubted."

The power is there, and it simply cannot be doubted. It is a peripheral pathway finding whose dimensions are awesome. I doubt, however, that except where self-healing is concerned, this same measure of power is available to everyone. The point I make in revealing what Fools Crow has accomplished is only that of showing how such power is available and that it can be acquired. What each person will be able to do with it will only be known as his or her relationship with the Above Beings unfolds.

The essentials, Fools Crow says, begin with both the healer and the patient believing absolutely in the power and in the way it is dispersed. Without this, there can be no effective treatment. Accordingly, he does not accept every patient. He is astoundingly perceptive and can look into the mind and heart of those who come to him and request his services. If he does not see what he wants to see in the way of faith, he will send them away. If their condition is in an extremely advanced stage, he may decide — for reasons known only to him and which he may reach in prayer — to offer them only that healing which helps those people lose all fear of dying and to graciously prepare for their deaths. He will teach them that once they learn what life beyond physical death holds for them, they will leave here joyfully and in great anticipation.

Mutual Faith

"Sioux healers have known for a long time . . . that most all illness begins in the mind."

Sioux healers have known for a long time what modern medicine is just now beginning to assert — that most all illness begins in the mind. They learned from the Above Beings that psychological factors can cause cancer, heart disease, arthritis, and even premature death. Fools Crow learned that stress weakens the immune system and lowers our defenses against illness and allergy. He knows that mind power can build greater immunity. Thus, it is that, in most instances, he holds carefully to the traditional four-day, four equally spaced times a day, approach to healing. Healer and patient begin with mutual faith — just as Cherokee healers — then carefully build that faith over the four-day period. Relaxation comes, blood pressure lowers, heart rates stabilize, peace enters in — at the end of the fourth treatment on the fourth day, the faith is so great that the majority of healings come resoundingly to pass. Now and then, the healing process takes a while longer.

One interesting detail about his method of healing is that, surprisingly enough, the patient determines how many of the 405 good spirits will come to the sweatlodge or other place when Fools Crow heals him. (When he does not use the sweatlodge, he always forms on the ground or in a house a small square whose corners are marked by four flags — one for each of the Four Directions — made of cherry-tree branches with pieces of colored cloth attached. These are stood upright in tin cans filled with dirt.) The patient prays to Wakan Tanka, asking how many of the tobacco packets he should make, since each one will represent one of the 405 good spirit helpers. When this answer has been received, the patient then fashions the offerings, ties them to a string, and wraps the string up in a cloth. On the day the ritual begins, he places these within the flag-square or the sweatlodge. Only after the ceremony begins does Fools Crow unfold the cloth and learn how many of the 405 good spirits will be present to help him.

When Fools Crow heals in the sweatlodge, he will have singers and relatives of the patient assist him when the patient is present, and he will do the ceremony alone when the patient cannot be present. Fools Crow said that on four occasions he had heated the rocks without using the fire. Each time, people were there to witness this feat. While everyone sat in darkness, he chewed his sacred medicine up fine and blew it on the rocks four times. After each time, he poured a little water on the rocks, and they made a sound. By the fourth time he poured the water, the rocks were red hot and glowing. Everyone present could see the glow clearly and feel the heat.

The sweatlodge door flap is opened three times during the ceremony. When it is closed the third time, the fourth and final part of the ritual begins. Water is poured on the rocks, of which there are always twelve — with the first one having a red circle painted on it — and the sacred songs are sung again. It was at this point on each of the four occasions that the rocks could be heard speaking Lakota in joyful sounds and whoops, like "how, how." All of the people in the lodge joined in with this and made happy sounds until the lodge rang with the noise.

While the rocks make Lakota sounds in the sweatlodge when people are present with Fools Crow, they actually talk to him when he is in the sweatlodge alone. Fools Crow thinks the spirits feel freer when he is the only person present. Usually, as soon as the door flap has been closed for the first time and he begins to pray, the spirits in the rocks speak to him. They tell him what he needs to know about the patient and the medicine. During each of the four stages of the ceremony, he talks to both the rocks and the tobacco offerings and listens intently for an answer. He also sings a sacred song. If, as sometimes happens, the spirits do not at first speak to him through the rocks, he repeats the song until they do. The spirits in the tobacco offerings hear him, but they do not answer him.

When the rocks do speak, they ask him why he is having the ritual and for whom. Then they ask him whether he knows what the ailment is. During the fourth period of the ceremony, they ask him what the patient desires, what he or she wants the Above Beings to do — to heal physically or to prepare the patient for death. In all, the spirits ask four main questions, and the spirits in the rocks eventually tell Fools Crow what medicine plant to use and how to apply it.

In explaining exactly how they do this, he refers to the rocks as the Workers. There is always an item in the sweatlodge that belongs to the absent patient. The rocks ask Fools Crow where the patient is and how far away he lives. Then the rocks sniff the article as a hunting dog does an object to get its scent, and after this, "traveling like Wakan Tanka does, they go immediately to where the patient is. They examine the person and quickly return to the sweatlodge." They tell Fools Crow they have found the patient, how the patient is faring, and that they know what is wrong. They tell him what the right healing medicine is and how to apply it. Fools Crow then goes to the patient and follows to the letter the instructions given by the spirits. "The patient," he declares, "is always healed."

Fools Crow told me about a time when, at an Indian celebration in Flagstaff, Arizona, he was called upon to prove his power by doing a feat of magic. Under this pressure to perform and not knowing what would happen, he went to a small tree that had been set up in the middle of the arena and prayed. In a few moments, four flights of brightly lighted birds came from the Cardinal Directions and, to the spectators' delight, landed and turned the little tree into a brilliantly decorated Christmas tree! After a minute or so, the birds flew up and away, and something that looked like fire blazed out from the tree without burning it.

"Why did Wakan Tanka do this?" I asked.

"Because," Fools Crow answered, "he honors us in such instances, so long as we do not abuse the privilege."

He added that he did not ordinarily perform things like that, but in this instance, others volunteered him. For everyone's sake, he had to do something. But he does not like to do such things because it reduces his healing power, and healing is far more important to him than having fun.

"I could," he claims, "do many things to satisfy and astonish curious people. I could even take a baby and make him dance or do some of the other things only adults can do. But I don't really want to. I would rather confine my power to healing. I have met numerous people who have asked me to do feats of magic or miracles, but most of the time, I have not chosen to do so."

Fools Crow says that learning to love yourself is extremely important. When you do this, you feel good about yourself and what you are doing, and you accomplish things that otherwise would be impossible, including self-healing.

" . . . they believe thanksgiving to the Above Beings . . . is an essential component of healing and of survival."

In concluding the material about the Sioux and Fools Crow, we should never forget that they believe thanksgiving to the Above Beings and the powers who assist them is an essential component of healing and of survival. Fools Crow is profoundly careful to give thanks for the work the Above Beings do through him on extraordinary occasions, and he gives thanks for the daily gifts needed for ordinary existence. He always prays before eating, saving a small portion of his food for added thanks to be given after the meal. He takes this gift outside and uses a stick to draw a small circle on the ground. The circle represents the Above Beings and the Sioux people. Then he draws a vertical and a horizontal line through the Four Cardinal Directions. Finally, he scoops a little hole at the point where the lines intersect and, as he prays in thanksgiving, deposits the food-gift in it and covers it over. In this way, something of what he eats is given back to the Above Beings, and they respond by making certain that he will have enough food in the future. He thinks only of needs, not of abundances. If it weren't for his exposure to the world around him, I don't think he'd know what an abundance of anything was. Never, in all of the months we have been together, have I seen him fail to make this thanksgiving gesture — even after restaurant meals in towns and cities. He takes the gift outside and searches until he finds some cleared earth to deposit it in. Passersby often look at him as he does this and wonder about his soundness, but he doesn't care. His relationship with the Above Beings is far more important than what any human thinks.

THE NATIVE AMERICAN WAY
AND YOUR WAY
TO LASTING INNER PEACE:

SEEK TO ENTIRELY ELIMINATE
THE CAUSES OF STRESS
and
RESIST THE CAUSES OF STRESS
BY DILUTING THEIR FORCE IN ADVANCE
and
SEEK TO MANAGE INESCAPABLE STRESSES,
AND TO CONVERT THEM TO USEFUL ENDS
and
IMPROVE THE MANNER AND
QUALITY OF YOUR LIFE.

Love yourself
Get outside yourself
Take action
Focus on the solution
Be at peace

Following the Pathways

CHAPTER TEN

Active Meditation for Inner Peace

N ow we are going to do what the ancient Native American priests or the present-day medicine persons or holy men would tell you to do if they were going to help you adapt the essence of their ancient pathways to the present time and your life. The material in Part Three is primarily addressed to the individual, but it should be noted that some of the Native American pathways are particularly applicable to the present-day problems associated with groups, small businesses, and corporations.

For example, the steps followed in the Hopi nine-day approach to ritual adapt naturally to the contemporary workplace, for they have a group thrust. Recall that an entire society performed these steps and that each ceremony in the cycle was done for the welfare of the entire village — the goal being to foster long-term motivation, cohesiveness, creativity and accomplishment. When you couple these achievements with Cherokee organizational and end-state techniques, as well as with certain ideas of the Apache and Sioux, the end result is what all groups and industries hope for in terms of rewarding social relationships, cooperation, happiness, service, and productivity.

Acting and Imaging

As you begin to follow the Native American pathways, keep firmly in mind that while you perform the various actions I describe, you will be analyzing your problems in a manner that will produce positive results. Acting combined with imaging is infinitely better than imagining alone. Acting enhances and makes vivid the imaging. For example, as you make a ritual item to use in a pathway rite, you will be carefully thinking through the problem as you fashion the item. By the time you have completed the item, you will have a good understanding of the problem, and you already will have come a long way toward solving it. The completion of the solution is accomplished by putting the item to its suggested use.

Remember that different approaches will suit different people. In this respect, we are more fortunate than the Native Americans were, for while they had their own pathways to follow, we can choose from those of four different tribes. (If space permitted, I could have included the pathways of other tribes, for many of them have had marvelous pathways to follow.) Test the ways and make your own choices. It is not necessary for you to follow every pathway and use everything you discover. Employ different pathways at different times. If what you find touches you in some way, it will be useful to you. Be creative with it. I have by no means exhausted the pathways or their potential uses. I offer possibilities, but you can improve on them, making them more personal, or extend them.

Following the Pathways with Others

Be assured that you can follow these pathways by yourself, with a friend, or with a compatible group. Most people need strong ties with others to be happy. As word about the Native American pathways spreads, groups will form to follow the pathways together. Close personal contacts in which you will feel understood and accepted will result. This is a powerful gift. So take control of your life and improve your future. Use the pathways to forge friendships, find new interests, and enhance your sense of yourself as a worthwhile, capable person.

Know also that the pathways will serve persons of all ages, from teens on. Those who are retired and have extra time to give to the pathways will benefit greatly from their use. Pathways will accelerate your creativity and keep you moving forward with vitality, hope, and courage. Just recall the respected and useful positions that elders held in Native American society and recognize that the pathways produced this precious attitude.

We are aware that changes occur so rapidly today that our capacity to accommodate them is threatened. We are forced to cope with one new technology after another, and with ever-fiercer competition and ever-accelerating threats. Our adaptive system is overloaded. The situation promises to get worse in the years ahead. Stresses lurk everywhere, constantly threatening to leap out and do us harm.

While the Native Americans did not face the milieu of rapid change we do, they did face the maximum threats of intrusions: epidemic diseases, non-Indians, bewildering ideas, the unexpected and unknown, and fierce competition. Death by the hand-held weapon was as quick and final as that by the nuclear bomb. Smallpox raged, a swifter executioner than AIDS. The pathways the Native Americans followed addressed these stresses and are useful to us today. I have every confidence they will be equally useful a century from now. Our overall environment will change drastically, but the essential nature of human beings will not.

Permit me to say again that the pathways, and some of the uses of them that I am about to set forth for you, might seem strange and unorthodox. Recall, however, that the point for us is not to attempt to duplicate what the Native Americans have done. We only want to capture the essence of the ceremony and to understand and make use of their thought patterns. I do not in any instance give you enough guidance to duplicate any of the rituals. The Native Americans would be rightfully displeased if I did, and I would be violating confidences. The only ritual details I set forth are those given personally to me by medicine men for this purpose and which are in every instance those that are regularly seen by the general public.

Since the mind is highly susceptible to the power of suggestion, the value of the pathways is self-authenticating. The thought patterns will easily prove their worth as you use them. But how are you going to do these sometimes strange things I suggest in the presence of an unsympathetic or scoffing spouse, parents, or siblings? This is a question I can't answer. I have no way of knowing what your situation is. But I do know that once you begin to experience what they offer you personally, you will find a private place and a way!

Action Focuses Thought

Let me emphasize again the Native American conviction that *doing something* to deal with a problem is far more effective than attempting to handle it by thought alone. They discovered that a person is too easily distracted while thinking, and that the mind has an ever-present and disgusting tendency to go astray.

Most books dealing with stress and survival spend a considerable amount of time detailing what stress is and putting it into categories. No doubt you will have read some of them and already know what I am talking about. So, rather than duplicating their work, let me just say that stress is what results from whatever curtails your potential, upsets you, invades you, gnaws at you, undermines you, frustrates you, panics you, or causes insecurity or raw fear in you. In effect, it is anything that persistently attacks your mental or physical well-being, and distracts you from more healthy things.

Be discerning where stress is concerned, for not every problem is stressful or negative. Some problems are just the challenges of everyday life that hone us by testing our mettle and capabilities. Try to discern the difference when things happen to you. Recognize that your answers will often depend upon the way in which you view obstacles and the way in which your vision colors what you see. What are opaque walls for some are windows for others.

Perfection Not Required

As we move into the following material, never forget that success with the Native American pathways does not ask for or require perfection on your part. The Native Americans knew that perfection was not something finite man could achieve. So the effort was what mattered and paid dividends. Keep in mind the Apache Sunrise Girl who becomes Changing Woman and a seed. You are about to become such a seed that will bear wonderful fruit.

In the Christian tradition, Jesus does not demand a kind of perfection that we can accomplish on our own. He does say that we must be perfect, but adds the qualification, " . . . as my Father in heaven is perfect." What does he mean by this? That when we are fused with him through Baptism and Holy Communion, we have taken upon ourselves his perfection. Consequently, when the Father looks down upon us, what he sees is the perfect Jesus, and when he blesses him, he blesses those who are within him. But so long as we are in this world, we remain at the earthly level imperfect people, and must accept ourselves and one another as such.

The Native Americans were taught this same important lesson by the Above Beings, and except for their establishing laws to protect the welfare of the whole group, the Native Americans set no standards for individual perfection. On the contrary, the recognition of imperfection was actually a leveler, a maker of equals among men. The Native Americans were not nearly so judgmental as we are or so quick to lay blame. Authority and position came to those people who were chosen to lead, not because they were better or more perfect than others, but because they subordinated their own good to that of their fellow man.

Justice is not always done in today's world, but for the most part we can, in the long run, still profit by subordinating our own good to that of others. At the very least, it allows us to stand before our mirrors with our heads held high, and it brings to those who practice it many other worthwhile benefits as well.

Active Rituals to Eliminate Stress

If you are filled with power, there is no room for stress. Consequently, you cannot be overcome by stress.

You will recall the Native American view that divinely given power pervades the universe. Therefore, it is everywhere, waiting to be drawn upon. Think about this. Set your mind on it and know it is so. When you are ready to accept it, or better still are certain of it, you will then be ready to discover how you obtain this power for yourself and how you can dispense it to others.

PURIFICATION

The next step is to make yourself a fit vessel — a channel or tube — for power to work in and through. This step begins with purification. Cleanse yourself wholly, inside and out, to get the self out of the way and to remove anything about you that would impede the work of the Above Beings and their helpers . . . doubt, distrust, reluctance, wanting to do things your own way, and negative personal options all must go. Naturally, the Above Beings will help you accomplish this, but you must do it according to traditional ways.

Prayer Messengers

Begin by sending up prayers for the Above Beings' assistance. To do this, you will need a messenger to carry your prayers. Messengers can be smoke from a fire, a feather from a high-flying bird — you cannot use eagle or hawk feathers since government laws prevent your obtaining them — Hopi pahos or prayer beads. If you use any of the latter three, hang them up on a wall after you have prayed with them or place them outside in a private shrine you have built. They will continue to offer up your prayer for you, as do the prayer cloths for the Sun Dance.

Water Purification

Then use the Cherokee method of water purification. Go to the ocean, to a lake with incoming and outgoing outlets, to a river, or to a stream. While you concentrate your thoughts upon what you are doing, face east toward the point of the rising sun, and, as you pray, immerse yourself completely seven times. If possible, in addition to your bathing suit, wear something made of cloth that you have owned for some time, and let it represent anything of the past you want to rid yourself of . . . guilt, bad memories, acts you'd like forgiveness for. A neckerchief, scarf, handkerchief, shawl, or just a strip of cloth will do fine. As you immerse yourself, let go of this so it can float away. Concentrate upon what it is taking with it. But don't litter. Retrieve it before it goes too far and dispose of it. In ancient times, a Cherokee priest stood downstream to do this for the people, collecting what they let float away, then burying the whole in a common grave.

You can also purify yourself in a sauna, in a steam bath, or if nothing is available, in a shower. In these cases, face east and use your cupped hands to slowly pour water over your head seven times while you pray for assistance. Use simple words like "I am being purified. I am being purified." After you pray, let the old cloth drop onto the floor, then retrieve it and get rid of it. The way the immersion is done is not the most important thing, although some ways are mentally more helpful than others. It is what you believe that counts. If you believe it is so, it will be so.

Thanksgiving Offering

Now make a sacrificial offering of thanksgiving to the Above Beings. A general way for all seasons is what Fools Crow taught us — take a small piece of food outside, draw a cross in the earth with a stick, make a small indentation in the center of the cross, place the food in the indentation, and then, as you speak a thanksgiving prayer, cover the offering over with dirt. In winter, should you have an open fire, toss a small piece of meat onto it, Cherokee style. The Above Beings appreciate our recognition of them as the original givers of all things. When we give back to them, they bless us accordingly. The size of the offering does not matter, for we could never return to them in equal measure anyway.

CALL DOWN POWER

Remember that the numbers four and seven are sacred numbers that in and of themselves possess special powers. Use them in all of your ritual performances. For example, repeat each prayer four or seven times.

Once you are purified and a fit vessel for the Above Beings and their helpers to work with and through, call the power to yourself. You can do this in either of two ways: by meditating in the Sioux questing manner or by using a portion of the Apache Sunrise Ceremony. Of course, power is also called down by the cycles of rituals performed over the course of a year. But we must distinguish here between the initial call and, after you have received a response to that call, the continuing calls to retain it. The ceremonial cycles apply to the latter.

Prayer Offering

Begin this process by making an elaborate prayer offering after the manner of the one described on page 85, except include in your offering things that are personal to you and which represent your hopes in connection with what you are doing. When the prayer offering is ready, take it outside and hang it on a bush. Since you are to leave it there as a continuing prayer, put it where other people are not likely to notice it and take it.

Make a Questing Place

To meditate properly, you must choose a time and a place when you can be alone and uninterrupted. When you have found your place — outside in your yard or in a room you have selected — arrange a six-by-eight-foot open questing place, similar to that of the Sioux as described on page 177. Orient the long direction east and west. Set up the colored flags on the four corners and in their proper cardinal directions. You can use regular flag stands, branches, or even one leg of each of four chairs. Remember that Fools Crow filled coffee cans with dirt to use as bases for the flags. Then connect the flags or legs with a string or cord, so that the area is defined and closed in. Hang some small item as an offering at the middle of the string on each of the four sides, remembering that when you are finished, you will take these offerings outside, hang them on a tree or a bush, and leave them to be consumed by the elements. They will pray for you until they are gone. Strips of new cloth, in the colors of the four directions — red, yellow, white, and black — are excellent for this. You will recall that the Sioux used both cloth strips and small bags of tobacco.

Now make a symbol that represents what you are praying for and place it at the west end of the questing enclosure. A section of cardboard tube, which symbolizes what you are about to become, will serve well, but make it attractive. Add color and other symbolic items to it. Be creative. If you have a better idea than mine, use it.

Using Your Questing Place

When the symbol is in place, remove your shoes and stockings, step into the questing place at the east end, and sit down flat on the ground or floor with your legs extended in front of you; you may use a pillow if you wish. Place your hands on your thighs with the palms up and cupped. Close your eyes, relax, and begin to breathe deeply in and out. Multiples of seven are good, and twenty-one breaths should prepare you. Archie Sam told me that Cherokee medicine persons breathed to achieve relaxation by feeling the incoming breath enter through the fingers and palms, then move slowly up the arms and into the chest. When the chest was full of air, the air was released to pass down through the abdomen, through the legs, and out the feet and toes. Try it — it works beautifully!

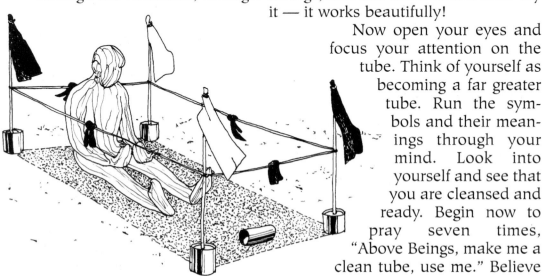

Now open your eyes and focus your attention on the tube. Think of yourself as becoming a far greater tube. Run the symbols and their meanings through your mind. Look into yourself and see that you are cleansed and ready. Begin now to pray seven times, "Above Beings, make me a clean tube, use me." Believe that you are becoming one.

Making use of the individual questing place and tube

Know that they love you, are grateful for your obedience and willingness, and are transforming you. Fix your eyes on the tube and keep it in your sight until you feel the power invading you, warming and blessing every part of you. Feel yourself opening up to become a more perfect channel through which the power the Above Beings will send to you can be dispensed to others.

Do not struggle with this or work hard at it. Never demand anything from the Above Beings. Flow with it. Drift into it. Don't try to force it. They read your heart and mind, and the power will come to you at its own pace.

An alternate and less complicated way of calling down power is to do it in the manner of the Apache Sunrise Ceremony Girl.

SUNRISE CEREMONY
Day One

Make the elaborate prayer offering as described above and place it outside on a bush as directed. Fold four blankets in half or quarters, and place them in a pile on the ground or floor. Wear some of your best clothing. Tie on your forehead or to a forelock of your hair a piece of abalone shell that is attached to a cord. Play rhythmic music, preferably without words, on the stereo. Indian music is perfect for this — especially when it features throbbing drums. Now kneel on the blankets in the manner of the girl, face east, and hold your arms and hands out to your sides as she does, with elbows bent. Begin to sway back and forth in tune with the music. Breathe in deeply and exhale seven times. Then close your eyes and begin to pray the prayer given above in the questing material. Use multiples of four or seven for this. Follow the rules previously given regarding attitude and conviction. Keep this up until you feel yourself tingling and the power coming. Then sit on the blankets with your feet extended in front of you and your hands upturned in your lap. Recall that, as they are for the girl, your hands are your purse. Feel them being filled with power by the Above Beings. The warmth of your hands will be their warmth. Soon you will know your purse is filled with power and overflowing.

Day Two

The next morning, awaken before sunrise, put the abalone shell on your forehead, and go to a place you have previously selected where the sun's light will strike you as it rises. With your arms and hands held loosely at your sides, face east and wait. Breathe deeply as you concentrate on what is happening. Close your eyes. When the first ray of light strikes your forehead, it will pierce through the shell and enter your head and body. You will feel a burning sensation as it does so. This is the seal and affirmation of the power you have received.

The Above Beings have come, touched, and entered you. They love you. Oneness with them and their helpers has been established. You are a tube.

In recognition of this, put any thoughts to the contrary aside. Refuse to listen to them. Send them politely away. Recall how well these procedures have worked for the Native Americans. Wear something that will serve as a constant reminder of your having become a tube. A small section of wooden or brass tubing on a necklace or bracelet will do. A crystal is excellent, since it represents enlightenment and clarity — and the light that has pierced through — and thus the fact that you have been similarly pierced and have enlightened understanding.

You are ready to put the power to work, and this is where the proof shows itself and the fun really enters in.

You will begin to feel different — more buoyant, more radiant. You will sing more as you go about your work . . . you will worry less . . . you will have a feeling of energy you didn't have before and a new sense of heightened awareness. You will begin to see things you have missed, which others aren't able to see. Look for this to show itself in your daily activities and even while you sleep.

PAHOS

Take comfort in the knowledge that the pahos and other offerings you have placed out in the sun or hung on the wall are prayers in themselves, continuing to offer up their designated prayers for you so that you do not need to pray constantly — although we will want to discuss shortly the amount and kind of prayer the Native Americans found to be truly beneficial.

How the Paho Works

If your prayer offerings have been placed outside, believe that as Sun traveled overhead for the first time, the spirit of the offering was picked up and its prayer was carried to the Above Beings. The prayer is with them, and they are answering it. The offering continues to send up the prayer, not so much to remind them of it as it does to remind you of what is happening because of it. It keeps these facts in your consciousness and helps you know that the prayer is working. Think about this while you drive to work on a busy freeway, and hang a small paho from your rearview mirror as a reminder of this. Offerings hung on the wall of your room serve as reminders, too, but they do not offer the imagery of Sun's having picked them up. Remember that it is what you teach yourself to believe that matters. The mind and body cannot discern the difference between what is imagined and real. What you convince yourself of will be so in every sense of the word. If you are convinced, the power will be yours, and your prayers will be fulfilled. If you are not convinced, the power will not come, and your prayers will go unanswered.

I cannot overstress how important it is to understand the way in which the paho works. While it is offering up your prayer, you go about your business. But as you do so, the Above Beings are fine-tuning you to constantly look and listen for their answer in what is going on around you. They will speak to you in events, in the elements, in what you see happening, or in what someone says to you. But

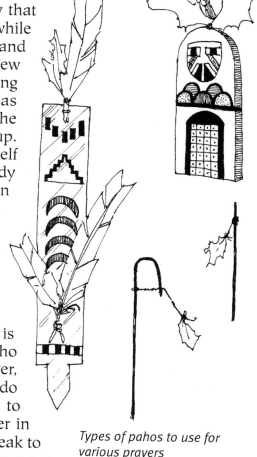

Types of pahos to use for various prayers

you will know it when it happens — that the Above Beings are answering your prayer. It may be only an ordinary thing someone else wouldn't notice, it may be unusual, or it may be a miracle. But you will know it. Only rarely do the Above Beings speak personally to someone, and when it happens it most often has something to do with the fulfillment of the divine plan for the whole of creation.

Although you may if you wish, you need not speak a silent or an audible prayer as you place a paho or other offering in its shrine — which can be any quiet niche or small altar of rocks or wood. The prayer is being inserted into the paho as you fashion it, in its carving and its designs and appendages, for you will have had to think about what you were doing as you constructed it. The same is true of any actions and

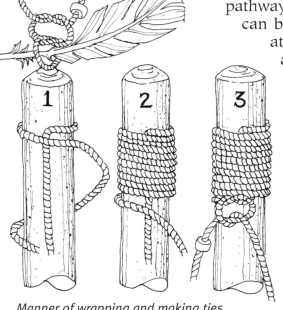

efforts you carry out as you make other things, such as masks or questing places. In effect, you will have prayed the prayer into it — prayed it into existence — and what you constructed contains the prayer and can offer it up. The more pahos you fashion and put out, the more powerful the prayers will be, because there is power in numbers. The cumulative voices are louder, carry farther, and are more insistent.

Designing Your Pahos

The symbolic designs placed on your pahos can be very simple. As the illustrations show, face, cloud and rain designs are common on Hopi pahos. So are corn symbols. You can use the same designs, but while the Hopi desperately needed rain and corn crops, you will probably want to think of the faces you use as symbolic representations of those persons you want to help you and of the rain symbols as raining down upon you the things for which you are praying. Focus your attention on the symbols and see these things raining down. They will soon be yours. The Apache and Hopi pathways material in Part Two of this book can be used as catalysts to your own creativity. The more personal your designs are, the more effective they will be.

Attitude for Prayer

Ordinarily, you will benefit the most when you think in terms of praying for needs rather than luxuries. Scripture gives us this guidance, and, as we should expect, the Native Americans were taught to think the same way. The Native Americans were grateful for abundances when they came, and they expressed their thanksgiving for these, but they let the Above Beings make the final decisions. The people were equally con-

Manner of wrapping and making ties on pahos with heavy string or yarn

tent and grateful when only needs were supplied. "What more," they would ask, "does anyone truly need than needs?" Keep all of your prayers simple. The Above Beings are impressed with what you feel and not with how you say it. Finite humans are not, with their most eloquent prayer and statements, likely to impress infinite Beings overly much.

MEDITATING
Vision Questing

It is the practice of those Native Americans who vision quest to carry out this meditative act either in conjunction with major ceremonies or when there is a serious crisis in their lives. They also meditate as part of daily prayer and in sweatlodge rituals. You should follow this practice of meditation as a means of keeping alive in your thoughts and heart the power relationship you have with the Above Beings. I suggest that each spring, when the new grass is just beginning to show itself, you either rebuild your Sioux-style questing place or do the Sunrise Ritual on your pile of folded blankets. Then in the interim between these annual repetitions, you can meditate whenever you wish by simply assuming the seated position on the floor, on the ground, or on a chair. With your hands cupped in your lap as directed, mentally rebuild in your mind the questing place, then do the breathing exercise, mentally place the tube before you, focus upon it, and think through the meaning of it and its symbols. This act will serve as a refreshing and renewing experience, and you can do it as often as you like, whenever and wherever you like. Bear in mind that the ability to call in and to dispense power accumulates and builds with practice.

In time, you will find that your main questing place will become associated with your center. It will be the place where you will root yourself in Native American fashion, the place to which your heart and soul and mind will cling even as you move forward in life in the crucible of the present-day world.

Centering

A person who lacks a center also lacks identity. Without identity, it is not possible to be balanced or to lead a balanced life. It is a matter of knowing who one is, of having a sense of place and self-worth. Without a center, we wander through life without moorings, and we are plagued by self-doubt and indecision. This is an intolerable situation, and our entire being rails against it.

In America's current melting pot of citizens and fluctuating religious and secular environments, those without a strong ethnic background often suffer an identity crisis and lack a center to hold on to. Children of mixed marriages usually find themselves envious of those citizens who have migrated here and continue to celebrate the national customs of their original homelands. We take great pride in our flag and in our nation's accomplishments, but beyond these things many people wonder who they are, for they have no center that serves as the supply source for their lives.

As we have learned, the ancient Native Americans were given a strong center to cling to; the best example of how this works was given to us by Fools Crow — although the whole of Native American ritual life was rooted in their individual centers.

What Is Your Center?

Just to review: The center consists of the empowered core of teachings given to the people at the time they first appeared on the surface of the earth. It is living and incredibly powerful, passing its power on to and influencing whatever it touches. The Indians of each succeeding generation apply it to every aspect of their lives and benefit accordingly. It is, in effect, their Bible and has the power to transform human beings.

Retaining one's center is in nowise a nostalgia trip in which the Indian desires a complete return to the past and to never-changing ancient ways. The center teachings are designed to be applied to changing circumstances and to help the individual and nation decide which changes are good and which are bad. Above all, the center teachings are meant to keep people attuned to the ways of the Above Beings. Drums draw the center up from the earth, rattles call it down from the skies, flutes sing of its beauties, and incense speaks to it in gentle and sweet-smelling tones.

The center principle as used by present-day individuals

The teachings in this book can become your center. They will be sufficient in themselves to be that center — although you can easily add them to any religious center you already have. For the teachings to function, however, you must recognize them as the center they are and make constant use of them. When you do this, you will no longer search for identity; you will have it, and you will have all of the security and confidence that comes with it. You will know who you are, what you are, and what you can become in the days ahead. Look at the symbolic diagram on page 181 and think hard about its meaning. Use it as a mental symbol while you meditate. Place yourself in it, and feel the core's power and heat as it pulses out to you.

Doing this — and reviewing the core of teachings — is your way of assuring yourself that the Above Beings and their helpers will continue to dispense to you the power that is everywhere present in the universe. Recall, however, that the Native American point of view is that while you were given power and became a tube in your first act of obedience, you can never take this privilege for granted. If you neglect or abuse it, you can lose it. You must remain forever conscious of the need to apply power diligently and to keep it fresh in your mind, heart, and soul. Remember that it is really the Above Beings' power that you have and are permitted to dispense. As such, what you possess is a privilege, not a right you will ever own in the sense of being independent from the Beings.

In this regard, the Native Americans thought of prayer as much more than words. Words are easily spoken and often just as easily forgotten. Reflect on how quick we are to pray loudly for deliverance when an aircraft we are riding in hits an air pocket — then how quickly we pass it all off as soon as the pilot rights the aircraft and we fly blithely on. Prayer does include words, but it is also an expression of relationship with the Above Beings, a relationship of love in which hopes and other information are exchanged.

I remember well a story about a missionary who had just returned from Africa. It seems he was riding his bicycle along a dirt road and passed a native woman who was on her knees in a prayer position. Assuming that she was a fellow Christian and was praying, he stopped and asked her whether that was what she was doing. "No," she answered, "not today. Today I am just visiting."

She makes a very good point for *visiting* is as much a part of what we do with the Above Beings as spoken words are, and every bit as important. You know what a warm experience visiting a friend is — how you relax and talk at a leisurely pace about all kinds of things, how easy it is, and how time flies. Well, our relationship with the Above Beings is like that, except that it is a love-relationship between parent and child. Just as children do, we sit close by to ask our questions and express our childlike thoughts with all of our wonder and with all of our dreams and hopes. And, like loving parents, they patiently respond and encourage us to go on and to seek fulfillment.

Listening is also important, and anyone who wishes to pray effectively will learn to spend as much or more time listening than he or she does speaking. How can the Above Beings answer if we fail to listen to them? One-sided conversations are seldom productive in ordinary life, and they are even less so in the Divine/human relationship. Jesus did a great deal of listening when he prayed, and to see how effective this was, just consider what he learned and was able to do with the answers he received.

I am not equating Fools Crow with Jesus, but Fools Crow also spends hours in prayer each day, and much of his time is given over to listening to what the Above Beings and the helper spirits have to tell him. By this, he too has become a power-filled, very wise, and productive man. Imitate him: Think awhile, pray awhile, and listen awhile. Then repeat the procedure. You will be amazed at what it does for you, and what you will learn from it!

Since your pahos and other offerings are in and of themselves prayers, you can use them in the same way as spoken prayer. Once they are constructed and you have set them out, you should spend some time thinking about what is going on as a result of your having fashioned and placed them. Let the answers that are forthcoming form and evolve in your mind, and in time, whole pictures will emerge to give you guidance or whatever else you need.

You are ready now to make further applications of Native American pathways for eliminating entirely the causes of stress.

A REVIEW

Let us review what you do as you begin walking the pathways:

First, you purify yourself to become a fit vessel or tube, and you continue to purify yourself on a regular basis.

Second, you make your questing place where you call down power and receive it.

Third, you wear symbols to remind yourself of what you have.

Fourth, you fashion and place pahos and other offerings that continue to pray for your ongoing relationship with the Above Beings.

Fifth, you establish and fortify your center and, at the same time, build your identity.

You will find that the stresses of everyday life are less upsetting. The stronger your center becomes, the more self-confident you become. Outside forces have less influence over you. Those walls that once were opaque for you will become your windows and doors opening into a splendid new world. Yet there are times when you will need to deal with stress and other outside forces in order to keep yourself centered. Two methods of accomplishing this are listed next.

REMOVING STRESS

The Native Americans removed from their presence those stresses they could by actually removing themselves. In effect, this was a kind of sensible surrender and the equivalent of our making that ultimate difficult decision to leave the job, person, or whatever else is causing a steady erosion of our lives. Here is an instance where one can win the war by retreating from one or more of the individual battles. As we have noted, both the stalwart Cherokee and the more passive Hopi were especially good at this; if they had not been, they would not be here today. We can safely assume that this sage advice was passed on to them as they listened to the Above Beings.

A second tactic is presented to us by the Cherokee in the use of their prayer formulas. You will recall that the formulas had as their basic nature the covering over of an enemy. In effect, what they did was to hide it or block it out from their view, so that it was gone.

You can employ the same device in a very simple way. Take a small box that has some dimension and form, and write on its surface the name of the individual or thing that is causing you unacceptable stress. Place the box on the top of a small table or shelf that is cleared of everything else. Then take a piece of black cloth that is large enough to entirely cover the box. As you drape the cloth over the box, say four or seven times, "I cover you over. I block you entirely out of my life." Then leave the cloth and box there on the table for four or seven days while, as time permits, you continue to contemplate it and reinforce the desire you are pursuing. You might make a paho to assist you. At the end of this time, whatever has caused you stress will no longer be a problem. Either it will be gone, or some aspect of it or of yourself will have changed so that it no longer troubles you. When that is so, remove the box from under the cloth and dispose of it. Leave the black cloth lying there flat for four more days as a reminder that the stress is gone. Then put it away and save it until you need it again. This method is by no means the equivalent of putting a

The control box

hex on something. It is purely and simply an application of the power that the Above Beings have made available to you, for it serves to transform your outlook at the same time as it works on the cause of your stress.

Other means are given in the material ahead as ways of developing further the "covering over" idea. As I said earlier, the Above Beings recognized the differences between peoples and wisely provided them with choices.

CHAPTER TWELVE

Calling in Extraordinary Power

Now that you are a tube with power and a center, I can present you with other Native American pathway findings you can make regular use of in your daily life. As a basic rule, when you wish to go beyond these findings — and you will — call upon the Cherokee material for adaptability, the Apache for perseverance, the Hopi for patience, and the Sioux for tenacity. Since the teachings of the four tribes as a whole comprise your center, review them regularly.

Should you do these things I suggest? If you have already carried out the preliminary steps, you will be anxious to do them. But if you have not, you may still be afraid or embarrassed to try. There are those who will wonder about me for having written and suggested them, but the pathways have served the Native Americans so amazingly well that I can't worry about what the hesitant or negative people think. The test of whether or not you should go on is a simple one — if you feel deep down inside that you ought to, you'd better. If stress is affecting you, shouldn't you do something before it does serious damage?

While I separate the following pathway findings, there is, for the most part, no fixed order for your applying them. Use them in any way you wish, and employ all or part of them as you think best. This must be a personal choice for you. I do recommend that you use them all and that you do so by selecting those ways that are designed to deal with what confronts you at any given time.

PREPARE IN ADVANCE

Prepare annually in advance so that you are ready to meet whatever comes. Follow the Cherokee central pathway for this preparation, and combine it with the essence of the Hopi ritual cycle and their nine-day ceremonial procedure.

You must choose a significant time and place to take this step for the first time. I recommend that it be done on either of the solstices, approximately December 21 or June 21, since these are important times of change and beginning in the universe. If you are not able to do it then, choose a time that has special significance for you — some date that holds a warm place in your heart. Remember that your attitude and the atmosphere are extremely important. Choosing a significant time will help ensure the right tone. Be alone while you prepare, for it is not a thing that can easily be shared. This is one of the times when solitude can prove to be a friend and offer certain advantages. People who are forever in groups and busy may find it hard to set aside the time or even to make the effort. Perhaps it will help you to know that the priests and medicine persons of the ancient tribes always preferred to be by themselves in some lonely place when they made medicine, prayed and meditated . . . for only then could they clearly hear their own thoughts and those of the Above Beings when they answered.

Writing as Meditation

When you have selected your time and place and are alone, sit down at a table with a large pad and a pencil, breathe deeply four times, and relax. Begin by mentally reviewing the past year and the situations in it that caused you discomfort. Using this as a basis, think through the year ahead of you. List on the pad every significant menace you think might confront you. Ask yourself whether you believe the year ahead is likely to be the same as last year. What new things might occur? Think about it. Write everything down.

Once you have the fully developed list, begin to consider ways you can deal more effectively with the stresses than you did before . . . ways that have been offered to you by the Native Americans. You will do well at this, because you now have new information, new insights, and special power. Write these thoughts alongside the items you have listed. Some of your answers may be specific actions you can take; others may be nothing more than random thoughts. For some discomforts, you may not yet have a solution. Don't let this bother you, for there are specific Native-American-based answers spelled out in the material just ahead. You can use these to fill in the blanks and to augment the answers you do have.

Now start at the top of the list and move slowly down it. Fix your mind for a minute or so upon each stress and the solution or solutions you have posed for it. While you hold all of these in your thoughts, mentally expose them to the six steps of the Cherokee — see these working and bringing the solutions to fruition. Begin with firm confidence that the Above Beings will answer the petitions you are offering up. Then acknowledge that there are no barriers to prevent your full union with the Above Beings. Next, express your unrestrained joy and thanksgiving for what you know you will receive. Now settle back and let winter and Cold Maker push you deeper into reflection and reassurance. Next, kindle in your mind new fires that show your faith in fresh new beginnings. Then see your spring of renewal and new birth, free of all stresses. End with a mental dance of rapture to celebrate your triumph and freedom. Finally, picture in your mind the stresses as completely overcome.

Remember that what you are doing gets your entire self ready to meet any stress situation that comes at you during the next year. The power of any stress you confront will be diluted and will not be able to do you serious or permanent damage. Recall that this is precisely what the Cherokee did in carrying out their central pathway, what the Hopi did and do in their annual cycle of ceremonies, and what the other tribes did also. Their attitudes were fortified, and they were strengthened in all ways. Millennia have passed, and the tribes have suffered countless tribulations, yet they are here today and still have their identities.

You will need to do this on an annual basis. Your power will not be strong enough to carry you for more than one year at a time. You will remain a willing dependent creature, but you will know this is for your own best good.

CALLING BACK THE DEAD

Whenever you wish to have counselors, call back the dead. I have explained how the Cherokee priests and medicine persons had techniques for calling back deceased individuals with whom they wanted to talk things over. But the ancient Cherokee could not write and did not have books. They, and other Native Americans, had no recourse but to pass on the ancient teachings and other knowledge by means of the oral tradition, legends, myths, and stories told by one person to another. Pictographic art was the only exception. So they augmented this information by bringing back the dead and discussing the central teachings with them, along with how they should make applications of it to the present day.

Our situation is significantly different from that of the Native Americans who could neither read nor write. The genius of our dead is available to us in books, letters, and memories, and we have an incredible and wondrous literary source that is as near as our storage cabinets, bookshelves, and libraries. You needn't have a secret chant to call back the dead, for many of the dead are already at your fingertips.

Masks and Pahos to Call Back the Dead

Yet there are those dead who can be helpful to you and whose knowledge is not recorded in books — mothers, fathers, friends, teachers, and other acquaintances. What of them? You can call them back by employing the Hopi method of making pahos — the crook for those who were old when they died and straight pahos for those who were young — and by fashioning a full, bucket-shaped Hopi mask that covers your entire head and wearing it as you meditate.

Another foolish thing? Try it, and see. The Native Americans aren't alone in calling back the dead. The people who follow the ancient ways of far-eastern meditation also have techniques for doing the same thing.

How to Make a Hopi Hood Mask

Decide whom you want to talk to. Then make your mask with a wire frame and cardboard in the form of the Hopi hood mask illustrated on page 223. If you want a more permanent mask that you can refurbish when you want to use it again, do as the Hopi do and make it of rawhide. Append to its exterior designs and items that add to the symbolism — things that represent the person you are calling back and the topics you want to discuss. The mask should be loose fitting, with small eyeholes for vision and a mouth hole for breathing. You must fashion your own mask, and while you can purchase the materials, resist any temptation to purchase a completed mask or to have someone else do it for you. The artistic quality of the mask is of no consequence. What is of consequence is that, as you construct it, you will be thinking through what you are seeking, and that is an integral part of the calling-back process. Your mind is engaged and working on the problem. For each use of the mask, you will refurbish the base with new designs and appendages. A mask that is worn out should be replaced with an entirely new one.

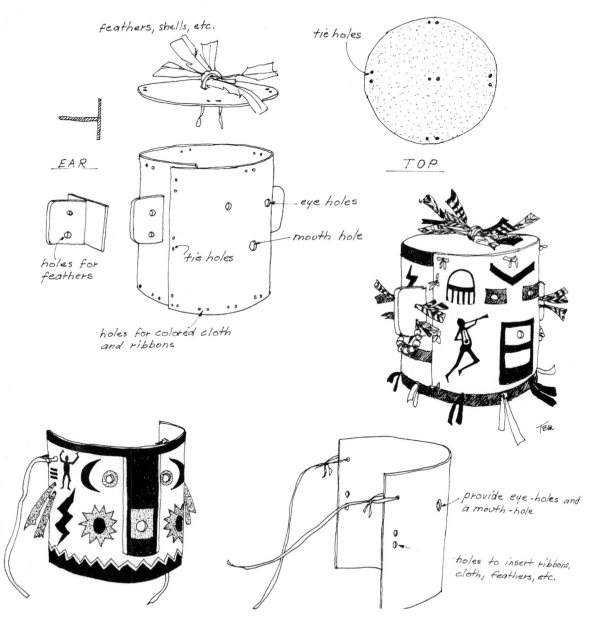

Making Masks: Above, hood mask; below, face mask using rawhide, cardboard, or heavy paper

Using the Mask

When the mask is ready, go at sundown to the quiet place you have found where you can be alone. Put on some pleasant music, playing it softly so it will nourish, but not interfere with, your thoughts. You may want to add to the effectiveness of the atmosphere with the aromatic smells of spiced teas, herbs, or incense. Turn the lights down low. Now put a chair in the middle of the room, sit down, and place the mask on your head. If you prefer, sit on the floor. Place your hands in your lap. Hold your paho in your right hand and turn the left-hand palm up. Breathe deeply, and relax in the way previously described by Archie Sam. Close your eyes, and as you sink ever and ever deeper into relaxation, letting each part of your body release its tension, begin to imagine that you are in an underground Hopi Kiva — in the womb of Mother Earth. You will be imaging now in the most effective way possible, for the mask will enable you to concentrate far better than you ever could by thought processes alone. When you are visually in the kiva and see it plainly, begin to think about the mask, and imagine the deceased person you want to talk to manifesting him- or herself before you. Open your eyes, and you will see the person. Now and then it is helpful to speed up the process by rising and dancing slowly to the music. The Indians do that a lot. Some of the deceased will arrive in your kiva in their typically human form as you remember them; others will come in ghostly fashion. When they do, they will exchange greetings with you in voices so familiar that they will clutch at your heart. Talk to them. Tell them why you have called them back. Visit about anything they bring up. When

Present-day person calling in the dead for counseling in both Cherokee and Hopi fashion

they are ready, they will leave, and the session will be over. Put the mask and paho on a shelf where you can see them to remind you of the experience. The effectiveness of this calling-back approach will increase with practice.

Why It Works

Now we will ask ourselves what has really happened. It is something like this: These people are stored away in our memory banks, and what we need is a means of recalling them as a computer calls its information to the screen. If we attempt to do this in an abstract fashion, it seldom works. All we receive is random and disconnected snatches of material. The mask, the paho, and the setting do a far better job, and you will receive in a warm and welcome way the recalling of the truly important moments of your life. These will stimulate your mind and enable the two of you — you and the called-back one — to enlarge in a pleasant way upon the subject at hand, just as if you were together on another day when the deceased was still here on earth. Rewardingly enough, there will never be any arguing or attempts to defend or justify positions. The thrust of the discussion will always be positive and toward the best possible future for you.

Just thinking about this now, I can clearly hear my deceased father's voice as he calls my name, and I am remembering how much I could have learned from him if only I had listened more to him while he was alive. I often call him back, for he was a very logical man, and I can use his advice. I'm sure there are people from your past that you would like to talk with again.

Sometimes a mysterious thing happened when the Cherokee medicine persons called back the dead, and it might happen to you. Archie Sam told me that his father experienced it fairly regularly and that it had also happened to him. On occasion, when the dead are called back, a person or persons unknown to you will come and talk with you. They may tell you strange things that can be frightening. They may just tell you things you need to know but have not thought of. Sometimes, Archie said, they float in the air and, without saying a word, just stare at you. Then they depart and leave you wondering. This is their way of disapproving of something you are thinking or doing.

The mask method is also useful when you would like to talk with living persons who are far away and can't be otherwise reached. Try it.

The Hopi belief is that when you put on a hood mask, you are becoming the person the mask represents and adding his or her power to your own so that you become more than you are. In the same way, after the Sioux vision-seeker has a vision in which a certain helper appears, let us say a bear, he then adds something of that kind of bear to his medicine bundle and puts the bear symbol on his war shield; he is no longer just a man, he is a bear-man. He will even, in some instances, act like a bear. He will fight like one, and he will study the bear to see what medicines he uses to heal himself. When you call back the dead, you become that person plus yourself — the Native Americans would say two merged powers — since in ancient days all persons would have obtained power.

Time Consciousness

I was interested to read in a newspaper some comments concerning time consciousness and the role this plays in our well-being. Among other things, it spoke of the result of a survey of several thousand people that was conducted by Stanford University professor, Philip Zimbardo, and Alexander Gonzalez, a psychologist at Fresno State University. It revealed that a vast majority of Americans are future- or present-oriented. Only about one percent of those they surveyed were past-oriented. Yet other cultures, they said, and particularly traditional ones, have a far stronger sense of the past "and the danger of not including a sense of the past in your time perspective is that you cut yourself off from your roots, it makes us a transient society. Families build unity by shared memories and repeating old rituals that bring them together; by sharing a past." They also found that those with sound identities had the most balanced perspective of any group, projecting themselves both into the distant past and the far future.

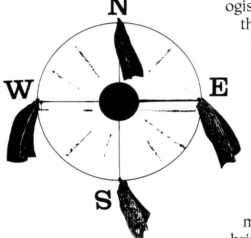

Manner of placing direction flags on the circle

In this connection, Native Americans found the calling back of the dead the most useful pathway in keeping their orientation and their perspectives balanced.

It is rewarding to know that one day, after you have left this earth, you too may be called back to serve this purpose by someone who loves you and will want to talk with you about their questions, needs, and desires. The thought of this possibility can add a new dimension to your self-worth and cause you to think about what kind of relationships you ought to be building right now with those you love. Leave behind your very best, and people will want to talk with you forever.

THE POWER OF DIRECTIONS

A Native American pathway finding for keeping order and a sense of purpose in your life is that of calling in power from the Four Directions. The Directions are called in by using colored flags — white for the north, red for the east, yellow for the south, and black for the west. As you have learned, when you add *down* for Mother Earth and *up* for the Above Beings, there are actually six directions. But the latter are called upon in most of the other pathways actions, and they need not be a part of this exercise.

You can fashion the flags in any manner you like, then hang one on each wall of your room or put them on the four sides of a stand or box that you can turn as you contemplate them. You can think about the flags in each of two ways, and you should look now at the Great Circle on page 226 as a guide for this.

The Great Circle

See the flags as directional points on a great circle that surrounds you and recognize that in the beginning the Above Beings gave to each of these Directions certain powers that the faithful can draw upon as needed. The Native Americans used these circles for education — to educate themselves and their children. They would, in effect, walk themselves or the children around the circle, contemplating and discussing at each cardinal point the powers associated with it. The color at each point indicated the kind of power that resided there, so once a person had learned the powers, he could simply use the color itself to represent the power. When he had a certain need, he knew what color was associated with fulfilling that need and would place that color out in the sun as his prayer offering. You will learn how to do this, too. Recall that in the Sun Dance, the Sioux tie to the base of the Sun Pole colored cloths that are chosen according to the prayers the donors wish to offer up.

Calling in Power from the Directions

As you make the first use of the circle, move clockwise. Begin at the south, and while you focus your attention on the white flag, call in the power from that direction. It will enable you to think wisely about the things of your life that are concerned with birth. Then move to the black west, and think about youth. Move to the red north, and consider adult life. Move to the yellow east, and consider old age. As you contemplate these things, you should see yourself fulfilling each role in your close relationship with the Above Beings and deriving the very best from it in a responsible way. Be ever conscious of consequences regarding the things you consider, for every thought and act has its consequences. Some are good, and some are bad. Emphasize the good ones.

Drawing in Wisdom

The second use of the directional circle is that of drawing into yourself wisdom concerning the development of your full potential as a human being. Begin at the south as you did before, but, this time, call upon the Direction to give you wisdom concerning physical health and healthy, productive mental growth. Don't be in a hurry. Think about these things, and you will learn a great deal. Now, move to the west, and call for enlightenment and perception. Move to the north, and call for a purification of your thoughts and desires. Move to the east, and call for renewal of body, mind, heart, soul, and spirit.

As you contemplate the circle and the directions, do not force an issue or make any demands. Be like the Apache. If you persevere, the guidance will eventually come, and you will grow in wisdom, strength, and grace. Anxieties and indecision will fade steadily away. You will feel so good about yourself, you will hardly believe it. Your orientation will be clear, your sense of purpose will be strong, and your goals for life in general will become attainable. It cannot be otherwise when you take the time to think them through and then resolve them to happen.

The Apache Attitude

Whenever you are weary or feel that you are aging, use the Apache pathway you learned from the Sunrise Girl and Changing Woman. Go outside to a place where you can be alone and walk toward the east. Fix your mind upon the view ahead until you see the image of the young Changing Woman coming toward you in her Apache clothing. When you meet her, let her merge with you, and imagine that you have become young again. You will find that this simple act restores your energy and hope.

When you want to determine your course in life and wish to have the assurance of protection and long life, think through the parts of the Sunrise Ceremony and apply their lessons to yourself. See their promises being fulfilled in your life, and they will be!

NATURE AS YOUR PARTNER

Accept nature as your partner and co-worker in life. This is especially difficult for those of us who are urban-bound and part of an industrial complex that, to satisfy burgeoning populations, chews up and despoils resources at a mind-boggling pace. The Native Americans were more fortunate for they lived in the midst of nature and were conscious of their relationship to it and its importance in their lives. Even with such an abundance of natural resources as they had, they learned from the Above Beings the sensibleness of conserving nature — of never depleting any aspect of it at any time. Enough of what they took was always left behind to produce what would be needed in future years. Of course, the Native American population was small compared to that of the modern world, and their ways would not house, feed, or clothe us. There had to be change, but the key question is whether or not the improvements have been truly beneficial. Nature seems to be angry with us and is justifiably turning on us today.

In essence, what we non-Indians have done is to adapt nature to ourselves, while the Indians adapted themselves to nature. The former approach does not seem to be working particularly well. Those of you who would like to see an excellent spelling-out of this should subscribe to an outstanding magazine for American Indians called *Winds of Change*. The publisher is Norbert S. Hill, 1085 14th Street, Suite 1506, Boulder, Colorado, 80302-7309. The June 1987, issue contains a chilling article titled, "When the Turtle Dies." It is a scientific report on the effects of the St. Lawrence River and other industrial pollution on the St. Regis Mohawk Akwesasne Reservation in New York State. Another powerful article details how a brilliant Yakima Indian named Russell Jim has become an extraordinary advocate in the fight for nuclear responsibility.

Be a Part of Nature

But what the Native Americans did, and would counsel you to do today, is to think of yourself as a part of nature, and to treat it as such. Think of everything in nature as being alive, and as making its contribution to the whole — which, in fact, it does. Is there any part of it that we do not make use of in one way or another? But the problem is, we abuse it as much as we use it; thus, we tear up other strands of the web that the Above Beings wove to hold us together. When the web is damaged sufficiently, we humans will be in bad, bad trouble.

So, to relieve your stresses in regard to pollution and depletion, do what you can to change your own attitude and actions. Take the time to look closely at the stunning beauty nature possesses, and ask yourself once more what it will cost us to be without each natural thing we see, smell, and touch. Go to where you can see animals in the wild, and smell the flowers, the trees, the grasses, the lakes, and the oceans. If it is possible, find some clean air. Touch what you are able to, feel the rich variety of textures, and remind yourself that each and every part of it is part of the great web of life woven over the ages by the Above Beings. Do not be surprised at what this effort does to inspire you, for as the worth of nature grows in your heart, your own worth will grow with it. The Native Americans knew this a long, long time ago.

The Sacred Place

In addition to thinking of themselves as a part of nature, each Native American tribe came to think of a particular area of land as associated with its center. They did this for two reasons: The first was that so much of their life was spent on it that they thought of themselves as sharing life with it; the second was that as the dead decomposed, they were received into the earth. That made that earth doubly sacred — the people were united with it. Whether or not you realize it, as you follow the pathways, you are now developing just such a place right now. What you feel regarding this place as the years go by will prove this assertion to be true.

MAKING A SUNRISE CANE

If you would like to live a long, healthy, and productive life, and if you would like to offer the same gifts to others, make yourself a cane like that of the Apache Sunrise girl. Be certain the wood you use is that of a fruit-bearing bush or tree. Decorate the cane with personal symbols. Then set the cane upright out in the yard, and, beginning from a marked starting point, run out to it, circle it, and return to the starting point. Move the cane out four feet further, and run around it again. Do this a third and a fourth time. Each time you run, believe that you are claiming for yourself a state of life: birth, youth, adulthood, old age. See yourself owning these stages in the belief that all of them will come to pass. As you run, consider this well, and see yourself as ever stronger and healthier. Remember that running around the cane is a prayer for the Above Beings to grant this. When you are finished, put the cane where you can see it, and be continually reminded of what you have done with it. If you have obtained a crystal, place it in running water, and look into it before and after you have made your runs. The pictures or images you see will differ from one another. For example, if, before you run, the crystal is hazy or the color of blue smoke, after you run it will be clear and sparkling. This is the precise omen you want to see for it forecasts a long, or at least a fulfilling, life.

I do not hedge my bets concerning the foregoing when I say that the long life offered by running cannot always be measured in terms of years — quality of life is equally or perhaps even more important than length. Beyond the quality, there is the eternal relationship with the Above Beings to be considered, since to be with them is to one day sleep, then to rise, but never to die.

USING FERTILITY SYMBOLS

To bring about or encourage fertility and procreation, use fertility symbols. When the earth is renewing itself and new growth is appearing, fashion for yourself each spring male and buffalo fertility symbols like those of the Sioux for the Sun Dance. When you place them before you and contemplate each one, carry out the kneeling and swaying gestures of the Apache Sunrise Girl as she becomes Changing Woman. Use music with this.

The symbols must include the phallus, since this will focus your thoughts on procreation. Think comprehensively about procreation and renewal and about all of the wondrous things the Above Beings have provided regarding it. To refresh your mind about procreation and renewal, reread the Sioux Sun Dance material in Part Two.

If you are a woman, while you do your contemplation, feel yourself being wondrously loved and impregnated by the rays of Sun — and at the same time by the one you want to be the father of your child. See yourself as splendidly beautiful and desirable. If you have a private place to do so, it may occur to you to be nude and position yourself where you are fully exposed to Sun, who in this instance fulfills a male role. The Sunrise Girl is always completely clothed in her finest costume as she performs the ritual, but she is in public view.

If you are a man, see any impotence or other problem removed and gone. See your wife being successfully impregnated. It will help you to remember and review the Cherokee sequence of ritual events and thoughts. They are extraordinarily positive and very productive. When you have carried out the use of this pathway finding, see clearly in your mind the child that will be born to you. Like the Apache girl, you are a seed giving birth. See yourself loving and caring for your child. See it growing up. Know that such positive thoughts will be releasing chemicals that can cause your body to respond to the directions you are giving it.

As always, there is another side to every ritual act performed by the Native Americans. In this case, the use of symbols will also increase your fertility where creative and productive ideas are concerned. The proof of this will show itself particularly in your work. Once again, your co-workers will notice the difference, and you can smile inwardly as you credit your secret source.

If you would like to carry this latter blessing a step farther, and I certainly recommend that you do, do what the Apache Sunrise Girl does. Fill a small basket with wrapped candy, nuts, and other small delicacies, and when you have finished the swaying for the ritual number of times, empty the basket over your head. As you do so, think of the co-workers or friends you want to bless with fruitfulness and productivity, and the next day, take the gifts with you to work or school, and pass them out. Do not tell the people why you are doing this; let them wonder and guess. Then wait for the results to show themselves.

CHEROKEE FACE MASK TO BRING GOOD TO YOURSELF

Use the face mask to control stress by bringing good things into your life. You will recall that this mask is a face mask only, not the hood type that is used for becoming or merging with someone else. The face mask can be made from a sheet of 8 ½ x 11-inch typing paper to which a band is attached, although a heavier weight stock will lend itself better to decoration and appendages. Papier mâché makes an excellent base. In preparing the mask, follow the directions given for the hood mask, including the small round eyeholes and the rectangular mouth hole.

Bear in mind the Cherokee belief that the mask itself has the power to control or to lure closer what it represents, so the symbolism used on the mask should represent what you want to control or to lure closer. I will make a few suggestions regarding the types of designs to use on the front of the mask, but it will be more productive if you think most of them up for yourself as a part of your preparation process.

If another person is involved, rather than drawing their face on the mask, use symbols to represent what it is about them you want to control. Black storm clouds can represent anger; a straight line, narrowness; a jagged line, pain; an empty cup, selfishness; a fog, gloominess; an iceberg, coldness; a closed door, a closed mind; a smile, happiness.

Using the Mask

To use the mask, you must envision what you want to control. Remember that the thing you may need to control is yourself — your emotions, your fears — anything that needs disciplining or is out of control. If this is the problem, let your mask symbols reflect it.

Now draw or paint a single symbol on a small piece of cardboard that best represents what you want to control. Put a paho out to assist you. When everything is ready, sit down in your private place. Position the single symbol in front of you, propped up where you can see it clearly. Then put the mask on. Breathe deeply the traditional number of times, relax, and focus your eyes on the image. In a few moments, the symbol will begin to move. If you are seeking to control what it represents, it will back away from you and grow smaller. Its power will diminish, and yours will increase. If you are seeking to lure it closer, it will come nearer and nearer until at last it reaches you and you possess it. Never allow yourself to have negative thoughts as you do this, for that drains you. Also, take one thing at a time. Don't try to deal with everything at once. Never blame others for behaviors or situations you are seeking to control, for as soon as you do that, you are actually giving control to them.

When, as it will be, your control is achieved, remember to make a thanksgiving offering to the Above Beings. Then put the mask and single symbol where you can see them as a reminder of what you have achieved. Don't let a single negative thought regarding victory enter your mind. Observe how you will begin to live comfortably with things you could not tolerate before. Why? Because they have changed.

I suspect you are realizing by now that over a period of time, your special room is going to be amply decorated with the items you have used — and will continue to use — as you follow the pathways. This should be an incentive to make attractive things. As you make them, your creative abilities will steadily improve.

MOLDING AND TRANSFORMING

Change Yourself Inside and Outside by Molding Yourself

Do you want to change your appearance and the way you interact with others? Would you like to be more beautiful, taller, more erect, more radiant? Would you like to be helpful to others and popular? Become Changing Woman as she walks to meet her youthful image. Be molded and transformed as the Sunrise Ceremony girl is.

Obtain some cattails and make yourself some pollen (grind some dried corn kernels to produce corn pollen). You can have an understanding friend help you with this pathway finding, or you can do it entirely on your own. As always, you will be wise to fashion a paho and put it out in the Sun before you begin. Put on one of your best outfits, and make your pile of four blankets. Put some inspirational music on. Rub the pollen on your cheeks and forehead. Tie your abalone shell on your forehead. Now, sit in the supplication position on the blankets while you go through your breathing and relaxation exercises. When you are ready, pray to the Above Beings, asking them to grant you the things you are questing for. Believe that as you do this, your prayers and those implanted in the paho will be granted. From this moment onward, you must not doubt that they will be.

The Ritual

Now, lie face down on the blankets with your arms at your sides and your head pointed toward the east. The Sunrise Girl is fully clothed for this pathway rite, but she is appearing in public. If you wish, while you are alone you can dispense with clothing. However, if someone is assisting you, be dressed. Slacks and blouse or shirt are fine. There must be nothing sexual about what you are doing, for that will destroy all possibilities of success.

Feel the power of Changing Woman enter through your abalone shell. Feel it move through your mind, and then follow it down into your body. Feel it move out into your arms, then to your legs and feet. You should be warmer now, perhaps even tingling. Close your eyes, and keep them closed throughout the rest of the ritual. Anticipate what is about to happen to you. See yourself as you want to be.

Molding

If you are doing this for yourself, feel the strong hands of the Above Beings slowly and tenderly beginning to mold you . . . starting at the toes of your right foot, then up along your leg, then your side, your arm, and finally, your face. Feel the hands move across your hair and head and down your left side to your left toes. Know that every lump, bump, and bit of fat or wrinkled skin, every deterrent to beauty, is being affected. Feel yourself stretching out, firming up, becoming more graceful, more assured. Know that the pollen is protecting you from everything unsightly or negative. If a friend is doing the molding for you, you must think these same things as your friend reshapes you.

Go through the entire molding process four times. Don't hurry. Concentrate on what is happening. Then stand up on the blankets, and, still facing east, by yourself or with your friend, go through mentally what the Sunrise Girl does when the Singer passes his hands alongside her body and head. Remember that he holds his hands about two inches away from her and does not touch her. This is because an aura of power is emanating from and surrounding her body by now, and he could not touch her if he wanted to. Your situation will be the same. As the Singer moves his hands, the Above Beings are redistributing portions of the girl's body so as to fill in what is needed in one place and take it away in another. In effect, the Above Beings are completely molding you. Feel your chest swell, your abdomen tighten, your body tone sharpen.

Experiencing the Change

Now open your eyes, but do not go immediately to a mirror. As you put the blankets away, change your clothing, and remove the shell from your forehead, have no thoughts other than positive ones. The aura that surrounded you is going to remain with you. You will probably see it as a glowing color when you do stand before a mirror. Different colors mean different things. Determine this by associating them with their direction. Recognize that you are going to behave differently now regarding your appearance and that other people are going to see the overall change in you. You will choose your clothing and accessories even more carefully than you did before. Expect to walk differently and talk differently. Expect to be more radiant. Expect compliments regarding the changes. Know that the Above Beings are looking down upon you with approval and pride. After all, you are their child, and they were the ones, really, who molded you and dispatched to you the kind of power you needed. No commercial beauty aid or treatment can touch this power for effectiveness.

The flipside of this ritual is that just as you have become more personally beautiful, you have become to others — and will continue to be in all ways — a more beautiful person. Where true beauty is concerned, the two go hand in hand. The transformation is both external and internal. Your concerns, actions, and attitudes will reflect this, for that is the way it is with Changing Woman and the Sunrise Ceremony Girl. You will recall that the girl does what she does and receives what she receives, not only for herself, but also for all of her people. Hers is a commitment with vicarious rewards. The beauty the Above Beings offer you and desire for you is not only a beauty to behold, it is a beauty whose richness is dedicated to the whole of life, and, like a fine wine, is to savor and enjoy. To make this aspect of your beauty its most effective, review the central teachings of the Apache.

TIPONI
To Measure Your Progress

Are you distressed over your lack of progress or over something regarding your behavior? Would you like a way to measure your progress in life now that you have power and can call in more power? Then make use of the Hopi tiponi, except that you will construct not one tiponi as each of their societies does, but two of them.

Since corn represents life, use two cardboard tubes or two glass jars of equal size, perhaps three inches in diameter and eight or ten inches tall, to make two tiponi bases that represent ears of corn. You can paint the kernel divisions with yellow and black colors on the tubes, or better still (and more permanent), you can obtain a sheet of small yellow tiles from a craft store and stick these on the jars.

Then obtain from a stationery store at least two dozen large cardboard tags that have strings attached. Make a list of the things you have done or achieved in your life that you are proud of. Include statements about your character that you believe are worthwhile. Do not consider your failures; these are about to take care of themselves. Write each one of these things on a tag, put one or more strings or rubber bands around one of the corn symbol tubes or jars, and tie the tags to these. Add to this tiponi objects that will serve as thank offerings to the Above Beings for what you have accomplished.

Now do the same thing with the other jar, except that on these tags you will write the things you hope to and feel you must accomplish. Be bold in this — like the man of La Mancha, reach for the unreachable star. Be sure to include things you know you ought to do for yourself and for others. Add to this tiponi either feathers or small cloth strips in the four colors to represent the four cardinal directions — east, west, north, and south. Then add a green item for Mother Earth and a blue item for the Above Beings.

Now place both tiponis in a small shrine constructed of rocks and flowers. Put the accomplished tiponi on the left, and the to-be-accomplished tiponi on the right. The shrine can be simple, but it must be beautiful, for you are going to have beautiful and positive thoughts about it. It can be placed on a shelf where you will see it often, or it can be set up in a sheltered and secluded place in your garden.

Now take a few minutes to consider what you are about to do with the tiponis. Kneel down facing them while you do this, for you are going to fix your mind and power upon accomplishing each of the things, one at a time, that you have attached to the right-hand tiponi. Decide which one you will tackle first. Make a small paho representing this, and put it out for Sun to work with. In the days immediately ahead, you are going to do it. No questions, no doubts — you are going to do it. And when you have done it, take the tag representing it off of the right-hand tiponi and transfer it to the achievement tiponi on the left. Then go for the next problem. In a much shorter time than you expect, the right-hand tiponi will be empty of its tags, the filled tiponi on the left will be a source of great pride, and you will be ready to pursue entirely new goals that have arisen.

To Remove Fear

The Native Americans made for themselves, and wore in various ways — the most favored of which was to append them to a neck thong — protective medicines. If there are things you fear about yourself or others, protective medicines will help you, too.

Recall that the Native Americans usually employed their medicines to guard them either against some forms of known potential harm or against the frightening unknown. The latter had the added worth of keeping people aware of their needs for the protection only a greater power could offer.

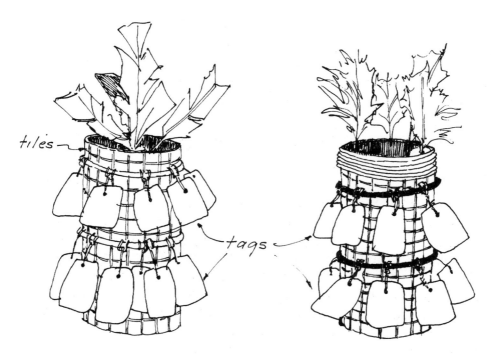

A pair of tiponis

PROTECTIVE MEDICINES

We need to protect ourselves from what are plainly real dangers — or, it is perhaps better said, to allow the Above Beings and their helpers to protect us — from accidents that are serious enough to be debilitating or to kill, and from violence, criminals, fires, storms, and similar menaces. For these, you should make use of Native American protective medicines by employing the medicines as a constant reminder that your best protection is to know and to do the things you ought to do to protect yourself. I do not mean obtaining a gun or other kind of weapon.

In this time and place in history, the Native American medicine people would provide us with medicines whose function is to remind us of steps we should take to keep from making foolish mistakes — mistakes like leaving ourselves vulnerable, being in places it is not wise to be, remaining in scenes that are explosive, or hating instead of loving.

You can do what the Cherokee did and exorcise your home . . . this action also acts as a catalyst to cause you to think about what needs to be done to the home to make it safe. You should regularly purify yourself, eat properly, and exercise regularly, not to keep invading problems such as viruses out, but to keep power and good health in — the fortress idea with a twist.

Crystals

Using crystals in the Cherokee manner helps you determine the true state of your health. If you see yourself as a shadowy figure lying down in the crystal, you are being told that you are not well and that you should do something about it. Improve your attitude, your nutrition, and your exercise program. Check your balance. Make sure you are giving equal care to both mind and body, the secular and the spiritual.

Turquoise

Wear turquoise as the Hopi and Apache do, not only to prevent stress from attacking you, but also to render it harmless and to avoid wasting your energies in attacking it. If you believe you can render stresses harmless, what can they really do to you? Now and then, rub pollen on your body, not to provide a barrier against harm, but to provide a barrier against your doing foolish things that may bring harm to you. This action provides the impetus to weigh situations and make sensible choices, and in any given instance to always ask what you might lose by going along with the crowd. It is the motivation to let go of grudges that could consume you, the motivation to forgive others and to forgive yourself.

Sage Bands

You can weave and wear the sage wrist, ankle, and headbands of the Sioux, not to keep evil from invading you, but to keep yourself from invading evil. Try this and see how reluctant you will be to do some of the things you would otherwise do without a second thought.

Draw a mental shield around yourself, as does that Apache Sunrise Girl when she is massaged, whenever you enter your automobile — not only to protect yourself from other drivers, but also to protect other drivers from you . . . to cause you to let up on the accelerator, to suppress your anger in volatile traffic situations, to avoid passing indiscriminately, to be more courteous and alert, and to keep your vehicle in prime running condition.

In effect, what I am suggesting is that in your use of protective medicines you reverse the flow of your thoughts from the usual outside in to inside out. Let other individuals be protected from you. This is responsible behavior where the welfare of the group comes first, and at the same time, your own best interests are also served. Think of how such an attitude would change the complexion of the work place if everyone adopted it. Of course, doing these things will not keep everything untoward from happening to you, but it will alter the odds substantially.

Thank Offerings

Daily thank offerings are in order. Do not neglect these, for the Above Beings will expect them. Your offerings are a direct measure of how much you appreciate what the Beings are doing for you.

To be effective, your protective medicines can and should be very personalized. They should be attractive and even exotic in their makeup, so that you will want to wear and display them.

CEMENTATION CEREMONY
For Your Unbroken Tie with the Above Beings

It is extremely important to your well-being that you know your love relationship with the Above Beings remains unbroken. Since we finite human beings will fail to measure up now and then and will wonder what this has done to the relationship, remind yourself that everything is well, in Cherokee fashion, by carrying out an annual mental cementation pathway ritual that Archie Sam told me about. New Year's Eve is a good time for this, or you can use the solstices or dates that are particularly warm and memorable in your life.

You may recognize as you read this that Holy Communion serves the same purpose for the Christian. As we carry out this act of obedience, we receive, as Jesus comes to touch us in the bread and wine, our *assurance* that having been forgiven at Baptism, the forgiveness remains, and no act of sin has cut us off from him.

To do the cementation pathway finding, first of all fashion and put out a paho. Then build a questing place in the Sioux manner and, when it is done, put on your finest clothing and stand in the middle of your questing place facing east. Perform the breathing and relaxation exercises in the traditional numbers, and then mentally see the highest and

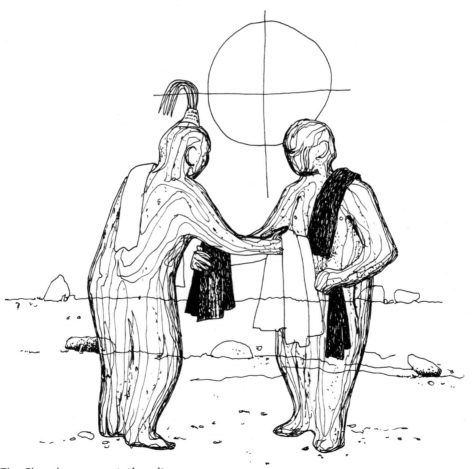

The Cherokee cementation rite

most holy Above Being manifesting himself before you. He will probably be fully clothed in white robes and bathed in dazzling light as Jesus was during the Transfiguration. Next, visualize the two of you exchanging your outer garments. You may want to add some gifts you would like to give. Embrace the Above Being, and know that the bond between you remains unbroken and strong. No spoken words are necessary. When he is ready, he will fade away and disappear. Put out a tangible thank offering. Go about your daily affairs with a light and joyous heart. Know that all is well with you and the Above Beings.

Following this pathway is not presumptuous. The Above Beings will only do what is acceptable and right. What they will reveal of themselves will be only what they wish to reveal. The point of the pathway is not found in what actually occurs. It is in what you are made to think. If in your own mind you envision or "image" the encounter and feel it is real, then the benefits for you will be just as real as if it actually happened.

Along the way, **as you make use of these findings, inner peace,** which is already there in the universe and waiting for you, **is going to come to you and enfold you.** There will be no mistake about it when it happens, for you will have a sublime feeling of comfort, ease, and joy. It will be the peace that passes understanding, a peace that is not like any the world gives. For the first time in your life, you will know what this peace is truly like.

CHAPTER THIRTEEN

Changing Stresses to Strengths

n the introduction to Part Three, I stated that the Hopi nine-day ritual format was primarily for the well-being of the entire village. In this respect, its most productive present-day use will be found in group, small business, or corporate management situations. This is also true for Cherokee organizational insights and certain Sioux and Apache life-way findings.

Nevertheless, individuals can make use of the essences of all the pathway findings. The following material reveals how to do this.

HOPI NINE-DAY RITUAL

You can make effective use of the Hopi nine-day ritual approach whenever a major crisis arises in your life.

For this ritual to be successful, you should recognize that once you decide to use it, you must devote a part of each of nine consecutive days to the ritual. The pathway findings won't work unless you do. You must recognize that it will be a demanding procedure — one that is justified only by a high degree of need. While its nature is preparatory — and it will prepare you to successfully meet future problems associated with the crisis — it will also enable you to manage and put to constructive use an existing crisis. I suggest that you begin it at sunrise on a Saturday morning and end at sundown on the Sunday of the following weekend. If you have a job, you can still do most of what is required on weekday evenings. In preparation for the nine days, on Friday night, purify yourself by one of the immersion methods previously described.

Day One: Entering

In your private room, you must clear away enough floor space to hold the rite. Pushing all of the furniture back to the walls should be sufficient. Purchase at least a half-dozen small but nice gifts to give to the special friends you will invite to dinner on the ninth day of the ceremony. Gather the materials you will need to construct the following: a small altar; a cardboard or plastic strip to make a ring that will serve as the sipapu hole; carved and stick pahos; at least two tiponis; colored sand and a cloth or board for a sand painting or markers and a large sheet of paper on which you will do a painting in lieu of the sand painting; a hood mask for calling back the dead; a medium-sized medicine bowl; a crystal; a whistle; incense; and a bunch of long grass or weeds.

Typical invitation sticks

Extend the invitations for dinner. Use invitation sticks for this as the Sioux did. The illustration on page 266 will serve as your guide in constructing these. The sticks will intrigue your guests and make them want to attend.

Once everything is assembled, make yourself a tiponi to which you attach one or more tags containing a written description of the crisis you face. Then make a carved paho whose symbolic painted designs spell out the prayer you are offering up to the Above Beings. Put the paho out where Sun can pass over it. You know by now what it will be doing for you while you perform the ritual. If you live in your own home, put the tiponi somewhere on the edge of the roof, where it too is exposed to Sun; it will serve as a notification to the powers in general that a nine-day ritual is underway and that you are calling them in to assist you. If you can't put it on the roof, put it somewhere overhead on a second floor or tie it to a ceiling fixture. The tiponi will watch over you and see that you do things correctly. Think constantly about what you are doing; understand that the doing is what is gearing your mind into the thoughts and acts necessary to accomplish your goal.

Let me emphasize again that the main point in our use of this pathway and its parts is not to achieve some magical result that causes the crisis to disappear in a puff of smoke. That might happen, but it probably won't. We aren't dealing with voodoo. The point of the ritual is to develop an attitude and enthusiasm that will enable you to cope with the matter and turn it to your advantage. As we proceed, you will see how this comes about.

During these days, keep your accent on positive thoughts, believing positively that the prayers you are offering up personally and through the tiponis and pahos, together with the obedient and trusting acts you are carrying out, will be fully answered . . . either in the way you hope or, as the Above Beings determine, in a better way. Remember that, for the Hopi, prayer is a form of willing something into being.

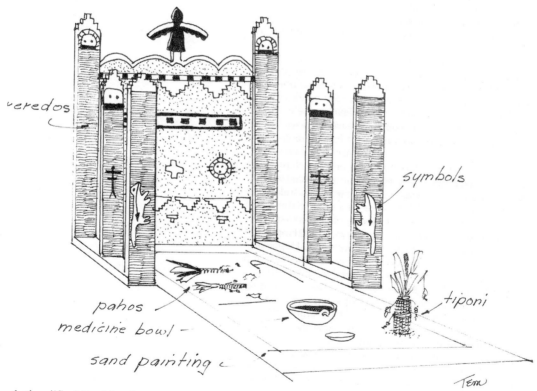

A simplified Pueblo altar made with boards that can be used as a design guide for personal purposes

First, construct your altar, using as your guide the illustrations on pages 82, 83, and 245 and the description given on pages 82 through 85 of the Hopi pathways material. The altar need not be large, and the symbolic designs can be very simple. Place the altar at the east end of your open space, facing toward the center. Put into it a great deal of thought, and remember that even as you fashion it, you are thinking through the things you should and are preparing yourself to meet the problem or problems head-on. Sing as you work, or listen to some music. Be happy. Great things are happening for you.

Next, think of the dead people you would like to call back as well as of the living people you would like to call in to help you with the ceremony and your thoughts. Determine which of them will be the best counselors to offer you the best advice. You want honesty now, not the encouragement of false hopes. Make pahos to represent these people — bent sticks for the older persons, straight ones for the younger. At this point, place the cardboard or plastic ring representing the sipapu on the floor at the west end of your open place and distribute the pahos around its edge.

Now, fashion another tiponi, adding to it feathers of the colors of the four cardinal directions and tags upon which you have described with care the crisis that you face. Use as many tags as are necessary.

Days Two through Four: Positive Preparation

Next, you will make your sand or marker painting. Follow as a general pattern the illustration on page 82, but be certain that the symbols apply to the problem or problems you want to address. The painting need be no larger than twenty by thirty inches. Place it on the floor directly in front of the altar.

On this night, you will go through the previously described ritual for calling back the dead and calling in the living. You will discuss with them the problem at hand. When they arrive, they will enter through the sipapu hole as ghostly figures. Talk with them. Solicit their advice and listen carefully to what they have to say. When you are finished, they will leave through the sipapu hole. It will help to write your thoughts down afterwards, and later, to review them from time to time.

The crisis should be well defined in your mind by now, and solutions should be beginning to form. You are dealing with it in a positive way, and you will be feeling better about it. It is time to offer thanksgiving to the Above Beings and to the powers that serve them.

Fill your bowl with water. Put something into it to make it sweet and sweet smelling; flower petals are excellent for this. Take the bowl outside and place it on the ground where Sun can shine upon it and empower it. Use your crystal to reflect light into the water. Believe that the insights and clarity are coming to you as you do so. Remember, this is "the light that pierces through," the light that will help you to see things you could not see before. Blow incense smoke and the whistle into the bowl. Realize that you are forcing yourself to come to grips with the problem in a way you cannot by abstract thought alone. Then take your grass switch and sprinkle a little of the water from the medicine bowl over the altar, sand painting, tiponi, mask, and pahos. This is a form of blessing that the Above Beings like. It releases power and puts it to work. It is potent. The room is filled with energy. The energy is alive. Feel it!

Day Five: Distribute Pahos at Shrines

The hardest work is over now, and whether or not you've recognized it, the harvest is beginning to come in. Take your stick pahos outside and place them in various places as thank offerings to those who came to help you when you called. On this night, rest and relax. Think warm thoughts about those who have helped you; consider ways in which you can be of help to others. Recognize that you are part of an inter-dependent community that can benefit greatly from your contributions.

Day Six: Nothing Left to Chance

Part of this day will be devoted to reviewing everything you have done and considering why you have done it. Examine the whole of it carefully to see what you may have inadvertently or carelessly left out. If you think of anything, do it now. Plug the gaps. Fill in the depression. Sprinkle more medicine water. Think again about why you are doing all of this.

Day Seven: Making Traditional Food

Prepare now to celebrate your success. Make a dish that includes corn as its principal ingredient. If you do plan to share it with others, make plenty. You will use corn because of its traditional significance. Think about this and think about the successful outcome to your crisis while you are preparing the dish and while it is cooking.

Day Eight: Supplementary Foods

Prepare the salads and other things — everything save those portions you will want to be hot for the victory dinner.

Day Nine: The Feast of Celebration

On the morning of this day, put away your altar and other paraphernalia, and then prepare the final things needed for the Feast of Celebration. You will be feeling very positive and warm by now, and your friends will notice this when they arrive. I suggest that you do not tell them why you are giving the dinner or why you are giving them the gifts at the dinner's end. They will see some of the things you have been fashioning for use with the Native American pathways, and they may want to know about them. If so, discuss as much of it as you like. But keep the secrets regarding the nine-day ritual you are just concluding between yourself and the Above Beings.

What you are doing is your secret. The Above Beings know the details, and they will be continually blessing you. The results will be known soon enough to those who are involved, who, to their amazement, will see you deftly handling the crisis. If any of the guests are among those who were called in to talk with you, give them each a stick-paho, and tell them that someday you will reveal why you are doing so. After dinner, when everyone has gone home, go outside and place a thank offering of food in the ground. Take for granted as you do this that the crisis is resolved. It is either gone, or you will have arrived at ways to handle it effectively.

Days Ten through Thirteen: Self-Denial

In a concentrated act of thanksgiving, you must practice abstinence from salt, fats, and sexual activities. On the morning of the tenth day, preferably at sunrise, you will take the tiponi down from the roof and put it away. At the end of the last day, use ashes in the Hopi fashion to purify yourself and your mask. Put the mask away and listen to some inspirational music. Look up at the sky. Know that the Above Beings are there. They are safely in their house, you are safely in yours, and all is well.

LOVE IS A GIFT . . .

Having a love no one can take away from you is a surpassing gift in the management of stress. Fools Crow learned from the Above Beings and from his center teachings that one's capacity to love and be loved in return is the most vital part of our nature. It is within us from the very beginning — a divinely implanted gift no one can take away from us. We instinctively know how to love. An infant has love that responds to love. This love grows and matures as it feeds on love. No one teaches us to love, but others can help us understand and expand love . . . and we can do the same for them. The love within us is like a seed. Without the proper nourishments, it does not grow, and it fails to express itself. So, Native American parents are expected to feed love to their children. When the children mature, the cycle repeats itself.

The Pathway of Love

The Native American way is to seek to live in an atmosphere of love. Even beyond personal relationships, each of the tribes we are considering has its own approach to this, although they readily admit that part of the time they fail or fall short. Perfection, they say, is not the nature of even those who have received power from the Above Beings.

Today, the Sioux use the colored prayer cloths they place at the base of the Sun Dance pole to serve as prayers for the well-being of all races of mankind. The Cherokee once had an elaborate peace-making ritual in which dancers, whose bodies were painted white, waved white swan-wing fans as a kind of benediction over the tribal leaders who were making peace to purify their thoughts and intentions. The Apache sought an atmosphere of harmony within their own groups, but they did not extend their efforts beyond that. The Hopi applied the "live and let live" theory to life; even when they were not let alone, they were either slow to strike back or did not retaliate at all. One of their tactics was to deprive themselves of possessions and land that anyone else might want and to follow austere customs that no one else would wish to duplicate.

But what do you do when others say or do things to hurt you? It should not surprise you to learn that Fools Crow, gentle and considerate as he is, has endured a considerable amount of hurt. Envy is goading, and more than a few Indians who have resented his serenity, his power, and his achievements have expressed their feelings in hurtful ways.

Fools Crow says that one response to this is to go to war. In earlier times, some of his people made war often. Then perhaps your enemy or you or both of you will be dead. This will end it — for a time at least. But revenge has a way of continuing. It feeds on itself as a fire feeds on a forest. Anger is equally destructive to those who allow it to fester inside. It solves nothing, and it multiplies unhappiness. Another possible response is to try to make peace. This succeeds only when your enemy wishes to do so, too.

Or you can follow the pathway taught by the Above Beings, applying love as the only saving answer. The Above Beings ask that we love our enemies and do good to those who hurt us. We may manage to accomplish reconciliation by this, and it is certainly possible — if the enemy has the same sense of decency and will respond in kind. But if they do not, then the best that loving them can do is allow us to feel better about ourselves, a little more dignified and warmed by the knowledge that we have done what the Above Beings asked us to do. The stress will, however, still be there. It won't have gone away.

Then again, there are those enemies who have learned what the Above Beings ask of us, and they play upon it, using or abusing it for their own ends.

I remember an incident that illustrates this reverse principle very well. Years ago, I was visiting a family who lived in Montana. We adults were in the living room, and the children were playing outside. Suddenly, their eight-year-old son threw the door open, burst into the room, and sobbed, "Daddy, doesn't the Bible say that when someone hits you, you should turn the other cheek?"

His father hugged him and proudly answered, "That is exactly right!"

"Well then," the boy sobbed on, "why is it that whenever I hit Billy, he keeps hitting me back?"

The air that went out of the father was quite discernible.

Meditation as First Response to Conflict

Fools Crow was not taught to turn the other cheek, but he was not taught to go to war either. What he does first of all is withdraw himself from the scene of action and go to his sweatlodge. Here he can put the situation into better perspective and place it in the hands of the Above Beings and the other powers. In the lodge, his spiritual helpers and the rocks speak to him. He asks them to help him evaluate the situation and to give him guidance. He stresses that he needs serenity, so that the information can be viewed in an atmosphere that is devoid of friction. He knows that emotions and stresses can warp judgments and distort vision; that they can balloon things out of all proportion to what they really are. Then in the atmosphere of calmness, he is able to hear even the still, small voices of the spirits as they speak. If in the end, he learns that he is wrong, he will say so publicly and will tell his opponent that.

How do those of you who do not know the secrets of using a sweat-lodge obtain this same serenity? The Native Americans might advise simple meditation — if they truly believed that would do the trick. Meditation is an action, but the Native Americans most often find their answers in forms more active.

Hopi Puppet Stage and Role-Playing

The Hopi have a fruitful technique to aid in quietly sorting out the truth of a situation. They build a puppet stage — sometimes a very impressive one in terms of its design — and put puppet protagonists, including themselves, on it. Then they use role-playing to carefully act out and analyze the situation. By this means — which includes the calling in of the Above Beings, other powers, and the dead — they reach clarification and a solution. As you would expect, pahos are put out to assist them.

You can duplicate this tactic in a simple fashion by putting on your own play. Place two figures — dolls or whatever — on a small stage. One will represent you, the other the person or persons you must deal with. Then play out the situation and roles. While it is admittedly difficult to do so, always attempt to be as fair with the opponent as you are with yourself. Examine motives, justifications, and actions. Ask of each player, "Who am I? What do I want? What are my strengths? What caused this difference of opinion? How do I want it to end? How do the Above Beings want it to end?"

Work everything into a perspective you can deal with. Once you have done this, the situation will be easier to handle. You won't know everything about the enemy, but you will certainly know more than you did when you started. You also will know a great deal more about yourself.

What Is Meant by Love

When you are ready to apply *love* to what you have determined, know first that when Native American holy men speak of love or loving, they recognize the physical aspects . . . that human beings — all nature for that matter — long for loving and being loved in return. Secondly, the holy men think of loving self enough to accept self and of loving others as ourselves — in other words, of loving people as they are, so that one may dislike the act but not the person. In its third and highest sense, they think of love as that which characterizes the relationship each believing person has with the Above Beings.

In making the application, and assuming you have learned that the enemy is truly wrong, you can seek to change their attitude by putting out a prayer cloth whose color represents them. Try using thought transference to influence them. You might try to reason with them. But none of these tactics will entirely solve the problem unless the other is open and receptive. Besides, the Above Beings will not change a person who doesn't want to be changed.

Dilute the Force of Evil Acts

Fools Crow says to focus yourself upon the act rather than upon the person. Dilute the force of the act or whatever the person has said by subjecting it to a kind of love that cannot be returned. The nature of what you do is such that your opponent cannot return it in kind. Let him believe that he has won. Let others think this, too — or whatever else they choose. Walk away. Resolve not to let the act or statement hurt you one iota more. Make for yourself a paho that says this, and know that before long, your true friends will see the truth and will give you whatever comfort and support you need.

Forgiveness

Authors who are active in the stress field say that *forgiveness* is a major key to the reversal of one's attitude and to the restoration of relationships and peace. I certainly agree with the need to forgive one's self and others. Scripture stresses how essential forgiveness is. But at the same time, I must tell you that forgiveness was not a part of the ancient Native American pathways. They were given no concepts of sin and forgiveness. There was a parallel for what we call "the condition of sin" wherein human beings were recognized as at times both capable of ignoring the Above Beings and capable of doing selfish and hurtful things to one another. Accordingly, the education of children included teaching them about proper deportment and the primary welfare of the group — especially tribal expectations. The soldier societies had as one of their main responsibilities the curbing of excesses and selfishness in adults. But so long as people were making their best efforts to comply with the village and tribal rules, they received sympathy when they made mistakes, and there was nothing to forgive them for. On the other hand, except where the peaceful Pueblo and a few other Southwest tribes were concerned, acts of intrusion or violence by other tribes were considered unforgivable, and retaliation was the accepted response.

EXPANDING YOUR MIND

To increase your power for stress control and survival, expand your mind. If you want to practice thought transference, this is an essential preliminary to it.

Today, we recognize that we use only a small portion of our mental capacity. Mind expansion is a process whereby we can use more of it. To expand your mind, follow Fools Crow's guidance regarding the use of the black pipe. But, since the pipe is peculiar to the Indians, employ instead a paho that you will paint entirely black. When you want to look deep within yourself or probe into a realm of consciousness that goes beyond the ordinary, take this black paho to a lonely place and meditate intensely. Place the paho on top of a red cloth on the ground in front of you.

Don't Give Up

As you begin, recall that Fools Crow is dogged in his pursuit of answers from the Above Beings, so be tenacious yourself when you seek to expand your mind. Don't give up easily. Recall also that he warns you to be brave when you do this, for when the answers do come, they will come in a startling way. It will help to set out your flags in the Four Directions, for the answers come from there . . . first in the guise of bright red lights and then in the form of messages. You will either see or hear the messages, and you will often be given a great deal of knowledge in a short period of time. Be prepared for a powerful experience that will nearly overwhelm you. Your mind will expand and contract rapidly as though you have been holding your breath for a long time. When it is over, you will be exhausted, yet wonderfully content. The more often you do this, the faster your mental powers will sharpen and increase.

Becoming

Another method of mind expansion practiced by the Native Americans has been that of *becoming*, which is actually a mind-stretching practice. While it is used in many ways, its primary purpose is to deepen one's relationship with the rest of creation. It is, therefore, an activity that builds harmony and is a great strengthener of inner peace. To do this, you must become something else . . . a rock, a spider, a tree, another person. A faceted crystal will help you consider the various aspects of the subject at hand.

Let us say that the subject you have chosen is a rock . . . something a person would not ordinarily think of becoming. Find an attractive rock you can hold in your hand, and focus your attention upon it. Imagine that you are becoming that rock. Feel its coldness, its firmness, its outer and inner texture, its durability. Reflect upon how some rocks appear to have lasted forever. Think about the ways in which rocks serve humans, and what humans have done with them. Think about the ways in which the Above Beings use rocks and what lessons rocks teach. Open your mind to another kind of consciousness. *Becoming* provides a unique growing experience and develops an appreciation of and closeness with other created things.

THOUGHT TRANSFERENCE

To manage stress by means of thought transference, you must first receive the power to do so through mind expansion, and then recognize the following basics about thought transference.

One of the purposes of thought transference is to let others see, as Fools Crow does, what the Above Beings are doing to and with us. Thought transference is one way we teach and pass on information; we can help others achieve things they otherwise would not or perhaps could not. We can send messages to them. Thought transference enables us to see happening around us what others are blinded to. After all, it is the primary way in which the Above Beings respond to us when we pray.

Remember that requests for this extraordinary ability must be preceded by purification, made in prayer, and intended for only the best purposes. The ability will be given to you in a direct ratio to your good intentions. The ability will probably not come with your first request. You can depend on being tested before this wish is granted. Once you have it, any negative misuse of it will result in the loss of the power.

For Healing

Thought transference is extremely effective in a healing situation wherein the healer wishes to transfer positive thoughts from his or her mind to that of the patient. I do not mean only physical healing; broken hearts and broken lives can also be redirected and restored by thought transference.

Remember that thought transference can only occur between believers. If your disagreement is with an unbeliever, thought transference is not likely to change his viewpoint.

THE SOURCE OF HEALING

In the Native American view, there is a dual source of physical and spiritual healing. The Above Beings are the primary source, and the professional healers and yourself are the secondary one. Recognize then, that thanksgiving for what is accomplished must go to the Above Beings. Whatever assistance you receive and render will have come from them, so self-congratulations are not in order. You should, however, think well of yourself for what you do; some authorities would speak of this in terms of loving yourself, and the Native Americans would not disagree with that point of view.

I have assembled from my research some fundamental teachings regarding Native American contributions in healing. Their similarity to modern health ideas is remarkable and recommends them all the more. As you consider them, do not forget that they complement and do not replace the services of trained physicians.

Begin by recognizing that illness can serve useful functions. For one thing, illness often forces you to think carefully about what is really important in your life. Those who survive serious illnesses seldom return to the fierce pursuit of status or material goods — other things become more valuable, and lifestyles are frequently redirected. Suddenly, the view changes from that of being optimistic about living forever and unhindered on this earth to a vivid realization that every moment counts and is precious. The survivors find more time for God, prayer, family, recreation, and for contributing those things that are truly worthwhile and lasting.

Positive Approach to Illness

Illness teaches those people who recover to recognize that however tragic and costly the experience was, it frequently leads to something worthwhile later on — something that never would have occurred had not the illness led to it. Triumph over a serious illness will teach the patient that when future illnesses do strike, they too can be overcome. Therefore, when the first symptoms of a new illness appear, do not panic and anticipate the worst. Instead, settle back and anticipate the best. Take the positive approach. Remember that you have been ill or hurt before and survived. Then, center your faith in survival again. Know that it will be so. Marshall your physical and mental forces, for this is what balance is all about — the two aspects of your person cooperate in restoration. One does not do the job without the other. The present-day concept of holistic healing supports this entirely.

Medicine Person Doubles Your Healing Power

Where do the holy man and the medicine person fit into this picture? They are an added dimension of faith wherein they share with you the belief that you can and will be healed. This doubles the power available to you. You see them as channels the Above Beings have provided and trained — as people who know the ways — and your own faith increases as it is coupled with theirs. The fear and anxiety you may experience can be incapacitating and can make it very difficult for you to keep a clear and positive mind. The healer is not so burdened and is able to supply clarity, calmness, and hope. As the healer works on you, the power flows through him or her and out to you. Your fear and anxiety subside. Your attention turns away from pain and fear toward optimism and motivation.

Fools Crow told me that every patient needs to know that as soon as an illness invades us, our minds and bodies join together to fight it and overcome it. Therefore, healing is going on even before a patient comes to the healer. In his four days of ritual and treatment, Fools Crow helps the patient focus attention upon this fact. During these days, the patient is turned away from negative thoughts and gradually but firmly toward a state of mind wherein he or she is assured that healing is going on. By the end of the fourth day, no other thought exists. The treatment with herbs, roots, therapeutic touch, and prayers builds steadily to a climax. The healing is accomplished the moment the last treatment is applied. Supplementary treatments may continue for weeks or months, but so far as the healer and patient are concerned, the main job is done.

Mind Is Healed First

In this method then, the first thing healed is the mind, since the patient's negative thoughts are replaced by positive thoughts. Somewhere within the four days of treatment, *inner peace* comes to the patient, and he takes control of himself and his illness.

Love Is the Key

I was profoundly moved to learn that Fools Crow considers love to be the key element in the healing process. What his patients learn is that he loves them, and that the most important medicine he is applying is his love and compassion. Even the application of medicine herbs on the patient's body is done lovingly and thus has therapeutic value. All treatments are gently and compassionately applied. He never hurts a patient by word or deed. The conversations between the two of them reflect this. In time, the patients begin to love him in return. Consequently, it is common for a lifelong bond to form between Fools Crow and his patients. The two become *hunka*. Where patients had once begun to wonder whether they should think of life as ending, they now think of it in terms of beginning and having a worthwhile future.

Just as the Cherokee priests taught, there is a joining, or merging, of human healer and patient in the healing process. In a greater sense, this merging symbolizes the loftier cementing together of the healer, patient, and Above Beings.

As previously stated, Fools Crow's four-day, four-times-a-day treatment does not always effect a complete cure within that period of time.

In these instances, his patients continue to take medicine and perform certain exercises until they are entirely well. However, the mental and spiritual healing that lies at the center of every healing rite does occur by the end of the fourth day. If any illness remains, it is only the physical aspect. This is true of the healing procedures of all of the tribes considered in this book.

BALANCE

It is vital to recognize that the balance of mind and body is an integral part of healing, as well as part of the general welfare of the person. Mind and body are interdependent; what one does affects the other in a positive or negative way. If, for example, the mind is negative, it will not assist the body. In fact, it will drain the body, reducing its ability to function. The reverse is also true, for the body can do the same thing to the mind. Review the Cherokee material on healing to see how they made good use of this principle. Notice that their harmonizing of mind and body was a primary key to success. When each of the two aspects of the person received the care it deserved, the two worked in concert to root out and dispense with the causes and complications of illnesses. If you properly care for your mind and body — and this includes such interrelated things as abstinence, proper nutrition, exercise, personal dignity, honor, and shared responsibility — then you will be balanced, healthy, energized, alert, and able to respond to any emergency.

Kinds of Balance

Balance has been a truly comprehensive term for the Native Americans. Among the tribes we are considering, there were several aspects to balance, and all of these were interdependent and interrelated. There was a need for balance between mind and body, for spiritual and physical balance, for balance in scope and pace of secular activities, in ritual performance and in warfare. When judiciously combined and executed, these balances assured for both individuals and the nation harmony, well-being, and firm inner peace.

By balance, the Native Americans mean that the two sides of each of the above aspects deserve equal attention. If either side is neglected or favored, if the attention is in any sense lopsided, balance is destroyed. The individual or the nation will suffer accordingly. We should pay careful attention to keeping balance in our lives. We must see that mind and body receive equal care and attention. Neither side should be in any way favored or in any way neglected. Both sides must be equally nourished with love and with all else required for their healthy function, today and in the future.

The amount of time we give to each side of each facet and the way we handle and think about time are factors of consequence. The ancient Native Americans learned that where heart, soul, mind, and body were concerned, time was best thought of in terms of seasons. They knew about sundials and solar calendars, but they recognized that things were best done within proper seasons or within large blocks of time, rather than according to tight schedules of set hours or minutes. This relaxed attitude reduced pressure and allowed them the space needed to think about what they were doing and why they were doing it. In our industrialized world, we cannot adjust entirely to this idea, but we can at least apply it to those times and activities we can control.

Procrastination as an Art

The Native Americans even practiced the fine art of procrastination, which is almost a lost art today. Whenever a task could be put off until tomorrow or the week or month after, it was put off, and the people indulged in recreation instead. "Burnout" was not a term they would have understood or sympathized with. The Indians were not compulsive doers. They didn't exhaust their strength before old age. They saved something for the last lap, enjoyed the full race, didn't drop out, and seldom suffered the debilitations so many of us do today. Were they wise, or were they lazy? As you think about that, consider this — they had stresses, but few of them were self-made. Most came from outside sources. With all of our conveniences, we are somehow busier than ever. We feel guilty about taking naps, we bring work home from the office, and we plan weekends and vacations with military efficiency. Not until our lives are threatened do we sit down to consider what really matters and ask ourselves what we should really be putting our energies into.

In August of 1987, *USA Today* carried a report on the subject "Your Time." In this report, they noted that the folks in Salem, Oregon, defied the ticking of the clock every day by squeezing in a few hours to fish or hike, by volunteering for everything from Scouts to schools, and by setting their watches ahead and keeping their calendars in line. According to the newspaper's poll, fifty-five percent of Salem's adults feel they haven't nearly enough time to do everything they want to do. Does this indicate a problem? Forthcoming articles would deal with "How the time crunch affects our relationships"; "How to take control of your time — hints for organizing your days"; "Readers' tips on making the most of your time"; and "Making your leisure time work for you." I noticed that there were no articles on procrastination.

The cover story concluded with the statement that as a nation we zoom through life in fast-forward. We are in a desperate race against time, a kind of temporal gridlock. Most people are constantly on the run, and by the end of each day, time will have taken entire families hostage. Time pressure, the article says, affects how we behave as families, as fellow citizens, as fellow workers; how we perform, spend our money, and most of all, how we feel about everything. Our highly automated computer culture is creating shorter attention spans in children *and adults*, impatience and greater hostility, intolerance and social alienation in us all. Workaholism has become so ingrained a habit that many of us don't know how to do otherwise. Some people have even convinced themselves that they like going at this pace . . . until the day arrives when suddenly they realize that their children have grown up without them and they've had no time to stop and smell the flowers . . . which will be rather hard to do from the underside of a grave.

Variation, sleep, relaxation, and play perform important roles in retaining proper balance.

The Native Americans learned from the Above Beings that variation in pace kept them alert and interested, since it reduced boredom. So they varied the pace and intensity of what they did during the day and during ceremonies. They made certain that nothing was entirely predictable, always including elements of surprise, mystery, and unexpected involvement. Sleep, relaxation, and play helped break the rituals of work, warfare, and spiritual pursuits, so that the rituals did not upset people's sense of balance.

Even with a simpler lifestyle than ours, there was never enough time for the Native Americans to do everything they wanted to do. So they took the time to determine what was important and what was not. Once this was established, they made certain the former was accomplished and worried very little about the rest. They also developed cooperatives to share the work, so that no one person ever had the pressure of having to do everything himself. This offered more free time to everyone and allowed for individual creative and recreational pursuits. Arts and crafts flourished, and beauty and happiness abounded.

Sleep

With few exceptions, waking and sleeping time followed the daylight and darkness pattern of nature. Other than on those enthralling nights when ritual, socializing, or story-telling was afoot, people went to bed early and arose early. Cherokee customs regarding this have much to recommend them. You will recall that they used the seven heavens concept to put themselves happily to sleep. You can do this, too, by imagining that at each of the seven levels, loving beings are thronging around you to care for your concerns and needs. Concentrate as intensely as possible on the idea that everything needful to your well-being is being attended to. Remember that the kinds of beings at each level will vary. In time, you will know them as concerned friends — like the 405 White Stone Men of the Sioux.

In the morning, follow the ancient Cherokee custom of setting your natural clock to awaken you early (you can use your alarm clock until the habit is ingrained) so you can prepare yourself for the coming day. Preparation for the day done during the morning is far more productive than attempting preparation before you go to sleep. The Cherokee would lie in bed and awaken slowly. They first stretched and luxuriated under their warm robes. Then they turned their attention to playing out in their thoughts what the day held for them and how they would accomplish the vital things. You can profit from this pathway. Play out your day. Consider especially how you will handle those things or persons who have proven difficult and how you want to encounter new challenges. Consider how you can remain positive and optimistic throughout the day. Call upon the powers of the Four Directions to assist you in this. Hang a string of tobacco offerings on the headboard of your bed and use it daily like prayer beads to call in good spirit helpers. This ritual need not take long, and the more you do it, the swifter it will proceed and the more effective it will become. But see what a difference it will make in your day. By the time you have risen and purified yourself in the shower, you will be refreshed, confident, and ready to go.

Thankful Meditation

While you play, take advantage of the opportunities offered to think about the Above Beings. Be conscious of their concern for your health and happiness, and stop to thank them for what nature contributes. When, for example, you sunbathe at the beach, close your eyes and think about spiritual and uplifting things. Recognize that the warmth that touches you is the warmth of the Above Beings who are nourishing, enriching, and energizing you. Soak that up together with the sun's rays. As the Sunrise Girl does, acknowledge that while the Above Beings are making you more beautiful outwardly, they are also giving you the power to be a more beautiful person.

NUTRITION AND EXERCISE

Nutrition and exercise are integral components of a healthy mind and body.

I say less about nutrition and exercise than other areas of life, not because I fail to see their immense value and necessity, but because the lifestyle of the ancient Native Americans was such that good nutrition and regular exercise were built into it. Their daily tasks required strenuous manual labor, and most of their play forms were vigorous. Their menus were simple compared to those of today and, for the most part, were comprised of wholesome foods. White traders commonly reported that prior to the adaptation of white ways, they seldom saw an overweight Indian; diabetes, ulcers, high blood pressure, and high cholesterol were unknown to the natives before the reservation period — as were birth defects and deformities.

Nevertheless, it is essential to follow sensible nutritional and exercise habits today, and while I say little regarding these here, I do heartily recommend that you make them part of your pathway findings.

OTHER HEALING TECHNIQUES

Recall the Apache view that the healing powers work best in a positive atmosphere of happiness. The opposite attitude conveys an impression of doubt and defeat. Therefore, avoid placing restraints upon the conduct of those who seek to assist and comfort you or others. Encourage them to socialize, laugh, and joke. Join in with them so far as you are able. Happiness is as much a treatment as anything else. Encourage all who are present to think positive thoughts. Recognize that they are present because they care. Someone should take the lead and give everyone something useful to do. Employ pollen blessings and music. Although I recognize why it is so, one of the great sadnesses I experience as a pastor is when I walk down pristine hospital corridors on my way to see a patient and am greeted by nothing but awesome silence. In Native American healing rituals, that has never been so.

Heal at Night

Try practicing your healing, self or otherwise, at night as the Apache did. Recall that this offers you the advantage of a time period when you will not be distracted by the usual things you would do and see in the daytime. Furthermore, the darkness forms an aura of wonder and inspires spiritual thoughts. Be certain also that the healing ritual lasts long enough to phase gradually in and out. How else can you think through all that you should? Make use of crystals and pahos; wear protective amulets. Recall that the Cherokee used the facets of the crystals to help them view every side of a problem or a hope. As you do this, remember that it is not the object itself that matters, but what you are forced to think through as you employ and fashion pahos, masks, tiponis, or like items. It is the clarity and effectiveness of thought that results from the effort that truly counts.

Touching

Do not forget that whether it is done with the hands or the mind, touching is a therapeutic force. One is not separate from the other; where one is used, the other is involved. When touching or being touched, the Native American takes for granted that a power transfer from the Above Beings is taking place. In other words, the Above Beings do the touching through a person or people who are tubes. Touching is looked upon as an expression of loving care, and it is essential in the healing process. The willingness to touch shows that there is no fear of being contaminated by the person being touched and that any forgiveness being offered is genuine. To see this more clearly, imagine a situation wherein two people have had a serious falling out. If one person comes to the other and asks for forgiveness, and the other person agrees but will not hug or touch the former, then the person making the overture is not likely to feel forgiven. If, on the other hand, there is touching, then both people will feel that forgiveness has really taken place. Touching is a remover of barriers, a restorer of relationships.

Cherokee Use of Acupressure

Archie Sam has told us that the Cherokee medicine persons practiced *acupressure* during his lifetime, and we know from historical research that its roots lie deep in Cherokee antiquity. He revealed also that his father, White Tobacco Sam, used acupressure to treat patients. In comparing what Archie said to present-day practices here and in other parts of the world, it appears that the Cherokee used fewer pressure points, but worked in the same ways. Essential in their application was first warming their hands over a small fire; they believed that through this act the Above Beings were sending the warmth of their person through the fire and the medicine person to the patient. The patient knew this and needed to believe it absolutely in order for the treatment to work. Sometimes the ancient practitioners simply pressed their warmed hands over the place where the pain was most acute. Other times, they would use pressure points and massage them in the same way as it is done today.

As Archie understood it, his father knew nothing of the meridians or blood-flow lines that are presently followed to relieve tension. But he did know about blocked blood flow and the problems resulting from tensing the neck and shoulders. To treat headaches, he either rubbed the patient above the eyebrows or found the point of tenderness at the base of the thumb or wrist and massaged immediately above or below that point. Other favored pressure points were above the shoulder blades and on the neck muscles just below the ear lobes.

White Tobacco Sam's favored massaging places for the relaxation of tension were the cheeks, up and down the insides and outsides of the arms and legs, and the entire back, including the back of the neck. He stressed to Archie that all of this should be done with utmost gentleness and love, that the pressure should never be applied for more than two minutes in any one spot, and that no harm would be done to the patient as long as the pressure was applied slowly and in a relaxed way. It was essential also that the patient be as relaxed as possible during acupressure or massage, with eyes closed and limbs limp.

Contemporary practitioners of acupressure believe that the technique works because it releases endorphins into the body, which are thought to be natural painkillers whose power is greater than artificial painkillers. Once you learn the technique, you can apply acupressure to yourself almost as well as a skilled professional. You must, however, observe the rules of caution just mentioned in order to avoid doing yourself damage. Properly applied, acupressure can serve as a daily recharging experience. When combined with meditation, it is known to provide an exceptional sense of well-being. There is much to recommend it. If a fireplace or pit is not available, use a heating pad to warm your hands. What matters is not so much the means you use as what you believe is happening. If you believe that the power of the Above Beings is coming to you through the heat source, then it will come.

Take Time for Healing Meditation

One other thing must be emphasized about those instances when you want to undertake self-healing — Fools Crow and his peers do not believe that you can just will away a physical problem by developing a positive state of mind about it, then going on about your business. Similarly, you cannot heal by sending an occasional healing message to the location of the problem. You must go to a quiet place where you can be alone, sit down, put aside all thoughts, prepare yourself, pray, and then concentrate fiercely upon the problem for several hours. Take hold of it, wrestle with it, and do not let it go until an answer comes. Many Native Americans who have done this report that ultimately they reached a point where the pain and the problem simply melted away — and stayed away.

In A.D. 270, the scholar Plotinus wrote, "And if you do not find yourself beautiful yet, act as the creator of a statue that is to be made beautiful: He cuts away here, he smoothes there, he makes this line lighter, the other purer, until a lovely face has grown upon his work. So do you also: Cut away all that is excessive, straighten all that is crooked, bring light to all that is overcast, labour to make all one glow of beauty and never cease chiseling your statue, until there shall shine out on you from it the godlike splendor of virtue, until you shall see the perfect goodness surely established in the stainless shrine."

Improve the Manner and Quality of Your Life

What Plotinus says is a kind of summary of what the Above Beings taught the Native Americans: The most effective approach to life at its best and worst is to consider it a reshaping process with an attainable goal. Included in the process is the distinct call for a change and improvement in — an upgrading of — the quality of your life. One who wishes to win the battle against stress and to have inner peace must give careful thought to the changes required here.

The Native Americans improved their quality of life by immersing themselves more deeply in spiritual pursuits. The greater the need, the deeper the immersion. This can certainly be a solution for you, and I recommend it, but there are associated avenues you can take in the secular realm.

Our affluent life — with its technological advances, tranquilizers, alcohol, drugs, frenetic music, gory films, frantic pursuit of excitement, and promiscuous sex — has brought no one inner peace and security.

Ask yourself if you should not seek instead regular periods of simple tranquility. Suppose you turn to music that is soothing and melodic, either classical or modern, and you become a student of restful art. Suppose you spend more time alone with nature and go to the great writers, past and present. Let your senses relax now and then. Work harder at understanding people. Improve family relationships and your relationships with good and trusted friends. Put the group ahead of yourself.

Remember the need for regular renewal. Recall how each of the tribes we have considered provided for that, how they considered renewal essential to their general health and progress. Remember to prepare in advance for what you know will come or may come. Etch into your memory the Sioux emphasis upon annual renewal, rebirth, procreation, and special thanksgiving. These are sustaining factors that will buoy you up and carry you. Above all, hold fast to the new center you have found.

While I emphasize that the Native Americans thought in terms of needs, the Above Beings also taught them to ask for what they wanted. If it was good, it would be given to them. Therefore, it is perfectly acceptable to follow the Cherokee pathway of using prayer formulas and masks to draw closer to you the things you desire. The Sioux, Crow, and Mandans had ways of doing this. One way involved a women's society whose secret rites gave them the ability to call the buffalo closer, thus making the hunters' task easier. To multiply what you hope for, save some of each year's grains in multiples of seven — like the seven ears of corn the Cherokees saved from each year's crop — and pray with these. Then add them to the harvest you receive during the next year and consume both together. This is a recognition of the Above Beings' faithfulness to provide. Be certain to define your wants — if you say you want money, you are asking only for a means to something . . . what is the money for? You must ask for what you really want.

The Indians would caution you to never get carried away with what you achieve to the point of pride or flattered ego. The Hopi have Sacred Clowns who share in all of their religious performances. The clowns play a dual role: They cheer the people up in times of depression or sadness, and they do ribald things to bring the people down to earth when they have become too enamored with themselves over what they are doing. Their foolish behavior shows the people what they ought not to do. You must develop that same mentality. Compared to the Above Beings, we are limited and dependent. Remember that whenever we make it to the top in whatever we are doing, we will not have made it on our own without their help.

Finally, bear firmly in mind that physicians and professionals in the psychology field are saying today that people who confront stresses head on and take action to solve their problems are proving themselves to be the best managers of stress. I personally know of no better nor more thorough approach to action than the Native American pathways. I have by no means exhausted in this book the number and kinds of Native American pathways. Were I to do that, the book would run to a thousand pages or more. What I have done is to lay out for you the main pathways of four tribes. As you follow these, you will come to understand the ways. Take it from there on your own. You will become creative in employing the pathways, and by going back into the body of the book, you will be able to make use of a number of the central and peripheral pathways that I did not discuss in Part Three.

Instead of following a pattern of life that amounts to a death wish, you must now make a life wish for a new and wonderful fullness of life. It is offered to you here, and it is yours for the taking.

Although you, as a non-Indian, will not become an Indian, you nevertheless will be able to think and feel like an Indian medicine person. Your stress demons will not like your doing this, and they will do their best to dissuade you. Listen instead to the Above Beings, and let them lead you to *positive action and a glorious inner peace!*

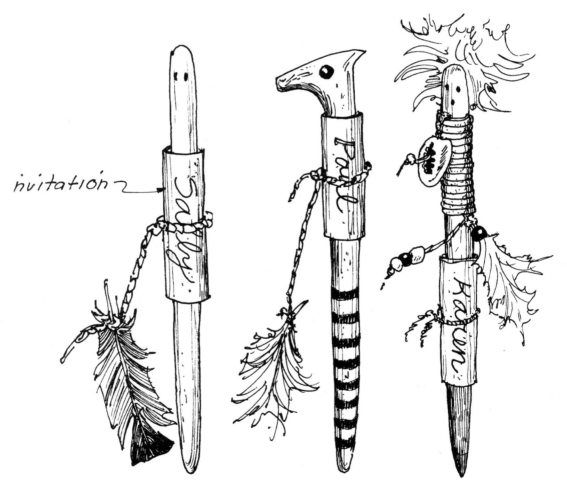

Typical invitation sticks

MUSEUMS AND RESEARCH FACILITIES

Please Note: Most of the Web addresses listed below will take users straight to the departments that are the subjects of this guide. However, please remember that due to the rapid pace of change in cyberspace, any and all of these Web addresses may change without notice.

SPECIAL ON-LINE RESOURCES

Oklahoma – Complete listing of Oklahoma Indian attractions:
http://greatspirit.earth.com/attract.html

New Mexico – Complete listing of museums and monuments in New Mexico.
http://www.nmculture.org/cgi-bin/instview.cgi?_cat=Native+American&_ext=+Museums+and+Monuments

United States – Complete listing of Native American museums around the country.
http://www.hanksville.org/NAresources/indices/NAmuseums.html

INSTITUTIONAL ADDRESSES & ON-LINE RESOURCES

Ableza Institute
1279 Mildred Avenue
San Jose, CA 95125
408-267-4609
Ableza@ableza.org

Ableza is a Native American arts and media institute dedicated to promoting, preserving and protecting traditional and contemporary arts by Native American peoples. http://www.ableza.org/

The Amerind Foundation

Off Interstate 10 take the Dragoon Road exit (318)

Texas Canyon, AZ
520-586-3666
Open: 10 a.m.-4 p.m. daily (fall, winter, spring)
Wed -Sun. 10 a.m.-4 p.m. (summer)

The Amerind Foundation, Inc. is a private, non-profit archaeological research facility and museum devoted to the study and interpretation of Native American cultures. Amerind is located in Southeastern Arizona in the beautiful Dragoon Mountains.
http://www.amerind.org/

Apache Cultural Center & Museum

Ft. Apache, AZ
928-338-4625
Open: Mon- Fri. 8 a.m.-5 p.m.
Sat. 8 a.m- 5 p.m. (summer only)

Established in 1969, the White Mountain Apache Cultural Center stands as a monument to the tribe's historical resiliency and ongoing commitment to celebrate and perpetuate Apache heritage. The Cultural Center serves as a repository for the tribe's cultural heritage through the preservation of oral histories, archival materials and objects of cultural, historical and artistic significance to the White Mountain Apache people.

Ataloa Lodge Museum

2299 Old Bacone Rd.
Muskogee, OK 74403-1508
888-682-5514 Ext. 7283
Open: Wed-Sat. 8 a.m.-5 p.m.
Sun. 1-5 p.m.

The historic Ataloa Lodge Museum is located on the scenic campus of Bacone College in Muskogee, Oklahoma. Ataloa Lodge Museum has one of the finest collections of American Indian artifacts in the USA.
http://www.wmat.nsn.us/wmaculture.shtmlhttp://www.bacone.edu/ataloa/

Cherokee National Museum

P.O.Box 515
Tahlequah, OK 74465-0515
918-456-6007
Open: Mon.-Sat. 10 a.m.-6 p.m.
Sun. 1-5 p.m.

A 20,000-square-foot building houses the Cherokee National Archives, the official archives of the Cherokee Nation, and the library, which consists of over 4,000 volumes related to Cherokee history and culture, including special collections of out-of-print bibles, books in the Cherokee language, and photographs related to Indian Territory. Approximately 55 hours of oral history tapes provide other research sources.
http://www.powersource.com/heritage/museum.html

Frisco Native American Museum and Natural History Center
P.O. Box 399
Frisco, NC 27936
252-995-4440
Open: Tues-Sun. 11 a.m.-5 p.m.

The Frisco Native American Museum and Natural History Center is a non-profit educational foundation created for the purpose of preserving Native American artifacts, art, and culture. Housed in a building with a 100 years of history, the Frisco Native American Museum & Natural History Center contains a nationally recognized collection of Native American artifacts, exhibits, and natural history displays.
http://nativeamericanmuseum.org/

Gilcrease Museum of American History and Art
1400 North Gilcrease Museum Road
Tulsa, Oklahoma 74127-2100
918-596-2700
Toll-free phone number: 888-655-2278
Open Tues.-Sun.10 a.m.-4 p.m. Closed Mondays & Christmas Day.

The Gilcrease archaeological collections encompass the Mississippi Valley (present-day Illinois and Arkansas), the Southwestern U.S. (Colorado, New Mexico, Arizona), and ancient Mexico, and include one of North America's most important collections of pre-Columbian projectile points (arrow and spear heads). Objects from 19th- and early 20th-century American Indian communities on the Great Plains are well-represented in the anthropology section, including important collections of moccasins, parfleches (rawhide containers), clothing, tools, and other items from the Kiowa, Comanche, Lakota (Sioux), Osage, Arapaho, and Cheyenne groups. Commissioned works by contemporary craftspeople and artisans preserve and develop traditional arts and techniques; and notable new collections document the arts of the Native American Church, the Native peoples of Mexico, and the Indian Nations of the Southeastern United States. Recent exhibitions have included Children of the Sun: Euchee Indian Culture and Tradition (1998) and Symbols of Faith and Belief: The Art of the Native American Church (1999). The museum's extensive archival collections include the papers of Cherokee Chief John Ross and those of Choctaw Chief Peter Pitchlynn,
www.gilcrease.org

Heard Museum

2301 North Central Avenue
Phoenix, AZ 85004-1323
800-252-8344
Open: 10 a.m.-5:30 p.m. daily

The Heard Museum's website contains information and history of the museum, information about current and upcoming exhibitions, a calendar of events, and an online store.
http://www.heard.org/

Indian City USA

Located 2 miles southeast of Anadarko, OK
Open: 9 a.m.-6 p.m. daily
800-433-5661

According to their website, Indian City is one of the Southwest's largest American Indian museums. The Indian City Museum was established to preserve items of Indian origin from the early years to the present.
http://www.indiancityusa.com/home.asp

Journey Museum, The

222 New York Street
Rapid City, South Dakota 57701
605-394-6923
Open: Mon.-Sun. 9 a.m.-5 p.m. (summer)
Mon.-Sat. 10 a.m.-5 p.m.; Sun 1-5 p.m. (winter)

The Sioux Indian Museum at The Journey Museum devotes its exhibitions to the past and present creative achievements of American Indian and Alaskan artists and crafts people.
http://www.journeymuseum.org/english/thecollections/sioux/

Museum of Indian Arts & Culture

PO Box 2087
Santa Fe, NM 87504-2087
505-476-1250
Open: Tues-Sun. 10 a.m.-5 p.m.

The Museum of Indian Arts & Culture, one of four museums in the Museum of New Mexico system, is a premier repository of Native art and material culture and tells the stories of the people of the Southwest from pre-history through contemporary art. The museum serves a diverse, multicultural audience through changing exhibitions, public lectures, field trips, artist residencies, and other educational programs.
http://www.miaclab.org/indexfl.html

Museum of Northern Arizona

3101 North. Fort Valley Road
Flagstaff, AZ 86001
928-774-5213
Open: 9 a.m.-5 p.m. daily

The Museum of Northern Arizona has created a dynamic and ever-evolving community where people of all ages, interests, and cultures come to build relationships with each other on a forested, nearly 225-acre intergenerational campus. The intergenerational campus includes the Museum and its treasure house repositories for more than five million Native American artifacts, natural science specimens, and fine art pieces.

Museum of the Cherokee Indian

P.O. Box 1599
Cherokee NC 28719
828-497-3481
Open: 9 a.m.- 5 p.m. daily

The Museum of the Cherokee Indian has just installed a completely new exhibit that combines computer generated imagery, special effects, and audio with an extensive artifact collection. This $3.5 million dollar project tells the story of the Cherokee and their ancestors from twelve thousand years ago through the present. Learn who the Cherokee are and why they are still here.
http://www.musnaz.org/http://www.cherokeemuseum.org/

Museum of the Native American Resource Center

PO Box 1510
Pembroke, NC 28372-1510
910-521-6282

The Museum of the Native American Resource Center contains exhibits of authentic Indian artifacts, arts and crafts. These items come from Indian people all over North America. The Native American Resource Center is a multi-faceted museum and research institute of The University of North Carolina at Pembroke. The Center's mission is to educate the public about the rich diversity of Native America.
http://www.uncp.edu/nativemuseum/

Museum of the Red River

812 East Lincoln Road
Idabel, OK 74745
580-286-3616
Open: Tues-Sat. 10 a.m.-5 p.m.
Sun 12 p.m.-4 p.m.

Some of the finest examples of American Indian art and artifacts are found at the Museum of the Red River. Housing over 20,000 objects in its collections, the Museum sponsors exhibits, lectures, and other programs, and supports ongoing

research efforts in the study of American native peoples.
http://www.museumoftheredriver.org/

National Museum of the American Indian
Smithsonian Institution
One Bowling Green
New York, NY 10004
Phone: 212-514-3700

This is the Smithsonian Institution's National Museum of the American Indian. The site has information about exhibitions (date, location, and topic), books, music, film & video, calendar of events, and more.

Palace of the Governors
POB 2087
Santa Fe, NM 87504-2087
505-476-5112

The Palace of the Governors, sit Native American artists and craftspeople who sell their handmade goods to tourists and local Santa Feans almost every day of the year, rain or shine. The 900+ vendors represent forty-one tribes including the Apache (Jicarilla & Mescalero) and Hopi tribes.
http://www.nmai.si.edu/ http://www.newmexicoindianart.org/

Red Earth Museum
2100 NE 52nd St
Oklahoma City, OK 73111-7107
405-427-5228
Open: Tues – Fri 9 a.m. to 5 p.m.
Sat. 9 a.m.-6 p.m.
Sun. 11 a.m.-6 p.m.

The Red Earth Museum has been home to the southwest's most extensive display of Native American cradleboards. The renowned Deupree Cradleboard Collection features outstanding examples of Native American craftsmanship representing Native American nations, tribes and bands from throughout the United States.
http://www.redearth.org/museum.htm

Southern Plains Indian Museum, The
P.O. Box 749
Anadarko, Oklahoma 73005
Open: June-Sept., Mon.-Sat. 9 a.m.-5 p.m.; Sun. 1 p.m.-5 p.m.
Oct.-May, Tues. – Sat. 9 a.m.-5 p.m.; Sun. 1 p.m.-5 p.m.
Closed: New Years Day, Thanksgiving, Christmas

The Southern Plains Indian Museum exhibits the creative achievements of Native

American artists and craftsmen of the United States. A permanent exhibit presents the rich diversity of historic arts of the tribal peoples of western Oklahoma, and a special exhibition gallery is devoted to changing presentations promoting the creative works of outstandingly talented contemporary Native American artists and craftsmen.

http://www.tulsaweb.com/spi-mus.htm

TRIBAL HEADQUARTERS

APACHE

Apache Tribe of Oklahoma
P.O. Box 1220
Anadarko, OK 73005
405-247-9493

Fort McDowell Mohave-Apache Indian Community
Post Office Box 17779
Fountain Hills, AZ 85269-7779
480-837-5121
http://www.ftmcdowell.org/

Fort Sill Apache Tribe of Oklahoma
RR 2 Box 121
Apache, OK 73006
405-588-2298
http://fsat.tripod.com/

Jicarilla Apache Tribe
P.O. Box 507
Dulce, NM 87528
505-759-3242
http://www.jicarillaonline.com/

Mescalero Apache Tribe
P.O. Box 227
Mescalero, NM 88340
505-671-4494 or 505-464-4494
http://www.newmexico.org/culture/res_mescalero.html

San Carlos Apache Tribe
P.O. Box 0
San Carlos, AZ 85550
928-475-2361

Tonto Apache Tribe
Tonto Reservation #30
Payson, AZ 85541
928-474-5000
http://www.commerce.state.az.us/pdf/commasst/comm/tonto.pdf

White Mountain Apache Tribe
P.O. Box 700
Whiteriver, AZ 85941
928-338-4346 or 877-338-9628 Ext. 373
http://www.wmat.nsn.us/

Yavapai-Apache Nation
2400 W. Datsi
Camp Verde, AZ 86322
928-567-3649
http://www.itcaonline.com/Tribes/campverd.htm and
http://www.yavapai-apache-nation.com/

CHEROKEE

Cherokee Nation
P.O. Box 948
Tahlequah, OK 74465
918-456-0671
http://www.cherokee.org/

Cherokees of Southeast Alabama (State Recognized)
2212 50th St.
Valley, AL 36854
334-756-2889
http://aiac.state.al.us/cherokees.htm

Cherokee Tribe of Northeast Alabama (State Recognized)
53 Buckworth Circle
Trafford, AL 35172
205-681-0080
http://www.tsalagi.org/

Eastern Band of Cherokee Indians
P.O. Box 455
Cherokee, NC 28719
800-438-1601
http://www.cherokee-nc.com/

United Keetoowah Band of Cherokee Indians
P.O. Box 189
Parkhill, OK 74451
918-431-1818

HOPI

Hopi Tribe
P.O. Box 123
Kykotsmovi, AZ 86039
928-734-2441 or 928-734-3000
http://www.hopi.nsn.us/

SIOUX

Cheyenne River Sioux Tribal Council
Post Office Box 590
Eagle Butte, SD 57625
605-964-4155 or 7275
http://www.sioux.org/

Crow Creek Sioux Tribal Council
P.O. Box 658
Fort Thompson, SD 57339
605-245-2221
http://www.travelsd.com/history/sioux/crowcrek.htm

Flandreau Santee Sioux
Post Office Box 283
Flandreau, SD 57028
605-997-3981

Fort Peck Tribal Council
Assiniboine & Sioux Tribes
P. O. Box 1027
Poplar, MT 59255
406-768-5155
http://tlc.wtp.net/fortpeck.htm

Lower Brule Sioux Tribal Council
P.O. Box 187
Lower Brule, SD 57548
605-473-5561
http://www.mnisose.org/profiles/lwrbrule.htm

Lower Sioux Mdewakanton Community
RR 1 Box 308
Morton, MN 56270-9801
507-697-6185
http://www.indians.state.mn.us/lowsioux.html

Oglala Sioux Tribal Council
P. O. Box H #468
Pine Ridge, SD 57770
605-867-5821
http://www.mnisose.org/profiles/oglala.htm

Prairie Island Community Council (Minnesota Mdewakanton Sioux)
1158 Island Boulevard
Welch, MN 55089-9540
612-388-2554
http://www.prairieisland.org/

Rosebud Sioux Tribe
PO Box 430
Rosebud, SD 57570
605-747-2381
http://www.rosebudsiouxtribe.org/

Santee Sioux
425 Frazier Ave N. Suite 2
Niobrara, NE 68760
402-857-2302
http://www.santeedakota.org/

Shakopee Mdewakanton Sioux
2330 Sioux Trail NW
Prior Lake, MN 55372
952-496-6173
http://www.ccsmdc.org/

Sioux Valley Dakota Nation
P.O. Box 38
Griswold, Manitoba
R0M 0S0
204-855-2671
http://www.dakotanation.com/

Sisseton – Wahpeton Sioux Tribal Council
P.O. Box 509
Agency Village, SD 57262
605-698-3911
http://www.swcc.cc.sd.us/swst.htm

Standing Rock Sioux
P.O. Box D
Fort Yates, ND 58538
701-854-7201
http://www.standingrock.org/

Upper Sioux Community
P. O. Box 147
Granite Falls, MN 56241
612-564-2360
http://www.indians.state.mn.us/upsioux.html

Yankton Sioux
Post Office Box 248
Marty, SD 57361
605-384-3804
http://www.travelsd.com/history/sioux/yankton.htm

ANNUAL EVENTS

Sources for Powwows, Concerts, and Other Events

Crazy Crow Trading Post
1801 Airport Road
Pottsboro, TX 75076
800-786-6210

http://www.crazycrow.com/ This website has a huge selection of Native American merchandise. In addition, you will find calendars with information about powwows and reenactments sites across the country.

Earth Circles
3320 E. 54th Street
Minneapolis, Minnesota 55417
612-729-2014

http://earthcirclesminnesota.com/ A Native American store in Minneapolis selling one-of-a-kind native artwork and crafts, as well as music and supplies. This site has information on powwow, concerts, and miscellaneous events, and also offers useful links to other Native American sites.

Gathering of Nations, Ltd.
3301 Coors Blvd. NW, Suite R300
Albuquerque, NM 87120
505-836-2810
Open Mon.-Fri., 9 a.m.-5 p.m.

http://www.gatheringofnations.com/ This site offers a calendar with information on powwows from California to Florida, the opportunity to sign up for free email, create your own web page, add your name to their mailing list, listen to Native American music, shop, see photos, and much more.

National Congress of American Indians
1301 Connecticut Ave NW, Suite 200
Washington D.C. 20036
202-466-7767

http://www.ncai.org/ – Founded in 1944, the National Congress of American Indians has been working to inform the public and Congress on the governmental rights of American Indians and Alaska Natives. The website has information on the history of the organization, a national calendar of events, a tribal directory listing contact information for all Native American tribes.

powwows.com
803-361-1160 (phone)
734-902-6547 (fax)

http://www.powwows.com/ Probably the most thorough listing of powwows across the country. Click on the calendar link and search for a powwow in your area (listed by month, year, and state). The information you receive will include the name of the powwow, location, dates, and contact information (either a phone number, email address, or website address). Also at this you can sign up to receive a newsletter, shop for Native American items, and more.

allpowows.com
http://allpow wows.com/ A new site still developing its contents. The goal of this website is to offer information on all the powwows (location and date) across the country. Includes information about the history of the powwow, current trends, dancing styles, and powwow etiquette.

OTHER USEFUL WEBSITES

Bureau of Indian Affairs (B.I.A.)

http://www.doiu.nbc.gov/orientation/bia2.cfm   This temporary website for the B.I.A. (which is http://www.doi.gov/bureau-indian-affairs.html) lists all 562 federally recognized Indian tribes in the 32 contiguous United States and in Alaska. The Bureau administers 43,450,266.97 acres of tribally-owned land, 10 million acres of individually-owned land, and 309,189 acres of federally-owned land held in trust status.

hanksville.org

http://www.hanksville.org/NAresources/ – Provides an index of Native American resources, including information on Native American culture, history, education, language, health, artists, galleries, museums, archaeology, books, video & film, non-profits & other organizations, governments, music, nations, jobs, and more.

http://www.hanksville.org/sand/contacts/tribal/ – Contact information by Native American tribe, a list of tribal colleges, and a list of Native American public radio stations.

http://www.hanksville.org/NAresources/indices/NAnonprof.html – Information on Native American non-profit organizations.

http://www.hanksville.org/NAresources/indices/NAmuseums.html – A list of Native American Museums around the country.

National Congress of American Indians

1301 Connecticut Ave NW, Suite 200
Washington D.C. 20036
202-466-7767

http://www.ncai.org/ – Founded in 1944, the National Congress of American Indians has been working to inform the public and Congress on the governmental rights of American Indians and Alaska Natives. The website has information on the history of the organization, a national calendar of events, a tribal directory listing contact information for all Native American tribes.

nativeculture.com

http://www.nativeculture.com The "Learn" section of this website contains links to numerous official, governmental, and organizational Native American sites, as well as Native American museums, libraries, schools, colleges and recommended sites for music, media, art, dance, literature, and more. The site also allows visitors to post messages on a bulletin board, sign a guest book, email the website, shop, and read Native American articles.

accessgenealogy.com

http://www.accessgenealogy.com/native/ Contains information on Native American genealogy. You can search by state and also obtain information on Native American cemeteries, census records, newspapers, a complete listing and history of tribes in the state, land and maps, roll numbers, message boards listed by tribe, links to other Native American websites, and more.

nativeweb.org

http://www.nativeweb.org/ Lists all news articles pertaining to Native Americans around the world, information about books and music, a resource section that contains numerous categories all devoted to Native Americans and a "Nations Index" which features websites categorized by tribe, a community center section with message boards to communicate with other Native Americans and an area to view job listings across the country, and much more.

INDEX

A

abalone shell or disk, 128, 132–133, 234–235
abdominal pains, 111
ablutions, 151
Above Beings, 9, 12, 13–18, 88, 202, 205–218, 220–221, 227–231, 233–236, 239, 241, 244–256, 259–260, 264–266; and lesser powers, 13–14, 26, 180, 250; primary source for healing, 254; and their helpers, 176, 186–188, 193, 205, 207, 215; as original givers, 207; in Anasazi beliefs, 22; in Apache beliefs, 152, 158; in Cherokee beliefs, 35–36, 97–100, 107–108, 114, 116, 118, 121–122; in Cheyenne beliefs, 185; in Hopi beliefs, 25, 27, 73–74, 91, 92, 95; in Sioux beliefs, 165–166, 168, 176–177, 179–182, 184, 186, 192–196; relationship with humans, 215, 251, 256; visiting with Above Beings, 215. See also God(s); Godhead; Immortals; Katcinas; messengers (between humans and deities); miracles; nature, and gods; power(s) available to humans; powers (supernatural); spirits; supernatural beings; supernatural objects; Supreme Being; Wakan Tanka.
abstinence, 63, 81, 84, 94, 107–108, 248, 257
accidents, 238
Acoma, 23–24
acorns, 130, 137
acts and action, 200, 245, 251–252, 266; control, 4; dilute the force of evil acts, 252; focuses thought, 201; and inner peace, 13, 18; and motivation, 13
acupressure, 4, 95, 109, 119, 262–263; blood flow, 263; massage, 263; meridians, 263; pressure points, 262–263; warming hands over a fire, 262
adolescence, 136
adulthood, 136
Africa, 215
the aged, 179
aging, 228
agreements, 116
AIDS, 201
Alabama, 32
Alaska, 47–48
Alcatraz, 54
Algonquin Sioux, 173
allotted land and goods, 61, 65–66
altars: for personal use, 244–246, 248; Hopi, 81–83, 94–95; Pueblo, 29; Sioux, 168, 175; Zuni, 83
American colonists, 153
American Horse, 66
American Indian cultures, ix
American Indian Movement (AIM), 64–65
American Judeo-Christian culture, ix
amnesty for criminals, 115
amputation, 109
amulets, 162, 262
Anasazi, 21–23, 27, 79, 87, 88
ancestors, 186
anger, 232, 239, 249
Anglo medicine, 155
animal dances, 42
animal ghosts and spirits, 110, 113
Animal Spirit Peoples, 183
animals, 2, 189; as Katcina types, 78; as supernaturals, 150–151, 177; humans taking on the shape and form of, 111, 120–121; in symbols, 157; on pahos, 85; reincarnated, 110; sacred, 56, 82; stone effigies, 83; use of animal parts in ceremonies, 157. See also antelope; ants; bears; birds; bucks and buckskin; buffalo; butterflies; deer and deerskin; dogs; does; elk; fox.
annihilation of Cherokee settlements, 40
annual cycle of ceremonies, for the Hopi, 27, 73–75, 220–221
annual cycle of festivals (Cherokee), 37, 97–100, 114